KNOWING OTHERWISE

FEMINISM WOMEN & RELIGION

ERIN WHITE & MARIE TULIP

CARTOONS BY JENNY COOPES

David Lovell Publishing
Melbourne Australia

Published by
David Lovell Publishing
308 Victoria St.
Brunswick, Victoria 3056
Telephone (03) 380 6728

Cover design by Peter Shaw
Cover illustration by Jenny Coopes
Illustrations throughout by Jenny Coopes
Design by Peter Shaw
Typeset in 10/11 Plantin by Optima Typesetters Brunswick
Printed and bound in Australia by The Book Printer, Victoria

National Library of Australia
Cataloguing-in-Publication data:

White, Erin, 1941–
   Knowing otherwise: feminism, women and religion.

   Bibliography.
   Includes index.
   ISBN 1 86355 005 4.

   1. Women and religion. 2. Social structure.
   3. Feminist theology. 4. Sexism in religion.
   I. Tulip, Marie. II. Title.

291.178344

Grateful acknowledgement is made to those copyright
owners who granted permission to reproduce extracts
used in this book. Every effort was made to trace the
copyright in each case — not wholly successful up to the
time of publication. Extracts: Constance Frazer, 'Stains',
in *Other Ways of Looking*, Kate Llewellyn, 'Lunch', in
Trader Kate and the Elephants; Valery Wilde, 'Singing the
Uncurling Woman' in Louise Crisp and Valery Wilde, *In
the Half Light*; all published by Friendly Street Poets,
Adelaide. Kate Llewellyn, 'Breasts' in Susan Hampton
and Kate Llewellyn, eds, *The Penguin Book of Australian
Women Poets*, published by Penguin Books, Melbourne.
Robin Archer, 'Menstruation Blues', in Robin Archer,
Diana Manson, Helen Mills, Deborah Parry, Robyn
Stacey, *The Pack of Women*, published by
Hessian/Penguin Books, Melbourne.

Contents

Acknowledgements

It was with members of the Magdalene collective and the Commission on the Status of Women of the Australian Council of Churches that I explored the questions of women's liberation and feminist theology through the 1970s and 80s. Warmest thanks to them all.

And my special thanks to Jim for his encouragement and challenging comments, to Libby for her joy and wisdom, and to my friends Jean Gledhill, Margot Mann, Joan Kirkby and especially Vicky Marquis for supporting this project and for their continued love on our journey together.

M.T.

My thanks to Graham English who often enough is willing to discuss religion and feminism first thing in the morning, last thing at night, and sometimes in between; and to Max Miles, our son, whose responses to feminism and religion frequently remind me that not everyone sees the world as I do.

to Sydney Women-church with whom I have thought and practised feminist spirituality for the past five years.

to Noel Rowe and Genevieve Lloyd for their critical readings of my text. As both friends and professionals, they have generously shared their skills of thinking and writing.

and to Joan Powell, a sister founding member of Sydney Women-church, with whom I have shared the feminist journey in religion over many years.

E.W.

Our thanks to Jenny Coopes whose cartoons pepper the text; to David Lovell, friend and publisher, for his ability to make a good-looking book; and to Margaret Munro Clark for her painstaking editing.

We thank too all the women who shared their stories with us, especially the following, many of whose stories appear under pseudonyms in the book.

Phyl Hulse	Helen Walmsley
Bernadette Harris	Susan Dickson
Irene Stevens	Elizabeth Mitchell
Elaine Lindsay	Cathy-Anne Grew
Pat Richardson	Ruth Mahoney
Lisa Ogle	Judy Crotty
Kathy Armstrong	Joan Powell
Ann Laidlaw	Isobel Bishop
Margaret Brown	Mary Lewis
Anna Blue	Heather Edgly
Roslyn Tinker	Pat Andersen
Mariana Moonsun	Michelle Scrimgeour
Mary Ellen Burke	Joan Doyle
Kath Lamoureux	Moya Merrick
Liz Rickman	Heather Tucker
Anne Byrne	Val Reid
Prue McPhillips	Trish Garland
Julie Garrard	Helen Choy
Vicky Marquis	Virginia Gawler
Margaret Knowlden	Cath Mullane
Theodora Hobbs	Ros Giles
Margaret Ogle	Mhairi Barnes
Marie Delaney	Lindy Kasen
Helen Simos	Gail Hewison
Dorothy Chaikin	Annalise Thomas
Maureen Gordon	

Finally, our thanks to each other for the serious fun of teaching, writing and generally exploring together.

M.T. & E.W.

Introduction

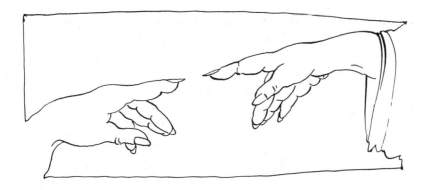

About Jesus people said, 'But this is Osiris! This is our Dionysus! We have known the suffering and dismembered god from long ago.' And they were half right: what they saw was the same general archetypal pattern. But the others were right too when they insisted that this was now a new cultural consciousness in a new specific form.[1]

Our reality is created through our stories and it is in stories that religious reality is contained and passed on. Myths of creation, history, poetry and theological re-creations, all come out of the experience of people and how they understand themselves in a context of meaning. Over long periods of time these stories change as the people encounter new events, new truth, new ways of understanding themselves. As the stories change, so do the symbols and structures of the community: a whole religion may wither if it no longer answers to the way people experience their lives.

Western culture has already seen several major religions grow and flourish, and then die, go underground or continue in constantly changing forms. From prehistoric times the Great Goddess, as Inanna, Ishtar, Isis, Asherah, Hathor, and many other names, was worshipped for thousands of years round the Mediterranean world.[2] Then the stories began to change. Hesiod, Homer and Ovid were among the poets and dramatists who wrote down the stories of the gods and goddesses of Greece and Rome. The Old Testament bears witness to the monotheistic God of the Hebrews, Yahweh, and it is in the Bible, both the Old and New Testaments, that the trinitarian God of Christianity is encountered. Today in many western countries the patriarchal God of Christianity and Judaism is increasingly being challenged, both by post-Christians (including feminists),[3] who no longer find that Christianity meets their experience, and by other feminists[4] who struggle to transform patriarchal Christianity into a religion of love and justice for all, based on relationships of mutuality rather than dominance and submission.

The stories on which this book is based come from women in courses Erin White and I have taught in Sydney since 1987. They are not big or even complete stories, but the recounting of small incidents, everyday happenings, words from the past which influenced these women's lives or affected them in some way. What they reveal is a women's reality which is not reflected in the Christian stories as we hear them in Australian life and particularly in Australian churches. Listening to these stories in our classes we saw the women who shared them come alive in a new way. It was the 'Yeah! Yeah!' experience that Judith Plaskow writes about[5], where each woman feels in her own way the truth of what another is describing. The vivid sense of a shared reality that grew out of these exchanges recalls for some of us an old sense of women's relation to the sacred, a sense of the divine in our lives. Coming from the context of our own experience in late-twentieth-century Australia, these stories nevertheless connect us with a very old tradition.

As far back as we can go in history and prehistory we find traces of a women's wisdom that continue to resonate for us today. It is in the rocks at Ubirr in Kakadu, with their glowing ochre image of Kalarrbiri the Rainbow Serpent. During her travels Kalarrbiri herself placed this image on the huge sandstone rockface there. The traditional owners who have lived in that area for over 40,000 years call her 'that old lady'.[6] It is in the figurines of Europe from 25,000 years ago such as the Venus of Willendorf and the Venus of Laussel,[7] honouring the life-giving powers of the female in societies who worshipped the Great Goddess until they were finally suppressed in 500 A.D.[8] In Jesus' time it appears as Sophia, the Divine Wisdom, the female face of God,[9] and it is reflected in the stories of the women around Jesus. Today I recognise the same tradition in the way my mother talks about friends and relatives and other women in the country town where I grew up, though they would be astonished to find themselves mentioned as part of such an ancient heritage. 'We think back through our mothers', Virginia Woolf said; and however much this tradition may have been interrupted and suppressed, burnt with the witches, ridiculed as gossip or dismissed as old wives' tales, it refuses to go away. Our mothers' wisdom surfaces in our recipe books[10] and in our gardens,[11] at times of death and childbirth, in ways of healing and laughing and weaving and story-telling. Although our lives depend on it, it is submerged and goes against the more public 'received wisdom' of our culture − like an underground river or maybe the Great Artesian Basin. It is a way of knowing otherwise.

In Australia a body of feminist scholarship now extends across various disciplines. It is to be found in books, research papers, journals and so on, and much of it is disseminated through women's studies courses. Significant numbers of women occupy leadership positions in most areas of public and professional life. The language and images of feminism have to some extent become part of everyday discourse, in however distorted a form, and some of the ways in which feminism finds institutional shape, in healing and therapy centres, refuges, women's studies centres, bookshops and government departments, are surviving even against successive backlashes and burnout. From being objects of patriarchy we have entered our own minds, our own bodies, to become subjects of our own experience and history. That is all cause for great celebration. However, because Australian political, economic, educational, legal, medical and religious structures remain largely patriarchal, women are inevitably in a situation of ambiguity and struggle. As individual women we constantly slide into a sense of isolation where it is easy to lose the confidence that comes from our presence to each other. We need to keep in touch, collect our strength, claim and maintain the ground we have gained.

In the area of religion, particularly in Australia, the male gods are so dominant and all-pervasive[12] that it sometimes seems healthier to abandon the field altogether, as many feminists have done. And yet that leaves the symbolic order, the meaning systems of our culture and the deep reaches of our psyches, as well as the more visible structures of society, stuck in the grip of patriarchal powers. There is in Australian culture, perhaps as a legacy from our colonial days, a strongly unified, hierarchical, monotheistic symbolic order which dislikes plurality or difference, and to challenge it or go outside it is to incur disapproval and can seem like entering a void. Women do this from desperation at the lack of empowerment and nurture within the patriarchal religions. And yet when women do act for ourselves, in the face of continuing dominance and rejection, we find a wealth of support. There is new life on the other side of the abyss. The artesian water spouts up.

The history of women's contributions to the life of Christian, Jewish, Moslem, Buddhist, Theosophist and other religious bodies and movements in Australia, though largely unrecorded until recent years, has many threads. These include political movements like the Christian Women's Temperance Union, the history of religious orders and the work of individual women, as well as that of many anonymous, hard-working women's groups around the country.[13] More recently as part of the second wave of feminism, one of the most active and articulate groups has been Christian Women Concerned,[14] which began in 1968 and transformed itself in 1973 into the Commission on the Status of Women of the Australian Council of Churches.[15] The Commission's *Enquiry into the Status of Women in the Church*[16] in 1974 was a breakthrough event, revealing to the Australian churches that women were no longer willing to remain silent. Rather, we were making our own assessments of gender relations in the churches, and were issuing a public challenge to the patriarchal church based on its own gospel of God's love for all.

The Commission's first conference, 'Women's Liberation and the Church', held at the Coogee Bay Hotel in 1974, brought an explosion of energy and vitality as women interested in feminism and religion came together for the first time after the long oppression of the 1950s and 60s and told their stories. The Commission's focus in the early 70s was on theology, language, biblical interpretation and church structures, as we explored together how to build a community that could be liberating for all.

Mary Daly's *Beyond God the Father* (1973)[17] spoke as clearly and powerfully to women in the church as to the women's movement generally and her devastating critique of the language of patriarchy was one of the areas of shared ground between us. Others were our common efforts in many struggles: for women's right to choose in the area of abortion; for women's autonomy in our bodies and sexuality as well as economically and socially; for lesbian and gay liberation; for Aboriginal rights and the rights of women from other cultures; and in the peace movement through the 1960s and 1970s and later at Pine Gap and Greenham.[18] And in the 1980s the Commission's work on particular social issues such as domestic violence,[19] the new reproductive technologies,[20] and women's poverty[21] has paralleled similar work in the secular women's movement. The Commission was always ecumenical, with women from the Uniting church (Congregational, Methodist and Presbyterian until their union in 1977), Anglicans, Baptists, Quakers, Catholics and the Salvation Army. The bonds of sisterhood crossed all denominational boundaries and even, to some extent, the boundaries between different religions.

This situation became more complex and varied in the 1980s. The women's movement in Australia became less hostile towards a concern with women's spirituality and religion; some denominational women's groups, such as the Movement for the Ordination of Women (MOW), became politically active; and the general public became more aware of the questioning of male domination in the churches, partly through such books as *The Force of the Feminine, Opening the Cage,* and *Sweet Mothers Sweet Maids.*[22] Discussion of feminism and religion came out of the church ghetto. The issue which put the struggle between women and the church on the front pages was the question of the ordination of women in the Anglican church. In 1977 many of us demonstrated with 'Equal Rites' placards outside Saint Andrew's Cathedral in Sydney as the Archbishop of Canterbury and members of the local hierarchy processed in.[23] The Synod, accepting a report from its own committee, ruled that there were no theological objections to the ordination of women. But thirteen years later they are still fighting a rearguard action which continues to prevent the ordination of women to the priesthood from actually taking place. Over the years the Anglican Women Concerned and more recently the Movement for the Ordination of Women have received such a bigoted response from the majority of bishops and priests that the Anglican church, in Sydney at least, has revealed itself as more sexist than even the Australian public thinks is a fair go.[24] A constructive side effect of the long-drawn-out campaign is that the women involved have acquired a much deeper theological and biblical understanding and will be in a better position to subvert patriarchal styles and structures when they are eventually ordained. The ordination issue is really the tip of an iceberg. It has revealed a depth of misogyny in Christianity, whose beginnings are apparent even in the New Testament. The struggle towards a more whole church and community is part of a very long healing process.

In the 1980s two strong movements of women have emerged in Australia from the Catholic tradition. One of these is Women-church (as opposed to the patriarchal church), a group with wide ecumenical and international links, which has a radical edge in its style of combining political activism with feminist ritual[25] in the context of a wide network of feminists with a diverse range of religious interests. The core group has a flair for innovative liturgy and action, which finds expression in the *Women-Church* Journal.[26] Another group called Women and the Australian Church (WATAC) maintains a consciousness-raising role among Catholic women in general. Although it appears to have the approval of the hierarchy, which implies a soft feminism, a real sharing of experience among the women has quickly become radicalising.

In the summer of 1989–90, two large conferences demonstrated a strong growth of interest in feminism and religion among Australian women. Over 450 attended the conference 'Towards a Feminist Theology'[27] at Collaroy in New South Wales, organised by the three groups mentioned above – MOW, Women-church and WATAC. And 280 were at the conference 'The Church Made Whole'[28] in Melbourne, organised by Uniting Church women, with over 100 more who could not be accommodated. I attended the former, and as one of the rather embattled activists of the early 1970s, when we were regarded with suspicion by both the church and the women's movement, I was astonished at the depth of bonding within this diverse group of women and the warmth and calm acceptance of even the most radical critiques of patriarchy and movements towards feminist community. Of course there was a great diversity of feminisms being articulated. But for many women there was a sense of coming home, of being in a community where each woman could be freely herself, at least for a few days. From the euphoria of women who were at the Melbourne conference, I gather they experienced a similar depth of shared connection, as did those at the recent Women-Church Convergence in the United States,[29] which was attended by 3,500 women.

Apart from those coming to feminism from a background in the institutional churches, feminists interested in religion are now to be found within various academic disciplines in Australia, including philosophy, art, anthropology, psychology, history and literature, as well as theology and biblical studies. Women's spirituality connects with an interest in ancient and eastern religions, as well as with contemporary ecology and peace movements and a range of healing and therapy centres.

The intention of this book is to look at stories and incidents from women's lives in the context of feminist theology. This involves both a critique of the patriarchal church and society in which we have grown up and now live, and the development of a feminist theology which affirms us as women and suggests a more inclusive and empowering context of meaning for our lives. The book grows out of a course Erin and I have taught for several years. It began as An Introduction to Feminist Religious Thought, in the Continuing Education Program of Sydney University, incorporating both the experience of the students and the work of feminist theologians and thinkers such as Mary Daly, Rosemary Radford Ruether, Elisabeth Schüssler Fiorenza, Phyllis Trible, and Carol Christ. Although we continued to teach it there, we also taught it at various other places in a form more closely tied in with various aspects of women's lives, under the name Feminism and Religion and the Seven Ages of Women. The seven ages were birth as a girl; menstruation and sexuality; production and reproduction; violence; women together; menopause; and death and regeneration. The first five form the basis for the five chapters here. The last two have not been included for reasons of time and space, and they, together with the many other aspects of women's lives which we would like to have discussed, must wait for another book. The 'ages' were based on phases of women's lives which do form a certain physiological sequence, but which also keep recurring in symbolic ways all through our lives. We make no claims to being comprehensive, either in our treatment of women's lives or in what we include of feminist theology. We leave out large areas of both, although many aspects do appear more or less en passant. There is an ad hoc, almost arbitrary quality in our choice of material, which comes from our decision to leap into the here-and-nowness of women's lives, taking examples from the stories of students, the daily newspapers, the life of the community and our own lives, and finding out what theology has to say about them. It is not a systematic treatment but does, we feel, have its own logic and flow.

The subjects are mostly very secular. It is commonly thought that talking about religion means talking about God. But what we are interested in is not some separate sphere called religion but rather the religious dimension of the everyday. We are interested in our lives here and now, our bodies, work, friends, survival, and the meaning of it all to us now.

Instead of starting with theological categories, as happens in systematic theology, we begin with present day reality in lived lives, and women's understanding of their own experience of the divine, of bodily and sexual reality, work, violence and friendship. It turns out that the Christian church, itself still a very patriarchal institution, has little to say to women that does not assume predetermined roles for us. What it offers that is affirming and celebratory has to be dug out, re-interpreted and recreated by feminist thought and reflection.

What does the church have to say to us about a female God? A God who loves women? How often does the church mention menstruation? Or consider women's work — other than in an exploitative way? Does the church support Equal Employment Opportunity (EEO) or Affirmative Action? What initiatives has the church taken in relation to domestic violence? Child abuse? Rape? Or to support a feminist interpretation of the Bible, or women's solidarity with each other over issues of poverty, inclusive language or inclusive liturgies? Most women would find it laughable even to hope that the church might take initiatives in these areas. It is like suggesting the local priest help out with a bit of baby-sitting now and then. Or that the Virgin Mary come down from her pedestal and join an International Women's Day march, not in her blue and white robes but maybe in jeans and sneakers. Or that we see the church organising a campaign for a more just evaluation of women's work and skills.

Given a slight turn of the faith and gender kaleidoscope, none of these things need be at all surprising. In fact they would flow naturally from looking at the world through the eyes of women, rather than only through those of men. From such a vantage point the divine energy and spirit may be seen not as an intellectual abstraction, a powerful father-figure or a judging, controlling God of anger and retribution, but as a presence here on earth, in nature and in all of us, in the interconnections within and among us, in our love and work and in our pain and pleasure, as we celebrate the wonder of the universe and the abundance of life that is here for us to claim. Maybe if the church listens more acutely to the stories of women, a more just, loving and joyful society will be brought closer. This book hopes to contribute to that process.

Knowing Otherwise, like the course it is based on, has grown out of Erin's and my friendship over many years and innumerable conversations round many tables. Our lives have been very different, but not without parallels. The fifteen busy years Erin spent in Brigidine convents teaching and studying and looking after the girls corresponds in some ways to the years I spent in producing and caring for four children in Epping. Before that I had an exciting four years in Chicago doing an MA in French language and literature at Northwestern University and then teaching at Roosevelt University while my husband Jim did his PhD at the University of Chicago. I emerged from the mothering years in Epping to an enthusiastic discovery of women's liberation and a job teaching English as a Second Language at Sydney Technical College. Erin, after leaving the convent, worked in Family Services, married Graham English, and gained a PhD on the work of the French philosopher Paul Ricoeur. Her Catholic background and culture are very different from my Presbyterian and Uniting church tradition, and where Erin's passion is for philosophy, my interest is in a literary-religious reality and activism. We find we energise and complement each other in our work on feminist theology, and our shared teaching has been a delight for us both. We both feel there is a need for more women to write and publish in Australia, particularly in the context of religious thought and experience. There is far more to say than we could begin to include here.

To divide up the work we have each taken different chapters. Erin wrote the chapters on menstruation, violence and women together, and I wrote those on being born a girl and work, as well as this introduction.

We realise our use of 'we' and 'they' is rather fluid. Sometimes 'we' means all women, sometimes a particular group, or feminists, or our students, or the two of us, or everyone. Sometimes grammatical exigencies lead us to use 'they'. We hope the context will make the meaning clear in each case.

Our use of 'we' also indicates our relation to what we say. We are not omniscient authors as in the patriarchal tradition; and we do identify with women, and are conscious of women-as-a-group. We do not, however, intend to universalise in a way that would deny difference or the particularity and uniqueness of each woman's experience and history. Nor do we intend to convey an assumption of biological essentialism, although occasionally we do wonder if there isn't something in it after all.

M.T.

Notes

1 Marie-Louise von Franz, *An Introduction to the Interpretation of Fairytales*, Spring Publications, Dallas, 1970, p.20.
2 See works by Marija Gimbutas, Merlin Stone, Charlene Spretnak and James Mellaart.
3 For example, Mary Daly, Carol Christ, Naomi Goldenberg, Starhawk.
4 For example, Rosemary Radford Ruether, Elisabeth Schüssler Fiorenza, Phyllis Trible, Letty M. Russell.
5 Carol P. Christ and Judith Plaskow, eds., *Womanspirit Rising: a Feminist Reader in Religion*, Harper & Row, New York, 1979, p.200.
6 These words are taken from the description of the rock painting on a notice placed nearby by the National Parks and Wildlife Service of Kakadu National Park. I visited the area in 1986. More recent archeological work suggests that Aboriginal people have lived there for 60,000 rather than 40,000 years. (*SMH* 14.5.90)

7 See Merlin Stone, *The Paradise Papers: The Suppression of Women's Rites*, Virago, London, 1976, and Erich Neumann, *The Great Mother: an Analysis of the Archetype*, Princeton University Press, Princeton, 1972.

8 Stone, *op.cit.*, p.211.

9 Elisabeth Schüssler Fiorenza, *In Memory of Her*, Crossroad, New York, 1983, p.134.

10 My grandmother had a recipe that began, 'Take an ox'. My mother still has a copy of *Mrs Maclurcan's Cookery Book*, published in Townsville in 1898. It begins with soups: 'For making soups of any kind, you must always have strong rich stock; having that ready you can make any soup you wish.' Looking in some of my own cookery books, as they were called, I find advice on how to cook an emu egg, how to dry herbs, how to use a bush oven ('First, dig a hole at least six inches larger in diameter than the oven . . . '), how to preserve eggs and what to do 'when eggs are scarce and dear'. There are lots of 'hints' on how to make meals that are nourishing and economical, what to do with left-overs, how to save time and energy in the kitchen − and how to make a gargle, or a remedy for constipation. There are menus for all kinds of occasions and seasons and numbers of people, and the *Woman's Mirror Cookery Book* of 1937, published by the *Bulletin* in Sydney, and which I inherited from my aunt, sums it up well: 'To collect the results of the experience of cooks and housewives for the instruction of others is the reason for writing any book on cookery. This keeps the modern housewife in the line of traditional procedure, and allows her to profit by the wisdom of her "foremothers".'

11 See Alice Walker, *In Search of Our Mothers' Gardens: Womanist Prose*, Women's Press, London, 1984.

12 See Anne Summers, *Damned Whores and God's Police: The Colonisation of Women in Australia*, Penguin, Melbourne, 1975; and Jan Mercer, ed., *The Other Half: Women in Australian Society*, Penguin, Melbourne, 1975.

13 See Barbara Thiering, *Created Second*, 1973 and *Deliver Us from Eve*, 1977; Sabine Willis, ed., *Women, Faith and Fetes*, 1977; Sally Kennedy, *Faith and Feminism*, 1985; Jill Roe, *Beyond Belief*, 1986; Hilary Carey, *Truly Feminine, Truly Catholic*, 1987; and the journals *Magdalene* and *Women-Church*.

14 *Magdalene*, May 1973, p.2.

15 *Magdalene*, July 1973, pp.5–6.

16 Sabine Willis, ed., *Enquiry into the Status of Women in the Church*, Commission on the Status of Women of the Australian Council of Churches (NSW), Sydney, 1974.

17 Mary Daly, *Beyond God the Father: Toward a Philosophy of Women's Liberation*, Beacon Press, Boston, 1973.

18 See issues of *Magdalene, passim,* for reports and comments related to all these areas of action.

19 *Breaking the Silence: The Church and Domestic Violence*, Commission on the Status of Women of the Australian Council of Churches, Sydney, 1986.

20 *Rock-a-Bye Test Tube: Reproductive Technology and the Churches*, a Resource Package on Reproductive Technology, Commission on the Status of Women of the

Australian Council of Churches, Sydney, 1986.

21 *Women, Poverty and the Church*, Commission on the Status of Women of the Australian Council of Churches, Sydney, 1986.

22 M. Franklin, ed., *The Force of the Feminine*, Allen & Unwin, Sydney, 1986; M. Franklin and R.S. Jones, eds., *Opening the Cage*, Allen & Unwin, Sydney, 1987; and K. Nelson and D. Nelson, eds., *Sweet Mothers Sweet Maids*, Penguin Books, Melbourne, 1986.

23 *Magdalene*, No.4, 1977, pp.3–5.

24 See for example *The Sydney Morning Herald* (13.11.90), *The Australian* (10.11.89; 29.11.90; 20.12.89; 13.3.90), *The Sun-Herald* (21.1.90).

25 Erin tells me that 'liturgy' was always the approved word in the Catholic church; 'ritual' was avoided or used disapprovingly as denoting pagan practices. In speaking of ritual, Women-church nods approvingly towards the denigrated pagan rites, paganism being literally the religion of the country people.

26 *Women-Church: An Australian Journal of Feminist Studies in Religion*, Women-church, GPO Box 2134, Sydney 2001. 1987– .

27 The conference papers are published in Elaine Lindsay, ed., *Towards a Feminist Theology*, Sydney, 1990.

28 The conference papers are published in *The Church Made Whole*, David Lovell Publishing, Melbourne, 1990.

29 See *Women in the Church and the World: An Annotated Bibliography*, CEO, Sydney, 1989, for lists and annotations of lectures and workshops given at this conference, *Women-Church: Claiming Our Power*, Cincinnati, Ohio, October 1987.

CHAPTER ONE

Being born a girl

Women have no territory in this country.
Jill Ker Conway

You just grow up knowing boys are where it's at.
Elizabeth

Eternal Father . . .

To be born a girl in Australia is to be born into ambiguity because we are entering two different and conflicting systems of meaning. The first is the system most Australians have grown up with and have been socialised into since birth. It is patriarchal, and has been the prevailing system in Europe and the west for about 5,000 years. Power is organised hierarchically, according to sex, race and class, so the people at the top tend to be rich white men, and the people at the bottom poor black women.[1] The second way of seeing reality emphasises mutuality between people rather than structures of dominance, and has emerged at many times and places throughout history to challenge the patriarchal system, though so far with only limited success. Broadly one could say that the ideological battle in relation to both race and class has at least been taken into the general discourse in the sense that although dreadful poverty and racial oppression still continue, they are widely recognised as destructive and inhuman. But sexual oppression is not yet widely condemned: in fact it is still justified and even promoted in our male-dominated society.

The major religions play a complex role in this oppression of women, since their scriptures and doctrines and prophets often call for the full equality of all people, but their practices perpetuate oppression. In Christianity, for example, all people are seen as equal before God, but the symbols and structures of the church are still largely and powerfully patriarchal and are oppressive to women as well as to some men.

Women today are caught between these two world views, one of which we may call patriarchal, since it is based on the traditional power of the fathers, and the other feminist, since it is feminists who are challenging the patriarchal system in relation to sex as well as class and race, and who are building a new way of living in the world in which sexist oppression is no longer tolerated.

Each of these two realities is strongly supported by the system of symbols and organisational and societal structures that underlies it and in which it finds expression. So long as the God of Christianity, for example, remains male in church language and symbols and in the public imagination, 'he' stays lodged deep in people's psyches as well as in the structures of church and society, and acts as an anchor against change. The changing of the gods is therefore important to the secular world as well as to churchgoers, since unless the gods change, the power relations in the secular world cannot be transformed either. So long as God is jealously male, women will continue to be oppressed.

This chapter looks at how women experience being born a girl in our still male-dominated society, and how this reflects the prevailing power of the patriarchal religious symbols. We then consider what happens when women construct their picture of the divine, and find a surprisingly different view.

Being born a girl

Most of us if we sit quiet for a moment can remember some of the dilemmas, the conflicting messages, the words from our childhood that touched us as we grew up. If we say them to each other now, we can be surprised at the power they still have for us – to make us cry, or more likely laugh, or maybe even touch off an old rage. Being born is an adventure for everyone. It is the points of becoming aware of having been born a girl in Australia that we are interested in here. What was it like? How do women remember it?

The responses quoted in this chapter are mostly from a group of about

20 women who were asked to recall a specific incident or memory related to being born a girl. The women were students in a course entitled 'Feminism and Religion and the Seven Ages of Women', with ages ranging from early twenties to over seventy. This exercise came at the beginning of the second class, the first class having been given over to introduction to the course and to each other. Considering the openness of the question the sharpness of the recollections is striking.

> I remember when I was about eight standing beside our car at our house. My father said half-jokingly, 'I wish you'd been born a boy' (he already had two daughters, and my mother was 40 when I was born). 'You were the last chance, and you were another girl.' In my memory he only said it once, but it stuck deep in my being, and I thought of that remark many, many times. I always felt second best . . .
>
> Jennifer

The father's words came as a blow and still carry the force of the rejection, and of Jennifer's feelings of hurt and inadequacy. We can recognise her direct experience of what it feels like to become conscious of oneself as a girl in a male-dominated society. Since a special value is put on boy children, the father is disappointed at missing his 'last chance', but his words have a deeper effect on his daughter. She accepts her father's authority, and the status he accords her in Australian society sticks, as does the hurt.

> Me being born a girl must have been a great disappointment for my parents. I was their fourth girl — or their fourth attempt to have a son. I was to be named Richard. Yet I was their last child, so my intrinsic value may have been recognised.
>
> Marion

Marion's birth is almost an absence — the fourth failure to have a son, the non-birth of Richard. Unlike Jennifer, who registers her own feelings, Marion's description is not from her own point of view but from inside her parents' feelings. Her recognition of a possibility of value in herself comes only by implication, through her parents not having risked a fifth non-event. Yet, in recognising their disappointment and loss, she can still refer to the concept of 'intrinsic value' in relation to herself, so her statement carries at least a possibility of hope.

> As a child I felt strong, tough, capable of anything, a real sense of my own female power, unique and special in a family with two brothers, sorry for my aunt that she had only sons and annoyed with my parents who did not seem to appreciate how lucky they were to have a daughter.
>
> Kate

In contrast to Marion, Kate's memory shows her as very much inside her own subjectivity, in touch with her own feelings, relying on her own power of judgment, accepting her own authority. She recalls a clear sense of her own worth, despite the realisation that her parents, like society generally, do not share her high valuation of girls. What is surprising is that far from internalising their attitudes, she delights in her own worth and locates inadequacy not in herself but in the attitudes of her parents. Her annoyance is the sign of a healthy self-respect.

These memories represent two kinds of response of girls to the realisation of being born into a sexist society — either to internalise the authority of the patriarchal society, as Marion did, incurring a measure of self-alienation; or, like Kate, to keep one's own authority and risk conflict. Kate's way allowed her to enjoy a lot of freedom in what we like to think of as a typical happy Australian childhood:

> I enjoyed my body especially in summer when I would run barefoot, my feet becoming hard and dirty, sunbaking to a deep brown, and letting my hair bleach in the sun, playing in the bush, dressing up, making up games, being part of a neighbourhood gang, playing football.

For Kate it was a specifically female freedom and power:

> Being female meant not having to go to war, hating people who made wars and endangered others' lives, putting boys like my brothers at risk for reasons of power. Florence Nightingale was my heroine. Being female also meant being a mother — and I was going to be a much better one than my own.

This autonomy ran the risk of incurring her parents' displeasure and anger and Kate knew she had to be careful:

> I like being seen as 'good' although I worried that God knew the times I didn't feel good inside — the times I wanted to be rude to my parents for instance; I think there was a strong sense of justice, of wanting to be treated fairly. I wished I had an older sister.

Kate had her own inner authority and moral sense and one feels a mutual respect between her and her parents — though she knew she needed allies! Other girls experienced not just the presence but the acting out of the father's authority, sometimes arbitrarily, or violently:

> I see a hand raised to hit me. I feel myself cringe and cower, raising my elbow to protect my face. I feel the pain and humiliation, the loss of respect and the

insignificance of 'who I am' at the expense of his wrath. I know I'm not strong enough to defend myself *and* he is my *father*.

Jill

We were all gathered in the kitchen. My 13-year-old sister commented offhandedly that our family doctor had suggested Dad was stupid in saying or doing something in particular (long since forgotten). Dad grabbed my sister and pinned her up against the wall and threatened her with a beating if she ever hinted at such a thing again. The anger and violence of this scene has stayed with me ever since and inhibits me still from telling my father what I really think about him − I am scared!

Ros

You couldn't even smile at our place. Dad would say 'Wipe that smile off your\ face.'

Penny

So the balance of mutual respect can easily be tipped into conflict and violence when the underlying structure is authoritarian. The other way, taken by girls who internalise the father's authority rather than resisting it, can lead to an 'If you can't beat 'em, join 'em' approach, identifying with the male:

I was the second child and second daughter and there were always whispers that my parents had hoped I would be a boy. I envied some aspects of boys' lives and still enjoy the 'male' sports of football and cricket. As a small child during World War II, I desperately wanted to be a soldier and badgered my mother until she made me a 'soldier suit' as a Christmas gift.

Helen

Helen puts on the clothes, the sports, the warrior image of the boys, identifying with and trying to satisfy the father's wish.

When I wanted to have fun I used to secretly go and get my brother's Scout uniform and put it on.

Sally

Sally wears boys' clothes not to fulfil her father's wishes but in response to the recognition that it is more permissable for boys to have fun than girls. She had to dress for the part to claim the privileges. But it is a process which intensifies the self-alienation.

I remember when I was about nine my family were going on holidays and I was out playing with my brothers and our nurse called me in to pack my suitcase. I was very angry because my brothers didn't have to do theirs. They could just go on playing. But I had to come in. That has always stayed in my mind.

Elizabeth

If it is the privilege of boys to have fun and be soldiers, the duty of girls is to be responsible for their own clothes and personal arrangements while boys can play and be looked after by others. The girls' world is inside, domestic, serving, being responsible for personal arrangements, while the boys' world is outside, the world of leisure and freedom. Elizabeth is angry not only because of the chores she has to do but because of the unfairness.

Girls who enjoyed boys' games, either because they were fun, like Kate, or because they were a way of identifying as a boy, like Helen, were called tomboys, and this was permissible, even desirable, up to the time of adolescence. Suddenly it became taboo. This is how a 15-year-old boy sees it:

I passed a girl who used to go to my primary school; she was a tomboy and always played cricket and footy with us and now her mother made her go to an all-girls school as some sort of cure for this 'disease'.

Stephen, speaking in 1988

And this is how Kate, who had previously had such a clear sense of her own power of being, describes the transition. Even her sentences break down into fragmented notes:

Adolescence – changed my sense of self. Taboos everywhere; boys were to be avoided, lots of homework, fear of sex, ignorance, sense of failure, of life not being fair; fear of punishment – God, school, parents; lot of guilt at not being good enough; being dumb, stupid, failing; sense of suffering. Pressure to be good all the time, to look after others, to be 'pure', clean, helpful, quiet, to please, be polite, neat, in the background, considerate, hidden, sense of not measuring up – clothes were never right, liking uniforms, being the same as everyone else. Wanting to be a nurse, to get married, to be looked after.

Kate

There is a terrible sense of failure, guilt, fear of punishment, inadequacy, of not measuring up, in fact there is a sense of the impossibility of ever measuring up because that is not part of the deal. Now she feels that one must simply be as good as possible, i.e. please and look after others, and become as invisible as possible.

Of course, it is not possible to be invisible and some of the worst embarrassments happen when one's body is noticed by others.

> I remember when I had to get my first bra. How embarrassing! Looking through the rows of bras trying to look as though I wasn't. Mum got a few, and then it was off to the change room. I thought OK, no worries, Mum only. Then an old lady came into the change room to see whether they fit or not. Then she goes and gets another couple and asks me to try them on. I'm blushing like crazy, trying to look serious, but it's almost impossible. I try another one on and the lady says 'That's perfect', then Mum and the old lady leave and I'm left alone trying to pale my face down. I cracked up and couldn't stop thinking about that lady. I go outside just glad it's over.
>
> Karin, 14 years old, 1988

And Stella:

> Puberty for me was a tricky time. I hated getting my periods and I didn't want to wear a bra. Most of my friends hassled me about not wearing a bra, especially my best friend. She constantly told me I'd grow up and have saggy tits. I didn't believe her. It was no big psychological deal, I wasn't depressed or confused. It was just a change in my life and I was used to changes, after all nothing stays the same forever.
>
> Stella, 15 years old, 1988

Stella has become philosophical, but not everyone can:

> My breasts developed when I was quite young, sooner than my sisters'. I can vividly remember my mother fitting a new frock on me and saying, 'You look dreadful, I'll have to buy you a bra.' Even as a reasonably mature adult, I still felt that a Size 34, B cup, was unusually large.
>
> Jan, 51.

A friend, Claudia, gave us the following incident as her memory of being born a girl.

> When I was four I went to school. One day a female teacher looked at another girl in my class who had very red cheeks and said to me, 'Why don't you have red cheeks?'

This didn't seem to me to be such a key story. It was only after I thought about it that I realised Claudia was pointing to another example of the impossibility of 'measuring up', when we are judged by such totally arbitrary standards. Why should she have red cheeks just because the girl sitting next to her did! Why should we be judged by our waist measurement or bra size or hair colour? Or the image that appears on magazine covers or page three? I understood why Claudia's outrage had lasted forty years.

Many women associate their adolescence with the word 'don't': Don't cross your legs, don't lead him on, don't beat the boys, don't be too clever, girls don't chew gum, girls don't swear, boys don't respect girls who do that, don't dwell on things, don't make a fuss, don't argue, don't answer back, don't disturb your father, don't be home late, don't talk to strange men. Many of the restrictions are to do with sexual repression:

> A symbol of Irish Catholic sexual repression in the early 1920s is for me an item on a school clothes list written in my grandmother's hand, and pasted on the inside lid of my mother's school trunk (which I later inherited): 'Bath Sheets (2)'. On questioning, my mother explained that this 'garment' had to be tied around the neck and draped right round and over the edge of the bath. Its purpose was to ensure that girls never caught a glimpse of their own bodies! Moreover, its use was strictly monitored by nuns who were likely to enter the bathroom at any time . . . School for me was also as a boarder with Irish Loreto nuns. Fortunately the bath sheet had been dispensed with, but modesty was still considered next to godliness and we had to dress and undress under our dressing gowns.
>
> Margaret, 55

But often the sense of taboo, of lurking danger, was conveyed without any information or reason for carefulness being given:

> The overall impression with which the young woman was left was that her condition (menstruating) was not only secret but shameful. If anything went wrong (and what did this mean?), it was her fault for being careless or wanton but, again, these words and their implications were not explained.
>
> Caroline, 67

Being good meant saying yes to parents and other authority figures (obedience), and no to boys (purity, self-respect). Girls were certainly responsible for male sexuality and for 'drawing the line'. 'He'll only go as far as you let him'. 'Keep yourself for your husband'. 'Boys marry virgins'.

Kate's evocation of adolescence catches the sense of urgency about solving one's future — 'Wanting to be a nurse, to get married, to be looked after'. In pre-pill days there were two reasons for urgency — sex was condoned only within marriage (and abortion was dangerous, expensive and a disgrace), and a woman's identity was bound up with a man:

I can never remember a time in my childhood or adolescence when I considered my future life without a man – marriage was always taken for granted and I moved steadily toward that goal at age 20. I never seriously considered any other options or planned a career for myself (despite having been an A student!).

Julia, 33

Although the convent school I attended was quite progressive for its time, the options for girls after leaving school were restricted. It was thought suitable to be a nurse or a teacher or a typist for a time before becoming a nun, by far the most desirable choice, or marrying. A few young women went to University, mainly studying Arts but a few studied Science or Medicine. The latter was considered daring and only for the cleverest and most gifted. Whatever was decided for us, it was quite clear that it was only for a time, that we would inevitably enter the convent, marry and have children or devote ourselves to good works as a virtuous single woman in the world. When I was a young child, many women I knew had been forced to accept the status of maiden aunt because of male attrition in the First World War. They did not have the dignity of nun or wife and were regarded as lesser beings who had no social position because they had no relationship to a man. Small wonder that if we rejected convent life, or were rejected by it, we hungered for marriage. A woman's dignity and livelihood was derived from the Church, either as bride of Christ or bride of man.

Caroline, 67

It would be hard for anyone born after the 1940s to imagine how strong this social and religious definition of a woman in terms of her relationship with a man was. Her whole social and economic status and identity was based primarily on her sexual status – as a nun or spinster, wife or widow, or, if she was sexually active outside those socially sanctioned roles, as whore. In the 1950s lesbians were so far from social recognition as to be almost unheard of. A profound change has taken place since the fifties in that social, economic and sexual autonomy are now at least theoretically possible for women, if difficult to actually achieve. But those questions will be taken up in later chapters. In Australia by far the majority of women reach what Julia calls the goal of marriage, and the whole cycle begins again:

I am the eldest of three girls. Our parents never even hinted that they were not delighted with their family, but we gained some impressions from our male cousins that we were in some way lacking. My mother came from a grazing family, and had let the side down by marrying a man from the city. She attempted to make amends by having us all taught riding, in case we married a grazier, but none of us did. We had a happy if rather sheltered upbringing – sheltered particularly in sexual matters, though intellectually we were all encouraged in every way. Looking back, I can say that the one part of my growing up which I would have preferred to have been different is that aspect of familiarity with the opposite sex. Even in that, our parents did their best: nearly every Saturday afternoon we played mixed tennis. Probably most people of my generation would have similar comments.

Giving birth for the first time, to a girl, caused me to fear that the whole cycle would begin again. My parents-in-law, too, showed a lack of enthusiasm for a female grandchild which caused me some distress. Fortunately, they were quite unconscious of their bias, and were happy to tell us that they were wishing for a boy, when our second child was expected (and that they had put a coin in the Trevi fountain in Rome, with this hope). The baby was a boy, and I was very relieved indeed.

I received one of the best and kindest letters I have ever had, from my aunt by marriage (a grazier's wife!), who had six daughters and one son, when our daughter was born. I have always been grateful to her for this.

Alicia, 58

Alicia takes pains to point out that her parents 'did their best' and 'never even hinted' that they were not delighted with their family. She attaches no criticism or blame to them, and we admire her spirit. But the message clearly got through. For her it came via some cousins, and for her mother, who didn't marry a grazier, who knows how she realised that she had 'let the side down'? Which side? It is like a game and whether the rules are conveyed by cousins, or referred to by one's father, or 'never even hinted at', families know what they are. For Alicia's family they were that you shouldn't have an all-girl family, you can use your mind, but you must be discreet or even silent about sex. She assumes that these were also the rules for society in general – 'most of my generation'. So when, on the birth of her daughter, Alicia reacts with 'fear that the whole cycle would begin again', she means the cycle of having only daughters, knowing that that is outside the rules, and yet 'doing her best' with what is seen as an imperfect situation. It is a situation for which she as mother assumes responsibility, which explains her relief at producing a son, and also her intense response to her aunt's letter of reassurance, and the solidarity between them as mothers who have suffered the pain of failure. Not that she would admit to such pain – she knows the rules. She simply evokes it by innuendo and double negatives, and her irony and humour keep it safely at bay.

This failure to meet the expectations of a patriarchal society reminds us of Kate's not measuring up, and Claudia's not having red cheeks. We are Eve's daughters after all, still guilty for biting the apple:

Mysterious reasons drove my mother to Confession quite frequently while Dad
hardly ever went. This was a puzzle – perhaps women committed more sins
than men or felt guiltier about them.

Caroline, 68

The symbol system of patriarchy

Perhaps this is the point to stand back from the sense of women's reality
suggested by these incidents and memories, and see how it corresponds
to the way Christianity and Judaism, the major religions in Australia and
in the western culture we have inherited, have structured the world. Of
course the traditional picture is changing, but until about 1970 it was almost
unquestioned in Australia; and in the general culture, though dented, it
still prevails.

The primary symbol is of God the Father, loving, powerful, male, monotheistic, jealous of his unique position. His will is absolute and arbitrary.
Of course sophisticated thinkers and mystics have always known and taught
that God is beyond male or female, but almost all of the imagery and
language used for God continues to represent 'him' in male terms and it
is the image of the divinity as male that is lodged in the collective psyche.
I know of no religious congregation or community in Australia, whether
Christian, Jewish, Islamic or even Buddhist, except for some small women's
groups, where the use of male imagery and language for the divine (or,
in Buddhism, the divine teacher) does not far outweigh the use of female
or ungendered words and images.

The Godhead in Christianity is relational, with Father, Son and Holy
Spirit comprising a complex unity but still all male. The risen Christ is
sometimes seen as including female and male, but as with God the Father
the image of Jesus as male totally overwhelms any real notion of the
feminine. The Holy Spirit also has female associations, but hardly in
sufficient strength to justify using a feminine pronoun, and it would, to
say the least, cause a mild surprise to refer to the Holy Spirit as She in
almost any church or cathedral or synagogue in Australia. Daughters are
totally absent from the Godhead, as are mothers (apart from Mary, who
in the hearts of some Catholics is a sort of de facto divinity, though not
of course du jure). So one has in effect a monotheistic male deity, attributed
with absolute power and authority, a transcendent being, above and separate
from his creation except through his grace and love which he bestows freely
when and where he chooses. The appropriate response to him from human

beings, i.e. the basis for Christian ethics, is love and obedience, to the extent, as Jesus showed, of suffering unto death.

This pattern is reflected in the structure of the church, with its power centred in a male hierarchy from pope to cardinals, archbishops, bishops and priests, set in descending order above the people, animals, plants, the earth. The family mirrors the pattern again, with a father as head, above the mother and children, and like the Father God he has power to exercise his will lovingly or with violence, as he chooses. As Mary Daly said, 'If God is male, then the male is God'.[2] The power of being, acting and naming is seen as belonging to the male, whether divine or human. Male subjectivity absolutises itself and sees women as other, not participating in the power of divinity but rather having the dependent status symbolised by Mary, associated with suffering and passivity, and a life of service and child-bearing, obedient to the will and the needs of the male − bride of Christ or bride of man. And if a woman is not 'good', i.e. dependent on and obedient to a man or male-controlled institution, she becomes 'bad', i.e. sexually independent and not obedient.

This may sound like a caricature, but it points to a strongly patriarchal pattern which, though it is now being seriously challenged, still reflects the prevailing power relations within the way church, family and society are constructed in Australia. And it corresponds very closely to the sense of reality revealed in the memories and incidents quoted above, where women reconstruct how they remember what being born a girl meant for them – the sense of being other, of not being Richard; the father as sometimes loving, sometimes violent; having to help in the house while boys play; having to be good; having expectations of marriage or the convent but not a long-term career; being an object of male observation and judgment; having to be dependent on a man for one's status; the sense of guilt and inadequacy.

Although a process of critique and deconstruction of the patriarchal structures has begun, it is still easier, safer, more comfortable, for women as well as men (black? poor? Jewish?[3] gay?) to identify with the dominant power structure than to see clearly our own inferior status within it. The sharing of these experiences of vulnerability and pain which happens only in a situation of trust enables women to move outside the mindset of the patriarchal system. Its values and structures are no longer simply internalised and accepted as the way things are, but can be recognised as a system which we have been socialised into, and which is not 'natural' at all. It is a construct within history. This system has been developed in a particular social and historical context and can be changed in response to a different context. To see this is to make a leap that becomes possible through sharing experience with other women so that what may have seemed individual inadequacies and doubts and loss of confidence come to be seen as the way other women feel, too, and an accurate reflection of the way women are constructed not only in the religious system outlined above, but also in society generally.

This shift in consciousness is an energising process and can lead women to contribute to the process of creating a new culture, in which women and qualities traditionally seen as feminine are celebrated and brought in to the centre, rather than denigrated and marginalised. This is not a reversal, changing patriarchy for matriarchy, but a move towards a community in which everyone has a part in making the decisions and naming the world.

Women's images of the divine

If women were asked now how they name the world, how they see the divine, what would they say? We asked a group of about 20 women to tell us how they image the divine. These women spoke with their own voices out of their own lives, 'hearing each other to speech',[4] to use Nelle Morton's words. They revealed not just the personal journeys and empowerment of individual women, but a collective process in which women are participating in a new adventure of the spirit, which Mary Daly calls participating in the unfolding of God.[5] It is a response to their sense of being absent from the patriarchal world. Even the word God is rejected by many women, not so much because it is a masculine word but because it evokes the patriarchal symbol, the God of our fathers.

In our class we asked the women to draw or use words to portray their image of the divine. After ten minutes we invited them to share their images with the group. The first to speak was a woman in her seventies. She held up a blank piece of paper and said, 'That's mine. One time I could have drawn an old man with a beard and so on – it's gone, all that vision I ever had. Once you get out of the Christian mould it's very hard to visualise – not that I could put it into pictures'. Barbara's blank sheet is not an unwillingness to participate but an eloquent no to a sexist God and to the sexist structures of a church which rejected her and which she sees as destructive to women. She empowers other women by affirming them, and by her refusal of that God. She is not interested in new names for the divine, but in living in new ways.

Margot wrote:

> Reject the image of a God in the form/shape of a person, and indeed a God who acts in ways acceding to human understanding. Reject an outside/third-person God. Believe more in some sort of energy flow of which we are all part, whether believers or not, and whether human or not. A quintessential life force which is expressed by all creation and in all creation.
>
> How to express something which is beyond language and human image-making and is infinite, beyond dimensions?

Margot said she 'also had a blank sheet; but unlike Barbara's, mine is full, not empty. It all depends how you look at it.' Where Barbara refuses to begin the process of naming and distrusts it, Margot expresses the impossibility of arriving at the name – the beyondness of the divine. This is a kind of transcendence, but it is a transcendence which is within us, some sort of energy flow of which we are all part'.

Two women drew spirals, an ancient female symbol, and this is how they described them:

> I see the divine as an active process, so therefore I've done a spiral, because a spiral you have to participate in, there's movement, there's colour, activity; and I see the divine as definitely a process of growth which you participate in, which is moving, and if you're lucky there's colour and meaning and pattern in it. But I covered everything with blackness because I think it *is* like that

most of the time and you don't know, you *are* groping in the dark, but through the darkness when you participate and you're active and moving, there is colour, there is pattern, you can sort of see the meaning of it all.

Rosemary

Mine's a spiral, with colour, strength, an aura. I just seem to be drawn forth from the earth around me into space, so mine's white, not black, and there's a centering and strengthening. It's not figurative at all.

Kath

Both of these images reflect a very close identification of the human with the divine, a strong focus on immanence rather than transcendence, and activity and movement rather than passivity or a static fixed reality. The person is called into being, growth, meaning.

Mary drew a big image of a leaf in many colours, with a big red sun and blue moon:

Mine's about interconnectedness, too, and energy, in the leaf and the flow of the pencil. It is also like a female sexual organ. I'm aware of the similarities between us and nature, and the life force that goes on in interaction between us and the sun, moon, love, thoughtfulness. It's all there, in here and in between. I suppose God is in the cracks somehow.

Again there is a strongly immanent and relational quality to this image, where the energy of the lifeforce is recognised in the creativity of nature, art and sex, as well as in human love and thoughfulness. Others also mentioned sexuality, the power of touch, the knowing that includes sexual knowing, and the electric charge that happens between people or in creating something.

Two women put question marks at the centre of their drawings. One said, 'We can only get glimpses of the divine and that's seeing anything in depth – in relationships, in nature. I usually live in a vacuum, but depth is happiness.' She wrote the words creation, love, truth, depth, next to her question mark.

Another said:

Mine also has a question mark in the middle, but I see it as a centering, drawing thing, almost like the light at the end of the tunnel. I've put the words beauty, love, nature, light, there. I see that as being the divine as the source of all these things. Everything's got a question mark over it. (On the drawing at the centre of the strong radiating rays is a faint picture of a face, as well as the question mark and words.) Maybe there's a sort of a human face that's got a loving nice smile in it. That's to ease me, to think God's got a human side.

> That's just a nice thought. It *would* be nice to find that loving face at the end of the tunnel.

It is as though this person has a strong sense of energetic life (the vibrant rays), but a reluctance to believe in such things as beauty and love, indicated by the question mark over them and the almost disappearing face of God.

Several women drew and talked about the bush:

> . . . the sudden sense of time stopping, and every leaf and twig seems to be in its own presence, and I'm part of it, it's all whole and it feels terrific.

Another drew an image of the colours of nature which reflect the divine – yellow, the aura, the energy each of us has, and blues and greens representing a movement going on, with no ending: 'it continually happens'. The centre of the image is red, an image of female sexuality. Another liked the bush as an image and spoke of the beauty of the minute, perfection, light, with some order. And others said the divine for them is like mist, or wind, or breeze, cloud, earth, or connections between earth and sea, earth and sky.

Jan drew the tree of life, which has 'a lot of life and activity in it, the source of life, sometimes it's Christ, sometimes it's me'. To Ros the divine is everywhere in and around her, and she sees striding along a bush track as her image of abundant life.

The image of no ending was picked up by a young woman in an image from maths and geometry. She drew a cube with 3 to the power of n in it, saying for her the divine accumulates and accumulates, is three-dimensional and expands and expands. There aren't any boundaries to it.

Another said that for her:

> . . . it's a feeling. It's very easy for me to have that in the bush, but I also like to have it when I'm in K-Mart and other places that are incredibly profane. I feel very close to whatever it is, I don't use the word God, I'm not a Christian, but it's a feeling of incredible mystery for me. I really don't understand it.

Margaret found the whole concept of the divine and 'those words like God' very limiting:

> Those limits are boxes around people and the church and we have this idea that God's somewhere up there but you're not really meant to get out of the box to get up to it or even be related to it. What I think of is some kind of an awareness, connectedness and openness and comfort, but with a solid base.

One woman talked about the power of sacred places, places that have been chosen for special ceremonies or celebrations in ancient Goddess-worshipping times, stone circles like Stonehenge and Avebury, places like Delphi and Eleusis for the Greeks, some sites of Christian churches, which are themselves often built on sites that were sacred in pre-Christian times, places which have a special resonance or beauty. She spoke of being with Aboriginal women on the south coast of New South Wales where the sense of the sacred and the power of the particular place and of Aboriginal Dreaming stories and recent history all combined in a very powerful way.

For Eleanor the sense of the Goddess was present in Crete:

> My image is the Snake Goddess from Crete. I was reading *Paradise Papers* [see Note 12], and I'm interested in archeology so I already had this mythological idea of the Goddess from ancient Crete. When I went there I had this overwhelming sense, it was really like Saul's conversion. While I was in Crete I just felt the Goddess was there, you know, it was really very strange. I'm a business woman, I'm not given to these things, and it was just amazing. The Goddess is there still, and I brought back the figure of the Snake Goddess and also Athena. I like the ones that are doing things, it's so far away from this droopy-drawers image of women, but it suits me, I like the ones that have a bit of activity, like Diana out hunting.

Another woman connected the Goddess with women's political activity:

> Perhaps I could just share my first experience of God as a woman. I had been participating in an occasional retreat given by a woman friend in the UK. Feminist interpretations/theology kept surfacing. Like a good scholar/retreatant, I was trying to redefine my traditional image/experience of a (male) God. 'Prayerful meditation' and intellectualising were not doing the trick!
>
> One day I visited some friends at the women's peace camp at Greenham Common. The presence of so many nuclear weapons emanates evil destructiveness. Standing at the gate looking in I felt first the cold wind of despair. I looked back at the silent witness of women and there She was.

Judith was the last to speak:

> It's life, it's love, it's living and loving, the life force. It has meaning and gives value.

These images of divinity point to a paradigm shift which is going on in our time.[6] It involves a deep change from the patriarchal values that have been the prevailing system for western societies for over 5,000 years to a new way which affirms women and women's values, a recovery of the feminine, the maternal, a system of mutuality and power-sharing rather than dominance and hierarchy. Signs of this change can be seen in every aspect of society – in the change in family structure as the father loses the right to rule; in the work place as women struggle for a just recognition of and payment for their work; in parliament and other decision-making bodies where women seek fair representation; in the recognition of our bodies and feelings which will no longer be subordinated to the rationalising of detached minds; and in the ecology movement, where the earth is striking back against centuries of pollution and exploitation.

In religious life and understanding, this shift is revealing itself in changes which the church fathers are only just managing to keep the lid on. The contrast between the way these women are constructing the divine and the prevailing religious symbol system of Australian churches and society is a story that need to be told.

As we have seen, the highly objectified and detached images dissolve into a passionate relational flow between subjectivities. Women are identifying with Ntozake Shange's intense expression, 'i found god in myself & i loved her/i loved her fiercely'.[7]. Figurative images such as Father, Son, Shepherd, Lord, King, Master, are replaced by images from mathematics, geometry, nature, the city, politics, sexuality, place, relationships, art, women's symbols. Rather than a fixed, static world with the hierarchical structure in place, there is an emphasis on fluidity, mutuality, connectedness, activity, the on-going. This links with Mary Daly's preference for verbs rather than nouns – the 'Verb of Verbs' in which we participate.[8]

Rather than being transcendent, the divine is seen as immanent, in and between us, nature and all that is. It is embodied, sexual, earthly. It is not all-knowing but open, growing, living, changing; not controlling but loving, calling us to be our fullest, most alive selves, calling us into responsibility for ourselves, for each other and the earth; not individualistic but communal; not judging but calling us into warm acceptance of ourselves and each other, challenging injustice and the structures of domination; using power not to dominate but to enable, accepting and revealing vulnerability and mortality; not the Eternal Father but the ever-renewed cycles of the earth, the seasons, our bodies, our communities, the people of the earth. Surprisingly, there is no sense of spirit versus matter, mind over body, the sacred versus the profane, or even male versus female, but certainly an awareness of the divine in the liberation experience, in the political struggle to transform the structures of domination and oppression into a new community, a new creation.

For women to begin to name the divine in this new way is a political, not to say revolutionary, act. Taking courage to experience and speak of

our childhood pain creates a liberating distance from experiences that have hurt and limited us, a freedom from their controlling power. Naming our pain as women in a patriarchal society enables us to move more fully into our own lives, our own subjectivity, our power to act. It involves refusing to be a victim, and it builds a sense of shared experience from which political and theological vision and analysis can be developed.

From the perspective of this new vision which women are developing, it becomes impossible to go on using the male language and symbols for the divine that are still so all-pervasive in Australian churches. Some are reluctant even to use the word 'God', since the accustomed words and symbols have become idolatrous, signifying a male divinity, represented in the church by a male hierarchy. Divine images always risk becoming idols, where they become identified or equated with the divine reality of which they are a partial image. Women are therefore calling upon the church to respect its own wisdom in resisting idolatry. A second reason is that words like Father, Lord, King can no longer be separated from the patriarchal authority-patterns of the church and society in which they exist. To use them is to collude in structures of dominance and dependency which are destructive not only to women but to everyone. Only when those structures have been changed and men no longer assume dominance over women will male words and symbols be acceptable, and whether that is ultimately possible in Christianity and Judaism remains an open question.

Feminist theologians and Women-church

This is not, of course, a new struggle but goes back to the beginning of Christianity, and thousands of years before that to the time of Goddess worship.[9] Feminist theologian and biblical scholar Elisabeth Schüssler Fiorenza reconstructs the struggle that took place in Jesus' own time between his vision of a community open to all, where women were fully included and played a leading part, and the patriarchal society and religious leaders of his time. In Jesus' ministry, Fiorenza says, 'God is experienced as all-inclusive love, . . . a God of graciousness and goodness who accepts everyone without exception' (1983, p.130). Fiorenza associates this God with the female divine wisdom, Sophia, and says Jesus probably understood himself as the prophet and child of Sophia. She is 'a people-loving spirit who shares the throne of God', and Fiorenza says it is as her messenger that Jesus calls 'all who labour and are heavy laden' and promises them rest and shalom (1983, p.134).

Fiorenza claims the Jesus movement was egalitarian, included women's leadership, and challenged and opposed the patriarchal ethos through the praxis of equal discipleship. In place of the patriarchal family it put a neo-familial community, one that does not include fathers, i.e. those who claim the authority of the father, because that is reserved for God alone. Men are present as brothers, sons, uncles, cousins, friends etc. Insofar as the new 'family' of Jesus has no room for 'fathers', it implicitly rejects their power and status and thus claims that in the messianic community all patriarchal structures are abolished. What Fiorenza argues through this reconstruction is that in the discipleship of equals the 'role' of women is not peripheral or trivial, but at the centre and thus of utmost importance to the praxis of 'solidarity from below' (p.152). As a feminist vision, she says, 'the basilea (or "Kingdom") vision of Jesus calls all women without exception to wholeness and selfhood, as well as to solidarity with those women who are impoverished, the maimed, the outcasts of our society and church' (p.153). In the face of the violence such a vision and commitment will encounter, it enables us not to despair or give up the struggle. It empowers us to walk upright, freed from the double oppression of societal and religious sexism and prejudice' (1983, pp.153-4).

Even in Jesus' time the patriarchal side won out, but feminist resistance and challenge has kept re-emerging ever since – in the Montanists,

Gnostics, medieval mystics, Quakers and many others. Like Fiorenza, Rosemary Ruether also stays within the Christian church, working toward a transformed Christianity which denounces all systems of domination and calls for mutuality among all people regardless of sex, race or social group and between human beings and the earth.[10]

Because of the church's continuing attachment to patriarchy, Fiorenza and Ruether have joined with many others to form Women-church,[11] a community of Christian women in many countries around the world who are making a profound affirmation of themselves as church, and a corresponding public challenge to the sinful assumption of power by the patriarchal authority-figures and male-dominated councils, the pope included. Women have moved from the margins to the centre. It is from such communities of women, acting together, and from the lives of women who live 'the option for our women selves',[12] that the new deep symbols will emerge.

Women's spirituality and Goddess religion

There is of course a multiplicity of ways in which women's spiritual experience is being expressed and named. Many women reject the possibility of transforming Christianity or Judaism or other patriarchal religions, and are constructing a more wholistic, life-affirming, joyful meaning-system from their own experience and from earlier and other traditions.

Charlene Spretnak[13] connects 'women's elemental power' with 'our power to form people from our very flesh and blood and then to nourish them from our own breasts', with 'the fact that we run on cosmic time, i.e. share the cycles of the moon', and with 'many moments in a woman's life wherein she gains experiential knowledge, in a powerful body/mind union, of the holistic truths of spirituality' (p.xvii). Referring to 'reclaimed' menstruation, to the 'peaceful, expansive mindstate' after orgasm, and to pregnancy, natural childbirth, and motherhood, Spretnak says 'the experiences inherent in women's sexuality are expressions of the essential, holistic nature of life on Earth; they are "body parables" of the profound oneness and interconnectedness of all matter/energy, which physicists have discovered in recent decades at the subatomic level. . . . In a culture that honored, rather than denigrated such "body truth", the holistic realities would be guiding principles of ethics and structure.' (p.xviii). Spretnak rejects patriarchal religion for many reasons: its emphasis on union with God after death; the divisions among people, with infidels, 'unclean people' and women not being considered to be full persons; its emphasis on the sinfulness of men, and even more on that of women; the judgmental Father God; and obedience to 'His will', with fear, guilt and alienation as some of its results. Spretnak accepts that some women are comfortable with the Goddess image and some prefer not to have any anthropomorphised image at all, but in any case she points out that the meaning of the Goddess is very different from that of God. No one, she says, is interested in revering a 'Yahweh with a skirt' – a 'distant, judgmental, manipulative figure of power who holds us all in a state of terror.' The revival of the Goddess, she says, has resonated with so many people because of what She symbolises: 'All forms of being are One, continually renewed in cyclic rhythms of birth, maturation, death. That is the meaning of Her triple aspect – the waxing, full, and waning moon; the maiden, mother, and wise crone. The Goddess honors union and process, the cosmic dance, the eternally vibrating flux of matter/energy. There is no 'party line' of Goddess worship; rather, each person's process of perceiving and living Her truth is a movement in the larger dance' (xvii).

Many women are interested in Goddess religion today as a way of finding out what our European heritage was like before the change to patriarchal gods took place. They are discovering what Merlin Stone called a 'vast and major religion, one that had affected the lives of multitudes of people over thousands of years.'[14] The period of Goddess-worship in Europe lasted over 25,000 years, whereas the time span of patriarchal religions, including biblical religions, goes back only about 5000 years. In breaking the huge silence about this long period of Goddess worship and its violent suppression, Merlin Stone, Marija Gimbutas and others are revealing the Judaeo-Christian tradition as constructed within history. Their work is thus having a profoundly relativising effect. Yahweh and the concept of male monotheism are de-absolutised, and alternatives become imaginable and possible.

The name Goddess is, I believe, not so much an image as a metaphor, a way of referring to the creative energy of the universe in a female way. As such, it is perfectly appropriate in some contexts, but in others still carries some of the limitations of personification and of separating out the 'divine' from the cosmic dance. It illustrates how difficult it can be to free our imagination from an inherited symbolic system, and many women prefer not to use it. Nevertheless Carol Christ makes a good case for keeping the Goddess symbol, in her article 'Why Women Need the Goddess'.[15] She argues that since symbols function at deep non-rational levels of the psyche, they must be replaced rather than simply rejected. Otherwise the mind reverts to them at times of crisis. Christ shows how Goddess symbolism 'undergirds and legitimates the concerns of the women's movement, much as God symbolism in Christianity undergirded the interests of men in patriarchy'(p.276). She recognises that women interpret this symbol in many different ways, and suggests the varying interpretations should be acknowledged. Of the many meanings of the Goddess, Christ chooses four to discuss: first, as a symbol of the 'legitimacy of female power as a beneficent and independent power'(p.277), in stark contrast with the view of patriarchy that women are dependent beings and that women's power is inferior and dangerous; second, the affirmation of the female body and the life cycle expressed in it, its connections with cycles of nature, and acceptance of aging and death as well as life; third, the positive valuation of will in a Goddess-centred ritual, encouraging the assertion of individual will, not in the arbitrary ego-centric way of patriarchy but in co-operation with natural energies and the energies created by the wills of others; and fourth, the celebration of women's bonds to each other, particularly the mother-daughter bond, which is missing or distorted in Christianity and other patriarchal religions and culture because the mother must socialise her daughter to become subordinate to men. In the four areas, Christ says, the 'mood' created by the symbol of the Goddess is one of positive, joyful celebration and affirmation of female freedom and independence, of the female body and will, and of women's bonds to each other, as mothers and daughters, colleagues and co-workers, sisters, friends and lovers (pp.277-286).

The struggle to be free of androcentric language and symbol systems and oppressive patriarchal structures in both church and society is continuing on many fronts. In poetry and art, conversations and stories, political action and women's centres, and in the unspoken self-understanding of many individual women, a new spirituality is being lived and articulated. Women who are rejecting the limitations and injustices of a male-defined world, and moving away from the transcendent male God, find that this releases an energy to live in new ways and discover a more powerful, just and life-affirming spirituality. For some, this energy and vision expresses itself in transforming the Christian tradition; others are reclaiming ancient women's symbols to construct a new languge and structure of mutuality; and many more are intuitively aware of a new and exciting spirituality without yet having the words or symbols for it. The naming of it, particularly in Australia, is hesitant and slow, and happens more in small situations of trust than on public occasions, particularly 'religious' ones. The process of developing our own autonomy, our own culture, has begun. Women are claiming our authority and our power to name. But the patriarchal structures and language are still in place. As women we are still being born.

M.T.

Notes

1 Elisabeth Schüssler Fiorenza defines patriarchy not as a system where all men have power over all women, but as 'a social-cultural system in which a few men have power over other men, women, children, slaves and colonized people' (*In Memory of Her*, Crossroad, New York, 1983, p.29). She describes it as 'a male pyramid of graded subordinations and exploitations' which 'specifies women's oppression in terms of the class, race, country, or religion of the men to whom we "belong"' (*Bread Not Stone*, Beacon Press, Boston, 1984, p.xiv). (Subsequent references to these two texts are indicated at the end of each quotation by the publication date and page references.)
2 Mary Daly, *Beyond God the Father: Toward a Philosophy of Women's Liberation*, Beacon Press, Boston, 1973, p.19).
3 In an ABC radio program on Memory (*Encounter*, 21 May 1989), Jewish people spoke of the continuing hurtful and damaging effect which Christian anti-Semitic statements have on them, especially the things they heard in their childhood. One man said that when he was a boy he was chased down the street by a group

of boys shouting 'Christ-killer!' He didn't know what Christ was, and certainly hadn't killed him, and he now feels the incident traumatised him in some way.

4 Nelle Morton, *The Journey is Home*, Beacon Press, Boston, 1985, p.205.
5 Mary Daly, *op.cit.* pp.13–43.
6 For an application of Thomas Kuhn's notion of paradigms to theology, see Elisabeth Schüssler Fiorenza, *In Memory of Her*, p.xxi.
7 Ntozake Shange, *for colored girls who have considered suicide when the rainbow is enuf*, Bantam Books, New York, 1980, p.67.
8 Mary Daly, *op.cit.*, p.34.
9 The following discussion of Elisabeth Schüssler Fiorenza, women's spirituality, and Goddess religion is developed more fully in my chapter, 'Religion', in *Feminist Knowledge: Critique and Construct*, Routledge, London, 1990.
10 See Rosemary Radford Ruether, *Sexism and God-Talk: Toward a Feminist Theology*, Beacon Press, Boston, 1983.
11 See Rosemary Radford Ruether, *Women-Church: Theology and Practice of Feminist Liturgical Communities*, Harper & Row, San Francisco, 1985.
12 Elisabeth Schüssler Fiorenza, 'The Will to Choose or to Reject: Continuing Our Critical Work', in Letty M. Russell, ed., *Feminist Interpretation of the Bible*, Blackwell, Oxford and New York, 1985, p.128.
13 Charlene Spretnak, ed., *The Politics of Women's Spirituality: Essays on the Rise of Spiritual Power within the Feminist Movement*, Anchor Books, New York, 1982. Page references are given at the end of each quotation.
14 Merlin Stone, *The Paradise Papers: The Suppression of Women's Rites*, Virago, London, 1976, p.14.
15 Carol P. Christ, 'Why Women Need the Goddess: Phenomenological, Psychological, and Political Reflections' in Carol P. Christ and Judith Plaskow, eds., *Womanspirit Rising: A Feminist Reader in Religion*, Harper & Row, San Francisco, (1979).

CHAPTER TWO

The issue of blood

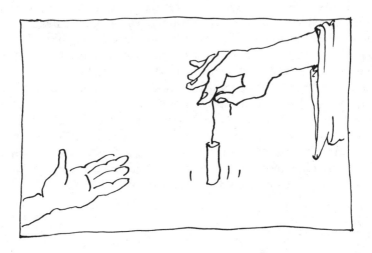

Is menstruation a blessing or a curse? In Christianity, menstruation represents the ultimate impurity; in common language, it's 'the curse'. Yet traditions more ancient than Christianity link menstruation with the most sacred period of the full moon, and some women today celebrate the menses as a blessing.

We can begin to explore the meaning of menstruation by telling our own stories about it and listening to those of contemporary women, stories which often betray ambivalence. Behind these stories are various traditions bearing the dominant voices of forefathers and the faint voices of foremothers. Even a brief exploration of these traditions uncovers the sources of our ambivalence. After listening to these voices ancient and modern, we can attend to contemporary feminist theorists who promote women's self-understanding by reclaiming healing traditions and critiquing harmful ones.

In this chapter I present a mosaic of women's stories, a sampling of traditional beliefs, and a taste of contemporary feminist thought. The chapter attempts to think through this regular, universal occurrence in the female world, so that we, late twentieth century women, may know and be more fully our centred female selves.

Our experience

To talk of menstruation is to break a taboo. Such talk evokes a rush of conflicting feelings: fear, embarrassment, shame, guilt, anger, confusion, isolation and loathing, as well as elation, relief, delight, fulfilment, excitement and solidarity. It evokes as well a welter of images like safety pins, belts, rags, tampons, towels, brown paper parcels, stains, sheets, backs of dresses, smells, clots and matted hair, and always blood. These feelings and images construct the personal, political, and spiritual agendas connected with menstruation, that essentially private, indisputably universal experience of women. In order to cover these interrelated agendas, I will consider the significance of menstruation for relations on four levels: with ourselves, with immediate others, with society at large, and with divinity. Listening to menstruation stories, we can hear how relations change as people accept and/or reject the inevitable female experience.

To begin with ourselves: menstruation is a body matter. Whether we like it or not, our bodies change dramatically somewhere between the ages of nine and eighteen. Menstrual bleeding appears along with breasts and hairiness of armpits, legs and genital area. We have no choice about these things, they are our fate. Impossible to ignore, this changed body can be welcomed with delight, accepted timidly, or roundly rejected. Most give it a mixed reception. Listen to this response to the question, 'how was puberty for you?', written in 1988 by a sixteen year old:

> Well let's see — what can I say? It came and went without me taking much notice of it. It's not that I didn't have any problems — I had my fair share — it's more that I didn't take any notice of the changes that were occurring. I accepted them without any questions, because after all what was happening was not unique to me, everyone experienced it. I can always remember my Mum, and how nervous she was when she told me about growing up. 'Do you know what a period is?' . . . her exact words. I don't know why, but I didn't — sure I'd heard people talking but I didn't take any notice of what they were saying. I was terribly naive. My first thoughts on the subject were disbelief, and of course revolt. What a terrible thing to happen — how could such an awful thing be 'normal'? Mum made me keep some pads and a spare pair of undies at the bottom of my school bag . . . 'just in case'. When I first got my period I used these. It was only two days after when I'd run out of anything to use that I told Mum. I can remember how I did it — I turned my back to her and told her straight out. I was embarrassed. Of course I didn't tell anyone else. Of course they didn't tell me. If the subject was brought up we'd talk about it, and be sympathetic and understanding. Maybe that is why puberty was quite easy. My friends were sympathetic and supportive as they too knew what I was going through. We all took it in our stride. After all, growing up is a part of life.
>
> Anna, 16[1]

What a range of feelings. From initial horror and revolt through a period of acute embarrassment, to feelings of solidarity and a comfortable acceptance apparent in the frank, easy style of writing. But the ambivalence, contradictions even, are encoded in the written account. On the one hand, puberty 'came and went without me taking much notice of it', but on the other, Anna can still, some years later, remember her mother's exact words, 'Do you know what a period is?', and her petrified stance when announcing that her own period had arrived. Such acuteness of memory sits uneasily with the stated matter-of-factedness. One wonders whether these 'I'm all right' assertions are closer to a certain resignation and a somewhat begrudging acceptance of one's fate, or to a thankfulness that one is normally female in step with one's friends and nature, a kind of pride in maturity and excitement in the possibilities.

Many stories express strong negativity towards the self, not just on the initial discovery of menstruation, but throughout one's menstruating life.

These words of novelist Doris Lessing recall many conversations with Australian women:

> I hear my voice shrill and I stop myself. I realise my period has caught up with me; there's a moment in every month when it does, and then I get irritated because it makes me feel helpless and out of control.[2]

And even more forcefully,

> I like the smell of sex, of sweat, of skin or hair. But the faintly dubious, essentially stale smell of menstrual blood, I hate. And resent. It is a smell that feels strange, even to me, an imposition from the outside – a bad smell emanating from me.[3]

So common are these feelings of hatred, resentment and self-disgust among women, that we may fail to recognise how extraordinary they are. Undoubtedly, these negative feelings arise from internalised misogynous traditions; they are indeed 'an imposition from the outside'. We can get in touch with their inappropriateness by comparing the female experience of menstruating with reactions to other bodily excretions and emissions. We all spit, sneeze, cry, defecate, urinate and fart, for example, usually in private, and sometimes, intentionally or not, in public. We may feel slightly uncomfortable, even thoroughly embarrassed, about these activities, particularly in front of others. The puritan lurking in most of us will always find the messiness of bodily emissions distasteful. Despite such passing distaste, we generally regard them with a measure of equanimity, if not private satisfaction, and we would certainly be judged as neurotic if we resented and hated them, seeing them as impositions from the outside.

These are appropriate comparisons, for, like menstruation, these simple bodily activities require a degree of submission to necessity. Being part of the human condition, they are our fate and as such are the subjects of myths and taboos. For all their being imposed on us willy nilly, none of them gives rise to disgust and resentment, or to hatred and a fear of contamination in the same degree as menstruation. Indeed, to find an adequate comparison, we have to think of diseases. Such a comparison may seem far-fetched, until we recall that today's middle-aged women can easily remember being described, when they had their periods, by the quaint, destructive, give-away term, 'unwell'. Most women today, like Sue, register annoyance at its continued use:

> 'You don't swim when you're . . . er . . . unwell?' my grandmother asked with well-intentioned kindness. 'It's not wise you know'. I felt irritated as much by

her coy use of the term 'unwell' as by my own inhibitions (no doubt inherited from her) at her intrusion into my privacy. But I also felt antagonism because I knew she had sent her daughter, my mother, to boarding school without even rudimentary knowledge of what lay in store for a developing girl. The onset of menstruation had been a terrifying shock indeed for my poor mother.

Sue, 55

The term 'unwell', which is just one step away from complete silence, may have practically disappeared but the stifling embarrassment which gave rise to its use remains. Reflecting on the attitudes of the succeeding generations, Sue notes the same inability to speak openly and comfortably:

When my mother proceeded to enlighten me, not wishing history to repeat itself, I feigned some surprise having already gleaned most of the facts from my friends at boarding school. I'm sure her information was very scanty – there were certainly no books or diagrams to explain why it was happening as in my own daughters' days – and the topic was not discussed with my younger sisters until they were deemed ready. I remember the consternation during a family picnic when one sister, idly looking through a women's magazine, asked: 'Mummy, what's Tampax?'. Visibly reddening, and with a hasty 'Sort of cotton wool, dear', my mother created a diversion!

The language has changed but the prudery, euphemistically called modesty, and the embarrassment have not. As much by what they did not say as by the inadequacy of their own faltering words, women from generation to generation have passed on a shameful secret, giving rise to guilt, anger and resentment.

Ignorance has undoubtedly been one of the major causes for the 'dirty secret' mentality. Deprived of language, women often did not know *what* to tell adolescent girls, not even what words to use. A profound ignorance appears in most older women's stories, a closet learning evoking fantastic fears and self-doubt.

When I was ten or eleven I would look at a book which was hidden in my mother's wardrobe; I suspect it was a medical or health book. Round thirteen when I was sick at school my mother told me I was going to get my period. I associated this with a diagram of a circular shape in the book. I did not recognise anything like this on my own body so I thought something would have to grow on me. I kept waiting. I was surprised when I got my own period as nothing had yet grown. Off and on over the years I have wondered what I saw. Just recently I saw a diagram of the cervical opening and I realised that was what it was.

Patricia, 48

Adolescent girls suffered from a condition called periods which, as they were described to me, I interpreted as bleeding, occurring once at about age 14 and once again at age 40 and that was all. I was not told what part of me would bleed. The single stricture was to be very careful of boys after menstruating began. It was difficult to see what all this had to do with those funny little pieces of cotton wool and elastic with which I was presented at age twelve whilst being told that I was now a young lady. Young ladies *never* soiled their clothes and were very careful to conceal any evidence of bleeding. It all sounded rather exciting and very secret, a secret to be carefully hidden from my father and brother. It seemed as if men didn't know about the changes which took place in a girl's body as she grew up or what these changes had to do with the men themselves. Questions were left unanswered. The overall impression with which the young woman was left was that her condition was not only secret but shameful. If anything went wrong (and what did this mean?), it was her fault for being careless or wanton but, again, these words and their implications were not explained.

Caroline, 67

I recall very vividly when my periods started. I had no idea what was happening and thought I was ill. When my mother told me this happened every month I was furious − I felt trapped and could see that my swimming was going to be spoilt. I also felt it was quite unfair that this should happen to girls and not boys. My mother came into the room at night, with the light out, to explain further about babies − God planted a seed in your heart! I remained embarrassed and uninformed for years.

Katherine, 59

Ignorance and secrecy distanced us not only from each other but from our own bodies. We were forbidden to examine our bodies, let alone take delight in them. Not knowing which part would bleed, expecting a growth to appear somewhere, or wondering how a seed would be planted, must have caused anxiety, and yet, written from the distance of many years, this fear received less emphasis than the quaintness of the predicament in which these women found themselves.

We may well judge the above accounts as interesting but irrelevant for post-60s generations. But today's adolescent girls, despite being generally better informed by parent-teacher nights, science classes and frank media coverage, still often find menstruation a 'major problem'. Embarrassment and ignorance remain common.

I was in Year 6 when I first got my periods. I knew what it was sort of but I wasn't really sure. I couldn't believe that I had them because it was only the tall girls in the grade that had their periods. And I was the smallest one.

I thought something was wrong with me. I remember thinking it was horrible and all I wanted to be was a boy. What made it worse was that we had swimming lessons at school for that whole week and I had my periods. I nearly died when Mum told me that I wouldn't be able to go swimming. I'd have to stay at school. I had to explain my MAJOR PROBLEM to my teacher. I was so embarrassed. I wouldn't let my Mum talk to anyone or tell anyone that I had my periods because I thought no one else I knew had them. Mum and I had big arguments over her telling other mothers. She was proud her baby had reached puberty but I wasn't.

Felicity, 15[4]

'All I wanted to be was a boy'. Felicity, like 16-year-old Anna quoted above, is initially horrified and rejects adult femaleness. She feels alienated from herself, from her peer group and from significant adults. She demands privacy from the imagined interest of her mother's friends. Yet, her unhappiness arises partly from her perceived isolation: 'I thought no one else I knew had them'.

The balance between respecting individual privacy and affording menstruation a public representation is always difficult to find. How to intimate to an adolescent girl both the specialness of menstruation for her as an individual and its ordinariness as a biological event? Menstrual bleeding is private and particular to each woman: she begins, continues and ends each cycle in her own way. What she wants to share of this experience and with whom is up to her. Menstrual bleeding is also public and universal. It is studied in science and medicine; it is the subject of law suits, of art, of literature and of education curricula; and it gives rise to primary and secondary industry, as well as to economic decisions. And this bodily event happens to half the population of the world for half their lives: to be human female is to menstruate.

Only personal stories have been quoted so far and there are as many of these as there are individual women. To sketch the public image of menstruation is far simpler. In the popular mind, menstruation is about sanitation. It is about cleaning up an unfortunate mess as quickly and quietly as possible. Advertisements for related products all announce: use this and avoid the restrictions, discomfort and embarrassment that go with this condition – with this product it will be as though it never happened. Divorcing us from our own experience, advertising images pretend to reassure while in fact they promote self-doubt: maidens in flowing white float through fields of flowers; robust women romp along the shore in bikinis or stretch to serve in snowy tennis-dresses; sophisticates in sleek evening dress glide through the night-club world. Nothing shows: nobody could possibly know. Why, you don't even know yourself!

The law is yet another public institution which deals with menstruation, differently from the advertising world, though no less deviously. The law usually relates menstruation to questions of responsibility: are women in general fit for some kinds of employment? To what degree was this woman guilty of a crime? Media accounts of individual law suits record delicate references to the possibility of diminished responsibility or impaired judgment at certain times. Beneath these references lie male fears of female hormones, a fear translated into the euphemism, 'women's problems'. Or perhaps it is not so much a fear of hormones as a fear of females and the hormones are simply an excuse for exerting control. Whatever the reason, legal pleading, at least as reported in the media, frequently gives the impression that women are at the mercy of wayward hormones in ways from which men and their hormones are immune.

A number of scholars, artists, dramatists and comedians have contributed to changing the public image of menstruation by breaking away from the coy terms enshrouding and mystifying it. Constance Frazer, for example, in her poem, 'Stains', clearly names the experience of menstruation with all its inherent ambivalence.[5] This public stating of private questions contributes to demystifying the experience while also beginning to remythologise it in a more positive way.

> My unmentionable
> secret — the blood
> my skin
> fails to hold
>
> and the small dread
> sensation inside-myself spreading
> intensifying
> into pain
>
> in and out
> of my life miserably
> inevitably
> but why
>
> anxiety
> tightening muscles
> into shackles?
> Oh go
>
> Shove a trusty tampax in! —
> just for
> convenience of course
> not to pretend

it never happens (is it
because
our highly-coloured stain
reminds them of butcher's blood?)

So many times
over and over
to endure this
harsh visitor

but why feel shame?
When men feel that
small damp spit of
seed — they are proud!

Asking the question is one way to exorcise shame. Another is to declare one's experience in the loudest voice possible. Robyn Archer's song 'Menstruation Blues', does exactly this.[6] At first glance, Archer may seem to have simply turned the idealised images of advertisers and the pussy-footing respectability of legal terms inside out. The lyrics may shock, by putting menstruation in the worst possible light. Melody and performance-style accompany lyrics, however, and must also be considered. Here first are the lyrics:

I got the menstruation, the menstruation blues
And I got 'em so hard I don't know how to lose them

I can feel my life blood flowin', flowin' down the drain
And the hardest damn thing to face is that next month it's all
gonna happen again

I got a pain in my guts and my head is spinnin' around
I feel like the lowest kind of animal crawling on the ground

I can't chuck, I can't even fuck
Honey this thing has put me out of luck

No one wants to mouth around that fishy old smell
Lordy I'm so lonesome and I feel like hell

I had to spend my dope money on a bunch of fanny rags
I'm 'bout to tell you that this thing is gettin' to be one hell
of a drag.

No purified, spiritualised, transcending images here. The animality of menstruation is on display and we may well recoil from the lyrics. But a gap opens between the starkness of the words and the rhythmic blues melody delivered in a raunchy, provocative, up-front style. Crudity of words, catchy attractiveness of melody, provocativenes s of style all announce that the secret is out, not in a whimper but a joyous wail. Essentially, the song is a celebration of female experience, though not without ambivalence. After all, the discomforts of menstruation are not good, while it is good to feel part of the community of women, and both kinds of feelings can belong to menstruation. By acknowledging pain and celebrating solidarity, 'Menstruation Blues' avoids both denial through romanticism and attention-seeking through wallowing in a degrading female fate.

Songs like this one, frank education programmes, and a measure of openness in the media, are all slowly changing the public image of menstruation. As public image and personal experience temper and inform each other, future stories will, hopefully, reflect less unnecessary pain. By means of the stories quoted above, I have pointed to the pain of being alienated from our own bodies. These same stories also bear on the significance of menstruation for relations with all significant others, with mothers, fathers, siblings, peers, lovers, husbands, and unborn children. Again there are millions of stories barely hinted at here, all part of that largely untold story of female culture.

Women frequently find their periods unwelcome for reasons to do with interpersonal relations: my mother embarrasses and angers me by announcing my periods to other mothers, putting my dates on the calender for all the family to see, or perhaps by ignoring me, letting me find out the 'dirty secret' as best I can; my father changes towards me, avoiding playful touching, deferring to me as if I were a stranger, over-protecting me as though I were a piece of china about to be broken; my sisters and brothers are curious, invading my space; boys taunt me, making coarse jokes because I am too big or too small; my girl friends are silent, making me think it's happening only to me; people in shops watch me buying Modess; sales assistants comment with their eyes when I ask for tampons; teachers expect me to go swimming or take part in gym classes and how can I possibly explain and I don't know what might be showing; a lover disdains me refusing to let his penis be bloodied, or he seeks intercourse when I feel bloated and uncomfortable; I've become pregnant when I don't want a child and I can't cope; a child has not been conceived this month, like all the endless months before; my children make demands on me when my body calls out for rest; my boss and my clients demand extra work; my doctor recommends a hysterectomy because the bleeding is too heavy or too frequent; I flood at unexpected times, when will this bleeding finally stop? Whether I am fifteen or fifty, everybody and everything can be affected because my body does this strange thing every month, thwarting my desires, and upsetting my relationships. I am no longer in control.

Women also celebrate their periods for reasons just as diverse: my mother answered all my questions and I'm excited; my father brought me a bunch of red roses; my brothers treat me with respect, letting me have the bathroom to myself; my sister showed me how to use tampons; we spent the whole recess time talking about our periods; I'm so pleased they've come, I thought it'd never happen; I rang my best friend to tell her I'd got them too; boys notice me now; I really want to have a child some day; I'm so relieved I didn't get pregnant; my husband and I enjoy intercourse knowing I won't get pregnant; my lover is always especially tender when I am bleeding; my family gets the meals and does the washing up when I've got my periods; my boss and I do extra work for each other on those days; all the female staff have their periods at the same time so we go out for lunch once a month; I feel close to all women, even ones I don't know; I feel linked with the moon and the tides, it's like a recurring mystical awakening; my body pulses in rhythm with nature. For many reasons both lofty and mundane, and at all ages, periods are celebrated. Often they engender intimacy between women, between women and men, and between women and nature.

The mosaic of stories presented in this chapter is typical in a Western Christian or post-Christian society. Details vary between individuals and groups, but a similar range of feelings and images always emerges. I have suggested that menstruation informs our relationships on several levels: with our own female bodies, with significant others as well as with strangers, with society, and with nature. It is both a public and a private event. I have not discussed the religious or spiritual significance of menstruation, though some will have read the above stories with this significance in mind. Menstruation, like all experience, does have spiritual significance; it is revelatory. Yet, some religious traditions have presented the menstruating woman, not as a revelation of life and death, of divinity itself, but as a symbol of defilement. Christianity is such a tradition. I will now look briefly at the ways in which feminist writers have re-evaluated and revised these traditions or gained from other traditions the impetus needed to move beyond destructive images.

Our experience and religious traditions

In Christian and post-Christian cultures, the menstruating woman is a symbol of defilement. How did this come about? Why did women collude in establishing an arrangement that harms us? Why do we let it continue? Feminists have asked these questions for a long time and with increasing urgency. Modern feminist scholars give various explanations, psychological, philosophical, anthropological and economic. I am concerned here with the ways in which religion, with its symbolic systems, has contributed to present arrangements, an area in which much scholarly work has been done. I begin with the work of two contemporary American theologians, Mary Daly and Rosemary Radford Ruether, both of whom have, for more than twenty years, analysed the role of religion in constructing patriarchy.

Dualisms: micro and macro levels

Daly and Ruether have pointed to a series of harmful splits or dualisms in contemporary Western ways of viewing the world.[7] According to their analyses, the most harmful split occurs within the self, in the alienation of the person from his or her own body, a split that is most evident in the fear of sexuality, both our own and others'.[8] This fear appears in the revulsion some women experience towards their bodies when menstruating, a time when they can become a stranger, or worse, an enemy, to themselves. Feminists have argued that this most basic form of alienation is replicated on a progressively larger scale until, in its most encompassing form, a transcendent, all-powerful, all-knowing father God resides in a heavenly realm totally removed from his lowly, sinful, dependent creatures, the most debased of whom is the prostitute, the woman defined publicly by her sexual activity. From a very great height indeed, this transcendent God reinforces a series of interrelated dualisms extending all the way from the split within the self, alienating us from our bodies to the divine-human split promoting an idolatry destructive of humanity.

Between these micro and macro levels of alienation, versions of similar dualisms find expression in myriad poetic and religious images, in symbolic structures and in the social order. Always one side is idealised and the other denigrated in what is essentially a pattern of domination and subordination. One classic example, possibly the earliest and most pervading, is the earth–sky duality in which the sky is imaged as Heaven, dwelling place of transcendent divinity, and the depths of the earth as Hell, the domain of Satan and all his legions, the kingdom of evil. In Christian mythology this image is well-nigh dead. Certainly it no longer commonly prevails. But it lingers in the Western imagination and we are just now beginning to recognise the destructive consequences of this domination-subordination model. That harmony between earth and sky has been broken is witnessed by the greenhouse effect and all its associated problems.[9] In some sense, the neglected and idealised sky and the abused and denigrated earth are taking revenge, or better, giving notice. In the long term, this patriarchal, dichotomising model destroys both poles of the duality.

Dualisms: male and female images of divinity

This Christian mythology with its roots in Hebrew religion grew out of, and eventually conquered, earlier less destructive mythologies, traces of which remain in Christianity. For thousands of years the great Mother Goddess along with vegetation and fertility goddesses were widely venerated as is evident from innumerable surviving artefacts.[10] The status of these Goddesses and their effect on societal structures and prevailing world views is a matter of lively scholarly debate.[11] What is certain, however, is that by the time writing was invented (about 3500 BCE) the patriarchal invasions of the Mediterranean world had begun and an ideology of domination-subordination was already in train, though nowhere nearly as firmly established and invisible as in our own time. It is also clear that innumerable and violent attempts were made over a lengthy period to extinguish all trace of the Goddess, and that as a result of this struggle male Gods systematically supplanted powerful Goddesses, a cosmogony which reflected the establishment of imperialistic kingships. With the gradual and violent establishment of Hebrew monotheism (1800–1400 BCE), the religion which shapes so much of our own cultural heritage, the Goddesses were eventually supplanted by a single male God, imaged as Father, King, Lord. Devotion to the Goddess was still being publicly enacted, however, when Christianity was establishing itself and the last of the Goddess temples was not closed until 380 CE under the order of Emperor Theodosius.[12]

Despite this highly significant patriarchal victory, female images of divinity have persisted within both Judaism and Christianity, albeit in drastically weakened forms. The virgin Mary, for example, is a remnant of divinity imaged in female form.[13] On the doctrinal level, she is infinitely inferior to Christ, since she is human and he divine, but on the imaginative level she is often preferred to Christ and even to God and there are images of her revealing an unmistakeable acceptance of the divinity in female form. But Mary is an ambiguous figure, being simultaneously over-esteemed and under-esteemed. In relation to other humans, she is far superior, warranting divine titles like Mother of God, Star of the Sea, Queen of Heaven, while in relation to Christ or God the Father, she is, as just noted, infinitely inferior being merely human. Sometimes human companion, sometimes Goddess, the figure of Mary is effectively split off from both the human and divine, unable to integrate the two levels. Oscillating between idealised humanity and dubious divinity, this figure can easily signify the denigration of women and has almost certainly functioned in this way. It is commonly noted, for example, that within Christendom, the oppression of women is greatest in cultures which especially venerate Mary, an observation that suggests a correlation between the idealisation of the mythical woman and the subordination of flesh-and-blood women.

Mention of 'flesh and blood' brings us back to the experience of menstruating women in the late twentieth century, and it is instructive to observe how far Mary, as mythical figure and even as historical woman, is removed from this experience. Mary's asexual purity has functioned, within the tradition, as substitute and compensation for human sexuality with all its messy bodily emissions. Mary alone remains immaculate. According to orthodox Christian tradition, she was exempt from all taint of sexuality: ever a Virgin, she never had intercourse with any man, Jesus having being conceived of the Holy Ghost; she is rarely, in modern times, imaged as breast feeding her divine child, despite an ancient heritage portraying her as suckling mother[14]; and she is never, to my knowledge, imaged as menstruating. In fact, a nexus of doctrines, myths and symbols specifically protects her from the uncleanness of menstruation.

The myth of the Fall as it appears in the Hebrew Bible and in later Christian interpretations asserts that Eve, because she succumbed to the serpent and disobeyed God, was punished by experiencing pain in childbirth and a desire for her husband.[15] This punishment fell on all women as daughters of Eve: women, like men, are born in the state of original sin, as a result of which we are condemned to die and both motherhood and sexuality are experienced as cursed or at least unclean. Mary alone escapes this fate, 'our tainted nature's solitary boast'. According to the doctrine of the Immaculate Conception, this unique woman, because she was to be the Mother of God, was conceived and born free from original sin, thus justifying her assumption into heaven, hence her escape from death, and her freedom from the uncleanness of sexuality and the pain of childbirth. By implication, Mary, unlike the rest of us, never had her periods, whereas Eve, whose name means 'mother of all the living', most certainly did. In the mythical figures of Mary and Eve the dualism of heaven and earth appears once again – a dualism reducing actual women to an undesirable choice between the stereotypical figures of virgin and whore.

This is an orthodox view of Mary, but of course myths, and even dogmas, are never so clear cut. Mary Immaculate is an extraordinarily complex figure. In Christian mythology, the Immaculate Virgin with the twelve stars around her head and the moon at her feet has conquered evil as symbolised by the serpent on which she stands triumphantly. This serpent, representing all evil, is that same mythical figure from the Genesis account of the Fall, but the serpent is not always a symbol of evil. In ancient Goddess religions,[16] in the gospels themselves,[17] as well as in mythologies of our own day,[18] the snake signifies wisdom, healing and sexuality. And even in the Genesis account, the figure is not wholly evil, being 'more subtle than all the beasts of the field' and knowing the secret of immortality. In the mythologies of many cultures, the snake, sloughing off its skin and appearing newly created, is associated with the waxing and waning moon, and both are symbols of the death-resurrection cycle, part of the Great Round. These two symbols are also widely linked with menstruation. Some cultures tell tales of women being bitten or penetrated by snakes, an experience that brings on menstruation,[19] and the moon has long been linked with the menses because of their common monthly cycle. Reverberations of these meanings remain in the image of the Virgin Mary decorated with the stars and the moon, and the serpent crushed beneath her feet.[20] Even this rarefied image of Mary at the peak of her chastity and most removed from all carnality cannot be entirely divorced from the serpent, about which linger these most ancient meanings. Ironically, the very association of the defeated serpent with this transcendentally pure female image, signals the immortality of wisdom and sexuality and the links between them. Immaculate Mary, unlike the ancient Cretan Goddess, cannot raise the snake triumphantly above her head, but at least the figure of the snake, although debased, survives.

Protected by modern scientific knowledge, we may well feel unaffected by, even scornful of, such ancient myths, but, as Mary Daly sees it, they are embedded in our psyches, liberating or oppressing us.[21] Scorned and suppressed, they do their work in the unconscious. To take an example:

the symbolism of wholeness apparent in the myth of Mary ever a Virgin with unbroken hymen even after childbirth, remains with us in a fear that using tampons will damage virginity, one's priceless maidenhead.[22] Consider this recent statement from a fourteen-year-old girl in a group discussion in a comprehensive school in England:

> We don't like to buy Tampax ourselves in case someone sees us – they might think we are tramps or slags or something. You know how people think – neighbours and all that. I ask Mum to get them for me. I'd never tell my boyfriend that I use Tampax. You know what he'd think don't you. I hope he'll never guess that I've got a period.[23]

The experience of menstruating is denied here. Conscious of others' opinions, her boyfriend's and her neighbours', this young woman is prime material for the advertisers' ploys as she splits away from her own body experience. So much remains unstated, for the 'dirty secret' mentality dictates that this female experience may not be named. This denial says clearly that periods are defiling and that using tampons, like having intercourse, is damaging; it says, 'I am defiled, I am damaged, but no one need know'.[24] And lurking in the unstated is the infamous double standard whereby girls are required to be virgins at the time of marriage and boys are not: boys are always whole and girls can never be, except for Mary who never menstruated and who remained a virgin before, during, and after childbirth.

Dualism: nature and culture

This discrepancy between female and male experience signifies another key dualism, the nature/culture split frequently analysed by feminist scholars.[25] Woman is to nature as man is to culture: she is immanent, material, inchoate, emotional and identified with the earth; while he is transcendent, spiritual, differentiated and rational and identified with the sky. She is partial, he is whole. Among the innumerable examples of this dichotomy, I mention only one, a recent survey of fifty-five students aged fifteen and sixteen who responded to the question, 'How was puberty for you?'.[26] While every girl in this sample wrote of having periods and nearly all of developing breasts, not one boy referred to erections or wet dreams. This discrepancy can be interpreted in many ways: in the present context I see it as a sign of female identification with nature and male distancing from it. If women's periods are a dirty secret spoken in whispers behind closed doors, male emissions denoting sexuality are not spoken of at all. If Mary is removed from the experiences of menstruation and sexual intercourse, Jesus, as both historical man and mythical figure, is even further removed from male sexual experience. Although my focus here is solely on women's experience and the effect of religious traditions, it must not be forgotten that the current dualistic arrangement is equally harmful for males.[27]

Culture-making male experience is overesteemed to the detriment of both males and nature-identified females, a detriment readily detected in the blood symbolism of the Christian tradition. Christ's blood, spilt on the cross, given in redemption for a condemned humanity, transubstantiated in the form of wine in the daily sacrifice of the Mass, devoutly received as the sacrament of communion between Christians and their God, is a most holy substance, worthy of adoration. Current rituals, rooted in the Christian scriptures and evolving from a long tradition, recognise Christ's blood as nourishing the soul, bringing the possibility of ecstatic union with the divine. The danger with such rituals, as Mary Daly points out, is that they feed necrophilic impulses, turning devotees from life to death.[28] Contemporary images of Christ, no less than earlier ones, are frequently tainted with a sadomasochistic focus on God the Father's demand for retribution, and on details of the Son's agonising death.[29] Blood, undoubtedly a provocative and potentially life-giving symbol, is easily debased.

What is the status of female blood in the Christian tradition? Mary, that figure most nearly approaching divinity, is generally divorced from blood symbolism. She does not menstruate, and blood is not associated with her giving birth to Jesus, nor with her own death. Belonging to a blue-white-gold world, she is rarely dressed in red. Various myths, traditions and scriptural incidents bring her close to blood, but this is usually on account of her association with Jesus, as for example, with the flight into Egypt, the circumcision, the wedding at Cana, and her position at the foot of the cross. Her title, Queen of Martyrs, also associates her with blood, but this role is filled only in Heaven where, one imagines, blood is less messy. Mary's own blood, except perhaps in the image of her sacred heart, is not venerated.

It is the blood of martyrs which, along with Christ's blood, receives attention in the Christian tradition. Detailed accounts of martyrs' deaths often betray a sadomasochistic interest, and some scholars argue that this is especially evident in the case of female martyrs.[30] Agatha's 'breasts are cut off from her bosom' as the Little Office of the Virgin Mary graphically relates each year on her feast day; Margaret Clitherow was pressed to death beneath a door; and Juliana was shattered on a wheel 'until the marrow spurted out'.[31] Such material, sometimes verging on the porno graphic, has been regular fare for generations of priests and men and women in religious orders, often read aloud at meal times! The same voyeurism appears in the intense interest that was shown as today's middle-aged Catholics will remember, in the death of eleven-year-old Maria Goretti, who was stabbed fourteen or was it twenty-eight times while resisting rape. For Catholic girls growing up in the first half of this century, Maria Goretti was a model. The choice was virgin or martyr, no blood spilt or all blood spilt, white or red.

So women's menstrual blood does not appear overtly in Christian symbolism, although it is there beneath the skin. Never celebrated, menstrual blood provokes either denial or ritual purification. It remains in the private domain, largely unnamed except indirectly as, for example, in the churching ceremony which in some Christian denominations used to be mandatory for women after childbirth. Daly's claim that the power of naming has been stolen from us accounts in a general way for the absence of women's blood from Christian symbolism.[32] As contemporary women reclaim the power to name, new images are emerging from female experience. Divinity imaged as a crucified female figure is one.[33] Like many female images in a patriarchal culture, this figure, the Christa, carries ambivalent meanings. For so long has the suffering of women given rise to sadomasochistic pleasure that we need to be wary of the Christa figure or it too will reinforce female suffering. Women's bodies, and particularly the blood of women, have become the raw material of the pornography industry, appearing in debased forms in restricted material as well as in all forms of the media. A necrophilic culture accustomed to feeding on the blood of women cannot quickly or easily recognise any spiritual dimension in female images such as women's menstrual blood. A biophilic religion and culture would, by contrast, associate women's blood with giving birth and life, with acceptance of mortality, and with the willing, active choice of necessary suffering. The imbalance becomes apparent when we reflect that patriarchal culture reserves these positive meanings for those, principally males, who have given their life in the event of war. Contemporary culture, of which religion is one dimension, esteems male blood almost exclusively.

Feminist hypotheses and analyses

The dichotomy, evident in Christian blood symbolism, between culture-making males and nature-identified females is encoded in language and symbolic structures, as well as in our social institutions. Yet there is widespread feminist resistance to this dichotomy. Feminists have shown that women have always contributed to the creation of culture, though this contribution has not been widely acknowledged. These theorists deconstruct the Christian-based cultures of the west, showing that many aspects of them are neither necessary nor natural, and certainly not desirable. They have suggested that the nature–culture dualism represents a projection of male fantasy which allows men to appropriate to themselves the overesteemed qualities of transcendence, rationality and immortality while allocating to women the unwanted underside of immanence, emotionality and mortality. Alienated male experience has reduced the menstruating woman to a symbol of defilement. In Daly's terms, woman is the 'primordial scapegoat'.[34]

A complementary hypothesis suggests that males, being unable to give birth, provided for themselves the substitute satisfaction of creating religion, and culture in general. Ruether points out that giving birth and feeding, two activities naturally and traditionally proper to females, are the basis for key religious rituals, Baptism and Holy Communion, and that leadership of these rituals is generally reserved to males; in fact in the Roman Catholic church to celibate men, that is to those most removed from sexuality and reproduction.[35] According to this hypothesis, religious rituals are compensatory activities, the product of unacknowledged male desire. Certainly, the violent opposition to the ordination of women, particularly to women of menstruating age, would suggest repressed fear and desire, thus giving weight to these two hypotheses.

Feminist visions of the ways to proceed are highly diverse. Consider, for example, the many feminist approaches to menstruation. Some advocate reclaiming the experience by celebrating and honouring menstruation, and bringing it into the public arena. Advocates of this position acknowledge women's identification with nature and are proud of it, seeing women as intuitive, aware of nature's rhythms and in tune with them in a way men are not. Male-identified culture needs to respect and learn from women and nature or it will destroy the planet. This approach highlights the differences between women and men, between nature and culture, while at the same time strongly denying that such differences call for the domination of women by men. Instead, difference is seen as gift, and the particular giftedness of women is desperately needed today.[36]

Other feminists judge that highlighting the specialness of women's experience is reactionary and undesirable. Emphasising the ordinariness of menstruation, they downplay the differences between the sexes and any notion of specialness or separateness. Women are perceived as having the full measure of human potential usually identified with the male and therefore as able to enter fully into what is deemed the important public work of the culture. This is not to imply that women are virtually identical with men, fulfilling the same roles in the same ways. All feminists are interested in structural change, and many believe that the entry of sufficient numbers of women across the spectrum of positions will promote more egalitarian structures. Women a:e seen as men's equals in every sphere, or perhaps as their superiors, but not as having any complementary role, even if it be considered a superior one. Ruether specifically warns against spiritualising female experience and turning our attention inward to the neglect of the public domain. Spiritualising menstruation, for example, might just divert female energy into the private sphere. Distracted by spirituality, women may tend to avoid difficult political struggles and leave the running of the world to men.[37]

The first feminist position outlined above requires that women and nature be more highly valued. The second requires that women not be excluded from certain roles on account of their gender or, put positively, it requires that the categories in which women function be widened. The first approach emphasises the value of the denigrated, underesteemed pole of the culture–nature dualism, and the second encourages women to occupy the forbidden, overesteemed pole. A third broad position can easily be identified. This approach looks to an integration of nature and culture in such a way that women and men can successfully live in the tension between necessity and freedom. Instead of identifying women with the necessities of nature and fate and men with the freedom of culture, we are all perceived as both subject to necessity and free to achieve full human potential. Undoubtedly, this is the most satisfactory vision, but it is almost impossible to live out in the context of the prevailing dualistic structures. Because of current economic, political, education, sexual and religious institutions, women, like men, are forced to identify with one or other side of the dualism for most of the time. Only with the breakdown of sharp distinctions between culture and nature, public and private, mind and body, heaven and hell, work and play, men and women, will women, and the menstruating woman in particular, be able to take their place wherever they choose.

Feminist historians and anthropologists generally agree that the foundations for our present patriarchal arrangements were laid in pre-history and that we can now only speculate on how they were established. Gerda Lerner, for example, hypothesises that men initially appropriated the labour of women as *reproducers*.[38] As humankind moved from foraging for food which was eaten immediately to gathering food which was stored and eaten later, tribes formed. Children were necessary for the survival of the tribe, so men protected nubile women whose energies in such harsh conditions had to be primarily devoted to bearing and rearing children. This led to the first sexual division of labour by which men did the big-game hunting and women and children the small-game hunting and food gathering. Lerner

thinks that both women and men agreed to this division which was biologic-
ally necessary at first, with neither group realising the long term consequences of such a choice. And by the time the division was no longer
necessary for survival, it had become culturally established, virtually
invisible and seemingly in the nature of things. Lerner argues that male
dominance, beginning in prehistory, was completely established and
institutionalised by 400 BCE. This hypothesis, emphasising women's
reproductive role, complements the suggestion presented above that patriarchal culture in general and religion in particular involve projections onto
women of the idealised and disowned parts of the male psyche.

Feminist historians and anthropologists are analysing the ways in which
patriarchy has been expressed in various times and places, and history itself
is gradually being subjected to a critique. Of particular relevance here are
analyses of Greek thought and Judaic messianic religion, the twin bases
for Christianity.[39] These analyses show how body-hating, neo-platonism
and triumphant, exclusivist messianism created a Christianity accommodating to ancient forms of patriarchy and becomes disastrous for women.
Feminist thinkers differ, though, on the question of whether these harmful
elements are essential to Christianity or a perversion of it. Daly, judging
them to be of the essence, becomes post-Christian; Ruether and Fiorenza,
judging them to be perversions, remain Christian. The latter theorists
provide an intellectual base for Christian feminists. Fiorenza, for example,
argues that the patriarchal elements in the Christian scriptures are actually
unfaithful to the liberating impulses of the early Jesus movement.[40]
Examining the Household Codes which prescribe that wives be subject
to their husbands, slaves to their masters, and sons to their fathers, she
points to their source in the Aristotelian philosophy which undergirded
household management in the Greco-Roman world of the first and second
centuries. According to Fiorenza, the transforming impetus of the original
Jesus movement was slowly eroded as Christianity established itself by
adapting to and spiritualising prevailing patriarchal arrangements.

Dangers of feminist critiques

Fiorenza's careful textual work and daring hypotheses provide a model for
feminist scholars reconstructing the past.[41] Displaying a fine balance
between respect for the integrity of the text and respect for the past and
present experience of women, her work avoids some of the dangers to which
feminist textual critique is prone. One of these is the selective quoting of
misogynist passages. A prime example in the present context is the quoting
of the Leviticus text concerning the impurity of the menstruating woman,
a text which reflects fear of defilement through contact with the female body.

> When a woman has a discharge of blood which is her regular discharge from
> her body, she shall be in her impurity for seven days, and whoever touches
> her shall be unclean until the evening. And everything upon which she lies
> during her impurity shall be unclean; everything also upon which she sits
> shall be unclean. And whoever touches her bed shall wash his clothes, and
> bathe himself in water, and be unclean until the evening; whether it is the
> bed or anything upon which she sits, when he touches it he shall be unclean
> until the evening. And if any man lies with her and her impurity is on him,
> he shall be unclean seven days; and every bed on which he lies shall be
> unclean.[42]

This text is frequently and appropriately quoted in feminist works, but
often without attention being drawn to the verses immediately preceding
these, which reflect a similar fear of defilement through contact with male
bodily emissions. The feminist work, *Menstrual Taboos*,[43] for example,
having quoted the above section, makes no mention of these verses:

> And if a man has an emission of semen, he shall bathe his whole body in water,
> and be unclean until the evening. And every garment and every skin on which
> the semen comes shall be washed with water, and be unclean until the evening.
> If a man lies with a woman and has an emission of semen, both of them shall
> bathe themselves in water, and be unclean until the evening.[44]

To quote Leviticus only on the sexual impurities of females while omitting
the prescriptions for males leaves a reader with the impression of a disgust
reserved for women rather than a more general fear of defilement by bodily
emissions. Perhaps it can be shown that the prescriptions for females and
the purification rituals required are more severe than for males, but this
would need to be argued on the basis of a close study of the original passages,
taking into account their context within Leviticus and the Bible generally,
as well as their relation to other texts of the period.

Feminist theorising is also beset by the danger of becoming ahistorical
and universalising, especially when the topic, like menstruation, is one
common to all women. Discussions of attitudes towards menstruation, as
with all feminist issues, needs to be grounded in particular times and places.
The danger of making ahistorical, universalising statements is heightened
where there is a lack of written records. Since the subordination of women
accompanied by denigration of the female body is evident in some societies
at the very beginning of written history, we can now only speculate on
how this came about.[45] This does not mean there are no records from
prehistory. The most ancient human communities have left all kinds of

traces suggesting how they lived and what they believed including thousands of female figurines. So feminist speculation concerning the subordination of women can be well-informed, but it needs to be stated with an element of tentativeness, since the evidence it relies on can never be conclusive. Imaginative constructs, suggesting reasons for this large-scale event, can carry degrees of likelihood but never certitude. They engage the logic of argument, not of proof.

A further danger is that of a reverse sexism. Arguments which claim the superiority of women's experience and which privilege our bodily functions to the detriment of male experience are narcissistic and sexist.[46] At its best, feminist theory assumes that menstruation is both an ordinary experience that can be taken for granted and an extraordinary experience to be celebrated and delighted in. Worthy of being mythologised and ritualised, menstrual bleeding has still a quality of dailiness. Similarly, ejaculation of semen, although on occasion messy and embarrassing, is nonetheless revelatory, delightful, and worthy of respect.[47]

Another shortcoming of some feminist theory is the assumption that women are only victims.[48] To write history, to theologise or to philosophise as though women were *only* objects of patriarchal oppression is to deny our subjectivity, thereby corroborating an entrenched masculinist assumption. Women's subjectivity is expressed and honoured when we write, read, or perform any other activity from our own female perspective, but this perspective must not be limited to that of victim. While the victimisation of women, underplayed or denied in patriarchal culture, must clearly be brought to light, it is just as important that women's culture-creating activities, also underesteemed and denied, be well documented by feminist theorists and artists, enabling such work to receive general critical appreciation and eventually becoming part of the collective imagination. This work of honouring female traditions is enormously difficult as each generation, actively seeking women's culture-creating activities, uncovers afresh the work of feminist forebears. The story of menstruation can, for example, be told from two perspectives: as a story of women's victimisation, and as a story of female power and potential. Cultural and religious practices honouring our experience as well as those denying and debasing it need to be documented, for menstruating women are both victims of culture and participants in its creation. Feminist theory, despite difficulties, must take account of both dimensions.

Creative responses

In this final section I shall consider current creative responses to the experience of menstruation. Again, even restricting ourselves to the spiritual/religious sphere, only a hint of what is taking place can be given.

One key development is the feminist renaming of sin and virtue within Christianity, with a consequent restructuring of the tradition and a development of new rituals.[49] As we women attend to our experience, we hear the past differently and ritualise the present in new ways. This current renaming within and on the borders of Christianity owes much to ancient Goddess-worshipping religions now being revived by increasing numbers of feminist communities.

Traditional Christianity has repeatedly called us to repent of the sins of pride, anger, impurity and lust and encouraged us to practise the virtues of humility, meekness, obedience and purity. But feminists have argued that in Western culture these are predominantly *male* sins, so that men do, by and large, need to foster the corresponding virtues. The same critique claims that women are, on the other hand, innocent of these particular sins, although, being the principal practitioners of Christianity, we tend to confess them constantly, both formally and informally. Born into patriarchal structures, we also tend to foster the qualities designated as virtues by patriarchy, thereby entrenching our own subordination and male domination. In response to our plight, feminist theologians have renamed male sins, designating as *virtuous* a female anger which rages against any denial of woman's full personhood, a female pride which asserts and delights in that personhood, and a female lust which eagerly and playfully lives out womanlife.[50] Feminist theologians have also renamed traditional virtues, designating as *sinful* a female humility and meekness which practises submission to patriarchy, and a female purity which denotes a denial, if not a hatred, of the body. So traditional 'virtues' are exposed as the destructive complement to male sins, fostering the puritan and the doormat in womankind, a state of virtual non-being.

Humility, obedience and purity, redefined as female sins, and pride, anger and lust, redefined as virtues, can be detected in certain responses to menstruation. The female sins of humility and obedience are in evidence when we internalise patriarchal attitudes belittling and denying our own bodies, denigrating the flow of menstrual blood. We are almost universally encouraged to despise menstruation, shaping our bodies to some pristine model of purity. The female virtues of pride and lust, on the other hand, involve respect for the experience of menstruation, one's own and others'. These virtues mean allowing myself to move into my own menstruating body to encounter myself in and through this experience. This is a time when the body demands to be noticed so that even the most distracted and unaware of us are called to pay attention. It is a woman-for-herself time. In Christian terms, it is a time of recognising the female made in the image of God, or, put another way, it is a time of recognising divinity imaged in the menstruating female. Pride allows, or rather delights in, the image of menstruating divinity, be it Mary or Ishtar or maybe even a depatriarchalised Christian God.

The God of Christians, often called God the Father, remains at an infinite distance from menstruation, and is certainly not at home with menstruating women. Feminist writers within Christianity have arged that this God *does approve* of menstruation since the Hebrew scriptures tell us that human females were created in his(!) image and that God found these females, along with human males, to be 'very good'.[51] Such approval is far from explicit, however, and is severely modified by other sections of the Bible, such as the Leviticus passages, denigrating female (and often male) sexuality. Innovative Christian theology searches for new images of divinity, but it may well be that the God of the Bible is too thoroughly male to be ever convincingly imaged as menstruating.[52] Mary too has trouble menstruating, for her image is as carefully guarded by the church fathers as that of God himself.[53] Nevertheless, widespread celebrations in song and dance, in art and drama, in poetry and scholarship, could still resurrect the image of Mary, and even of God, menstruating, for these images are nourished by traditions more ancient than Christian and Hebrew religions.[54]

Behind Mary, and surviving alongside her, are ancient Goddesses quite at home with menstruating women. The Babylonian Goddess, Ishtar (known in the older Sumerian religion as Innana), is, for example, depicted as menstruating at the time of the full moon. It is thought that when Ishtar was menstruating, when the moon was neither waxing nor waning, a day of rest was observed, a 'sabattu', and that this observance gave rise to the Sabbath of both Jews and Christians.[55] Modern Goddess-worshipping communities certainly differ significantly from traditional Christians in their understanding of menstruation.[56] The former honour the life-and-death tension within this experience, their rituals acknowledging menstruation as a symbol of constantly renewed life as well as of death and decay, and always celebrating the mysterious connections between these elements. Humans are, in some sense, mortal and immortal. This ability to accept human mortality gracefully differentiates Goddess-worship most sharply from God-worship. Christianity tends to deny decay by escaping into symbols of transcendence and infinitude; or to debase it as the outcome of sin, seeing it as equivalent to pollution and defilement, symbols of ultimate evil; or, surreptitiously, to find sadomasochistic delight in it, by giving way to the desire for titillation through suffering and death. Throughout recorded history, the menstruating woman in particular has been victim of these three destructive tendencies. Though there are life-giving counter-forces at work in Christianity, they are not generally associated with decay, or with the menstruating woman.

A notable exception, one that has had little impact on the Christian tradition, is Jesus' attitude to women, and to the woman with the issue of blood in particular. The story of Jesus' healing of this woman appears in the three synoptic gospels, always framed by the story of his raising of the twelve-year-old daughter of Jairus from the dead.[57] These interlocking stories are rarely read from the perspectives of the risen girl and the woman healed from haemorrhaging, though such a woman-centred reading is vital for female self-understanding.[58] Commentators, almost exclusively male, never seem to note, for example, that the Jesus of Matthew's sparse account is the most compassionate, for he, unlike the Jesus of Mark and Luke, does not demand of the woman a public confession regarding the reason for her action. There is something mildly titillating for the male in the image of the 'frightened and trembling' woman falling at Jesus' feet and telling him publicly of her very private illness. Matthew alone refrains from making her such an object lesson, an exemplary woman because of her faith; and surely such a Jesus is more admirable and the bond between him and the woman stronger for this sensitive silence on her account. While some commentators note the significance of Jesus' breaking with powerful and ancient taboos by actually *touching* the haemorrhaging and therefore ritually unclean woman, few, if any, note that it was this same 'unclean' woman who made the *first* move towards touching, thus displaying an equally courageous disregard for law and custom.[59] Jesus' admirable action was dependent on her equally admirable initial action. Some commentators also note that Jesus *touched* the dead daughter of Jairus, adding somewhat coyly that she was of marriageable age. What needs to be said quite clearly is that this girl was ritually unclean on two counts, being dead and being of such an age that she had just begun or was just about to begin menstruating, and that Jesus' touch is therefore highly significant.

A feminist reading of these and other scriptural stories can give emphasis to women as active participants, a fruitful exercise for Christian women. Another source of energy are menstruation rituals frequently celebrated now by Goddess-worshipping groups, as well as by Christian and post-Christian women. Unimpeded by patriarchal boundaries, these rituals are usually syncretistic taking from various traditions symbols that speak to the experience of menstruating. Most fundamentally, these rituals celebrate women's participation in the great mystery of dying and regenerating, a mystery proper to the universe itself. This intention is clear, for example, in the prayer recited at the Mikvah or Bathing Ritual, part of a larger menstruation ritual recorded in Ruether's *Women-Church*. The women stand naked by a pool saying,

> These are the waters of the primal sea, the waters of life from which all things came in the beginning and into which all things dissolve. Each month the powers of our bodies drain away and are washed back into the primal sea. Each month the powers of new life arise from this primal sea and empower us with the capacity to bring forth new life.[60]

Having entered the pool, the women immerse themselves three times saying as they rise 'Blessed is the dying away and blessed the regeneration'. When they come out they dress in bright robes made of new cloth. While this is an adaptation of a Jewish ritual, there are also echoes of Christian and of ancient Goddess symbols and rituals. In the case of Judaism and Christianity, these symbols have never, until the present, been appropriated in this way by menstruating women.

Numerous old symbols are reclaimed and new ones discovered as increasing numbers of women ritualise menstruation. Wine, for example, is sometimes drunk, intimating delight in one's life-giving powers and acceptance of one's bodily functions, and sometimes poured out, returned to the ground from which it came.[61] Rituals invoke the ancient Babylonian Goddess, Ishtar, or the Greek Goddess, Aphrodite, both of whom encompass every aspect of life, knowing that putrefaction is not necessarily pollution, and decay is not defilement. The Virgin Mary, utterly removed from decay and mortality, from the very earth itself, has not been allowed to image this. Swathed in blue and white and floating above our heads, she can hardly be invoked at a menstruation ritual. Only when Mary Immaculate dons red and puts her feet on the ground, allowing the moon and the serpent to rise above her head, will she be at home with her foremothers Ishtar and Aphrodite, as well as with today's menstruating women. Such is the rising of womanspirit, that this meeting will indeed take place. Already, Mary and Eve, as well as Lilith and Eve, are talking to each other.[62] In the mourning and celebration of womankind, images kept apart by patriarchal divisions for thousands of years are now beginning to interact.

Through ritual, through gossip, through theology, philosophy and psychology, women are gradually integrating mind and body. This act of integration has political consequences. Classic dualistic structures break down when women, no longer alienated from their bodies, allow themselves to be fully present in menstruation, and few human experiences can so effectively heal the destructive divisions of patriarchy. Intimately linking the mysterious events of life and death, regeneration and mortality, menstruation is an archetypal symbol. Women are recognising its power, consciously exploring its possibilities and submitting to its mysteries. This has led to an explosion of activity as women learn that everything patriarchy has taught us about menstruation is wrong and harmful. Rejoicing in our bodies, reflecting on the event of menstruation, expressing these reflections in art and theology, changing discriminating structures, women are now defying and thereby healing dichotomies between mind and body, culture and nature, public and private. Observing no dualism within, women can oppose, or better, ignore those from without, a shift which shakes the very foundations of patriarchy. One of our most revolutionary statements may yet prove to be 'blessed be women, blessed be our holy menstrual blood'.[63] Women know it can redeem the world.

E.W.

Notes

1 Unpublished survey conducted among students of a Sydney school, 1988.
2 Doris Lessing, *The Golden Notebook* quoted in *Menstrual Taboos*, Matriarchal Study Group, Flat 6, 15 Guilford St, London, W.C. 1, p.2 (undated). For another unfavourable view of menstruation see Simone de Beauvoir, *The Second Sex*, translated by H.M. Parshley, Penguin, 1972, pp.60ff.
3 *Ibid.*, p.8.

4 Unpublished survey.

5 Constance Frazer 'Stains' in *Other Ways of Looking*, Friendly Street Poets, Adelaide, 1988, p.31.

6 Robyn Archer, Diana Manson, Helen Mills, Deborah Parry, Robyn Stacey, *The Pack of Women*, Hessian/Penguin Books, Melbourne 1986, p.110. This song was performed on the ABC-TV show, *The Pack of Women*, 1986.

7 This theme runs through the work of both authors and both are prolific, Daly having published six books and numerous articles and Ruether twenty-three books as well as articles. Classic statements of their respective positions on dualism appear in Mary Daly, *Beyond God the Father: Toward a Philosophy of Women's Liberation*, Beacon Press, Boston, 1973, and Rosemary Radford Ruether, *New Women New Earth: Sexist Ideologies and Human Liberation*, Dove Communications, Melbourne, 1975, and the later, easier-to-read work, *Sexism and God-Talk: Toward a Feminist Theology*, Beacon Press, Boston, 1983.

8 See, for example, Beverly Wildung Harrison, 'Christian Feminism and Human Sexuality' in Judith L. Weidman (ed), *Christian Feminism*, Harper & Row, 1984, and Rosemary Radford Ruether, 'Sexism and the Theology of Liberation', *Christian Century*, Dec. 1973.

9 For the past twenty years feminist theologians have been pointing to the connections between abuse of women and abuse of the earth. A burgeoning eco-theology does not always acknowledge its connections with, or debt to, feminist theology. A local example of this lack of acknowledgement is Andrew Dutney, 'On Earth as it is in Heaven: An Environmental Awareness within Christian Theology' in *Chain Reaction*, No.57, Autumn 1989.

10 See, for example, Marija Gimbutas, *The Goddesses and Gods of Old Europe, 6500 to 3500 BC*, University of California Press, Berkely, 1982 (originally published as *The Gods and Goddesses of Old Europe, 7000 to 3500 BC: Myths, Legends and Cult Images*, Berkely, 1974); Monica Sjöö and Barabara Mor, *The Great Cosmic Mother: Rediscovering the Religion of the Earth*, Harper & Rowe, San Francisco, 1987 (revised edition).

11 See, for example, Carol Christ's 'A Spirituality for Women' in her work *Laughter of Aphrodite: Reflections on a Journey to the Goddess*, Harper & Rowe, San Francisco, 1987, pp.57–72. The notes for this chapter give the references for the lively debate between Christ and Ruether. A succinct statement of Ruether's view appears in her paper, 'Feminist Spirituality and Historical Religion', the Dudleian Lecture 1985–86, printed in *Harvard Divinity Bulletin*, 1986.

12 This summary of the destruction of Goddess worship does not infer that the ancient Hebrews initiated this destruction or that they invented patriarchy. In her article, 'On Not Blaming Jews for the Death of the Goddess' (*Laughter of Aphrodite*, pp.83–92), Carol Christ shows that the dominant tradition of the ancient Hebrews in the period of the monarchy and up to the Babylonian exile was polytheistic and not monotheistic. Most Hebrews worshipped numerous Gods and Goddesses including Baal, Anath, Asherah and El as well as Yahweh, and only some Hebrews worshipped Yahweh alone. After a long struggle, however, the monotheistic group violently imposed its will on the others, rewriting the texts so as to denigrate Gods and Goddesses other than Yahweh. Evidence of this struggle appears, for example, in books 1 and 2 Kings and 1 and 2 Chronicles of the Hebrew Scriptures. In the same work, Christ shows that patriarchy did not originate with the religion of the ancient Hebrews, or with Judaism or Christianity for that matter. All of these religions have simply maintained and further entrenched a violent and very ancient construction of 'reality' which probably arose during the fourth, third and second millenia BCE, well before the days of Abraham. Her thesis is that the largely peaceful societies of Neolithic times 'began to be transformed into patriarchal, militaristic, class-stratified, slave-owning state societies around 3500 BCE'.(p.88) The closing of the last Goddess temple is documented in many places. See, for example, Merlin Stone, *Paradise Papers: The Suppression of Women's Rites,* Virago and Quartet Books, London, 1976–7, p.211.

13 See, for example, Geoffrey Ashe, *The Virgin,* Routledge & Kegan Paul, London, 1976; Elisabeth Schüssler Fiorenza, 'Feminist Theology as a Critical Theology of Liberation' in *Theological Studies,* 36, Dec., 1975, pp.605–26; Rosemary Radford Ruether, *Mary, the Feminine Face of the Church,* Westminster Press, Philadelphia, 1977; Pamela Berger, *The Goddess Obscured: Transformation of the Grain Protectress to Saint,* Beacon Press, Boston, 1985.

14 Marina Warner, *Alone of All Her Sex: The Myth and the Cult of the Virgin Mary,* Quartet Books, London, 1978. See chapter 13, 'The Milk of Paradise'.

15 Genesis 3:16.

16 Merlin Stone, *When God Was a Woman,* Dial Press, New York, 1976 (first published as *The Paradise Papers).*

17 John 3:14 quoting Numbers 21:8–9.

18 The snake is still widely used as a symbol of the healing power of doctors.

19 Warner, *Alone of All Her Sex,* p.286, quoting Mircea Eliade, *Patterns in Comparative Religion,* Rosemary Sheed, New York, 1972, pp.165–9.

20 Warner, *Alone of All Her Sex,* chapter 16, 'The Immaculate Conception'. My discussion of Mary Immaculate is indebted to Warner's work.

21 See Mary Daly, *Beyond God the Father,* chapter 2, where Daly gives reasons for critiquing the Adam and Eve myth.

22 See an excellent discussion of the myth of female wholeness in Warner, *Alone of All Her Sex,* chapter 5, 'Virgins and Martyrs'.

23 *Menstrual Taboos,* p.19.

24 I am not saying that the use of some tampons is not harmful for some women. I am saying that patriarchal mythology, which promotes the pristine wholeness of the female body, denigrates all contact between the inside and outside of the body, including sexual intercourse and the use of tampons. This mythology does not concern itself with the physical harm which sometimes occurs to women because of this contact.

25 A classic article describing this split is Sherry Ortner, 'Is Female to Male as Nature is to Culture?' in *Feminist Studies,* 1(2), Fall 1972. Genevieve Lloyd, *The Man of Reason: 'male' and 'female' in Western Philosophy,* Methuen, London, 1984, provides a useful discussion of the philosophical tradition giving rise to this split from Plato to the present. Discussion of this dualism now pervades feminist work.

26 Unpublished survey.

27 Some examples of studies on the effects of patriarchy on males are Sneja Gunew, 'Male Sexuality: Feminist Interpretations', in *Australian Feminist Studies*, No.5, Summer 1987; and Gail Reekie, 'Feminism and Men's Bodies: More Thoughts on Male Sexuality' in *Australian Feminist Studies*, No.6, Autumn 1988. Gunew's article provides a useful review of relevant literature. Male scholars have not yet generally given attention to either the role of religion in promoting an image harmful to males or to the need for feminist theology for males.

28 Mary Daly, *Gyn/Ecology: the Metaethics of Radical Feminism*, the Women's Press, London, 1979.

29 See, for example, *The Nude Male: a New Perspective*, Penguin Books, 1978, pp.66–93. Freud's work is a powerful indictment against this aspect of Christianity.

30 Warner argues this is *Alone of All Her Sex*, p.71.

31 *Ibid.*

32 Mary Daly, 'God is a Verb' in *Women in a Changing World*, McGraw-Hill, pp.153–70. This theme runs through much of Daly's work.

33 There have been a number of Australian examples of the Christa. Arthur Boyd places a woman on the cross in his painting 'Crucifixion, Shoalhaven' reproduced in Rosemary Crumlin, *Images of Religion in Australian Art*, Bay Books, Sydney, 1988, p.159. Crumlin quotes Boyd's 1987 words: 'I do not believe it is enough to say *he* represented all of us. I do not wish to separate the idea of suffering by allowing just the male to be seen. There has been an awakening consciousness of the potential and force of women in our time' (p.158). A much earlier example and one possibly with different intent is Norman Lindsay's 'The Rosy Crucifixion'. The figure of a pregnant woman on a cross appeared in the local feminist journal, *Magdalene*, No.3, October 1982, an issued devoted to abortion. The figure also appears in a drawing by Graham English in *Women-Church* No.3, Spring 1988, p.40, and in drawings by Mary Leunig *There's No Place Like Home*, Penguin Books, Melbourne, 1982, and *A Piece of Cake*, Penguin Books, Melbourne, 1986.

34 Daly, *Beyond God the Father*, p.47.

35 Ruether, 'Feminist Spirituality and Historical Religion', p.2.

36 Women who tend to be separatist support this position. On balance, Mary Daly's work is not so concerned with political structures, as with celebrating the particular giftedness of women.

37 Marxist feminists support this position. It can be detected, for example, throughout Ruether's work.

38 Gerda Lerner, *The Creation of Patriarchy*, Vol.1, Oxford University Press, Oxford, 1986. This is one of a number of hypotheses. See Lerner's summary treatment of many other hypotheses in 'Origins', Chapter 1 of this work.

39 Rosemary Radford Ruether, 'Motherearth and the Megamachine: a theology of liberation in a feminine, somatic and ecological perspective' in Carol P. Christ & Judith Plaskow, eds, *Womanspirit Rising*, Harper & Row, San Francisco, 1979; Elisabeth Schüssler Fiorenza, *In Memory of Her: A Feminist Theological*

Reconstruction of Christian Origins, Crossroad, New York, 1984.

40 Fiorenza, *In Memory of Her* and *Bread Not Stone: the Challenge of Feminist Biblical Interpretation*, Beacon Press, Boston, 1984, especially chapter 4, 'Discipleship and Patriarchy'.

41 The relevance of Schüssler Fiorenza's reconstruction of early Christianity for feminist researches on the Goddesses is discussed by Carol Christ in her chapter 'Reclaiming Goddess History' in *Laughter of Aphrodite*, pp.161–180.

42 Leviticus 15:19–24.

43 *Menstrual Taboos*, p.3.

44 Leviticus 15:16–18.

45 Patriarchal history both privileges *written* documents and denies that there is an element of speculation in all historical accounts. It pretends to state the 'facts'. Feminist history, suggesting reasons for the subordination of women occurring in pre-history (i.e., before written records), engages in the interpretation of very ancient artefacts and a degree of speculation. But interpreting any event, no matter how recent, requires the same two steps: a consideration of the evidence and some speculation. So pre-history and history are on a continuum, both providing some evidence for what has occurred and both requiring a degree of speculation in order to be interpreted.

46 It is sometimes difficult to judge whether certain works are simply denigrations of male sexuality or expressions of a rightful rage against the misuse of this sexuality to violate females. The playful, over-the-top quality in Mary Daly's works places them, I believe, in the latter category.

47 New theologies reclaiming the sacredness of male bodies have hardly begun. Instead, many theologians are engaged in a rearguard action against feminist theology. See, for example, Patrick M. Arnold 'In Search of the Hero: Masculine Spirituality and Liberal Christianity' in *America*, Vol.161, No. 9, 1989.

48 In *Gyn/Ecology*, Mary Daly powerfully documents women's victimisation, but her work does not leave us in the depths. The final section envisages new modes of thought to which she contributes by constantly reshaping language.

49 This task was begun very early in the recent wave of feminism by Valerie Saiving in her article, 'The Human Situation: a feminine view', *The Journal of Religion*, April, 1960, reprinted in *Womanspirit Rising*.

50 This understanding of 'lust' is Mary Daly's in *Pure Lust: Elemental Feminist Philosphy*, The Women's Press, London, 1984.

51 Genesis 1:31.

52 For example, Sallie McFague, *Models of God: Theology for an Ecological, Nuclear Age*, Fortress Press, Philadelphia, 1987. This work images God as Mother, Lover and Friend and the world as God's body. It is still a long way, though, from imaging God as menstruating.

53 The meanings attached to Mary have been guarded by the church fathers for centuries. For example, the Council of Ephesus, 431, after a heated debate and the excommunication of Nestorius, proclaimed Mary, *Theotokos*, The God Bearer. Political wrangling continued until the Council of Chalcedon 451 gave her the title, 'ever Virgin' with her perpetual virginity being proclaimed a dogma at the First Lateran Council in 649. These two dogmas, as interpreted by the church, have negated each other and deprived women of authority.

54 The God of the Bible is largely protected from any contact with sexuality, female or male. So not only does God not menstruate, God does not ejaculate either. Though these sexual images cannot be forced onto an asexual God without doing violence to the biblical image of divinity, we can still note the enormous distance between the images. This distance, which is not a feature of many non-biblical religions, seems to signify a lack of ease with the body and with sexuality in particular.

55 *Menstrual Taboos*, p.1. Two Jungian books exploring the connections between the ancient Goddesses, Innana and Ishtar, and women's experience including menstruation are Sylvia Brinton Perera, *Descent to the Goddess: a Way of Initiation for Women*, Inner City Books, Toronto, 1981, pp.38 and 44; and Esther M. Harding, *Women's Mysteries, Ancient and Modern: a Psychological Interpretation of the Feminine Principle as Portrayed in Myth, Story, and Dreams*, Harper & Row, New York, 1976 (first published 1931).

56 See, for example, Monica Sjöö and Barbara Mor, *The Great Cosmic Mother: Rediscovering the Religion of the Earth*, Harper & Row, San Francisco, 1987, pp.176–199; and Judy Grahn 'From Sacred Blood to the Curse and Beyond' in Charlene Spretnak ed., *The Politics of Women's Spirituality*, Anchor Press/Doubleday, New York, 1982, pp.265–279.

57 Matthew 9:18–26; Mark 5:21–43; Luke 8:40–56.

58 Some of the best examples of reading the Scriptures from a women-centred perspective appear in Phyllis Trible, *God and the Rhetoric of Sexuality*, Fortress Press, Philadelphia, 1978; and *Texts of Terror: Literary-Feminist Readings of Biblical Narratives*, Fortress Press, Philadelphia, 1984. For a women-centred reading of this particular story (as well as other gospel stories), see Christine Burke *Through a Woman's Eyes: Encounters with Jesus*, Collins Dove, Melbourne, 1989, pp.5–8.

59 Francis J. Maloney, *Women First Among the Faithful: a New Testament Study*, Dove Communications, Melbourne, 1984, pp.10–12. This work, by giving a revisionist reading of the New Testament, seeks to raise the status of women in the text and in today's church. From a feminist perspective, the work fails, however, for it perpetuates the harmful dualism between male and female, by mythologising woman as a symbol of fidelity, thereby situating her exclusively at the overesteemed pole of the dualism. See my review essay, 'Woman – First Among the Faithful or Last Among the Demythologised?' in *National Outlook*, Vol.7, No.11, Dec.1985/Jan.1986, and *Compass Theology Review*, Spring 1985.

60 Rosemary Radford Ruether, *Women-Church: Theology and Practice*, Harper & Row, San Francisco, 1985, p.220. For another menstruation ritual see Z. Budapest, *The Holy Book of Women's Mysteries*, Part II, Susan E. Anthony Coven No.1, Oakland, 1980. For a comprehensive treatment of the folklore of menstruation and a plea that this experience be seen as a mark of the divine, see Penelope Shuttle and Peter Redgrove, *The Wise Wound: Eve's Curse and Everywoman*, R. Marek, New York, 1978. See also Dena Taylor *Red Flower: Rethinking Menstruation*, The Crossing Press, Freedom, California, 1988.

61 Carol Christ, *Laughter of Aphrodite, pp.183–205.*

62 The interactions between Mary and Eve have largely been manipulated by patriarchal religion: see Warner, *Alone of All Her Sex*, ch.4, 'Second Eve'. As we become conscious of Mary within the orbit of the Goddess, however, her interactions with Eve are necessarily changing. The figure of Eve is currently being reclaimed. See, for example, the two Australian poems, Judith Wright's 'Eve to Her Daughters' and Kate Llewellyn's 'Eve' both of which appear in *The Penguin Book of Australian Women Poets* edited by Susan Hampton & Kate Llewellyn, Penguin Books, Melbourne, 1986, and in particular the meeting between Lilith and Eve in Judith Plaskow, 'The Coming of Lilith: toward a feminist theology' in *Womanspirit Rising*, pp.198–209.

63 Readers with Roman Catholic backgrounds will recognise echoes of the old Divine Praises.

What *do* we do all day?

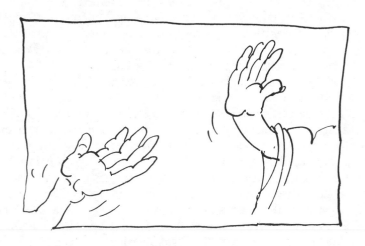

'Kept Women: They shop, they lunch, they take courses and they renovate. They don't work and they don't want to . . . ' This was the caption on the front cover of the *Sydney Morning Herald Good Weekend* magazine on 10 June 1989. The picture shows a blonde woman glamorously dressed in black, sitting on the bonnet of a red Ferrari along with a casually placed shoulder bag, a few books in French and German, and the words 'a gift from her husband'. The article is headed 'Ladies of Leisure: What *do* they do all day?', and the focus is clearly on the fact that they 'choose not to work'. As I was reading it I found myself getting angry. At the women for allowing themselves to be portrayed as disempowered, overindulged sex-objects; at the journalist, Jane Cadzow, for setting them up in this way, with no attempt to analyse the patriarchal and class structures of which they are part; at the newspaper for presenting this gratuitous slur on five women; and at myself for the ambiguities and inadequacies of my own work life.

In our society the question of women and work is beset by contradictions and ambivalence. It is hardly surprising that expressions of self-deprecation cropped up frequently in Cadzow's interviews, words like guilt, selfish, indulgent, apologetic, frantic, hectic, frivolous, sensitive to criticism, sarcastic, resentment, jealous, negative. But there were also expressions of self-affirmation and satisfaction with their lives, such as freedom, sense of fulfilment, worthwhile, a passion for study, lucky, leisurely. And if women who 'don't work' come under attack, so do women who 'work'. *The Sydney Morning Herald* (9.6.89) reported that the 'new head of Australia's 38,000 engineers believes providing childcare for female engineers with children helps them "abrogate their responsibility". Mr Skip Tonkin said, "Women who want to practise engineering and want children at the same time want the best of two worlds. They have to accept that they have to make a choice and that they themselves have to manage that choice".'

Of course the reason men like Mr Tonkin can happily accept 'the best of two worlds' for themselves is that they have 'kept women' at home managing the domestic and parental world for them. In fact it is often men with unpaid wives at home who think other wives should stay at home too. While many men believe that they themselves can have many roles and avenues of fulfilment, they want to restrict women to certain roles.

Both Mr Tonkin and Jane Cadzow imply that women have a free choice about whether to 'work' or not. Both put the full responsibility for that 'choice' on the individual woman, without any attempt to understand the social context in which it is made, or the power relations which make it anything but 'free'. They ignore the lived-world reality of women's situation. The use of the word 'work' to mean only paid work adds to the misrepresentation of who does what in our society, and to the confusion of attitudes and values in this whole area.

In Cadzow's article, the women themselves, although occupied with caring for children (one has four sons aged between four and nine, another two children aged three and five), running the household, teaching, studying, voluntary and community work, study and sport, cannot identify what they do. From the point of view of the paid workforce, the work these women do is invisible, in fact so invisible that they can hardly name it themselves. 'I love reading. But I don't read during the day. I'd feel guilty, you know. And I don't really have time. It's hard to explain why, but I really am busy.' And: 'Our days are so busy. I just don't know where the time goes'. What women do does not fit the categories of paid work by which people are identified in our society: 'When new acquaintances say, "And what do you do?", as if naturally you do *something*, that sort of daunts me a bit. I say, "Well, actually I don't work". And then the next question, immediately, is, "When did you give it up?" And I do find that a little bit difficult to answer. I feel guilty. Isn't that funny? I feel a bit inadequate.'

Of course it is class privilege that allows these women the option of not doing paid work, as well as allowing the journalist to see them as fair game. Under the guise of attacking the rich, she is actually trivialising and making invisible their very real reproductive, domestic and nurturing work as women. She would hardly dare do the same to wives of poor husbands. In fact a poor woman who had four children under nine, ran the household, kept them in touch with the neighbourhood gossip, helped her husband in his work and renovated the house would probably be seen as heroic. Probably, though, she would need and have a paid job as well. But no doubt she too would pause, with some feeling of inadequacy, before answering the question, 'What do you do?'.

An attack like Cadzow's could not be made on men, even rich men, because their work and money give them real power and status in our society. It is women's secondary and dependent status that makes them vulnerable. What do you do? is an identity question, and the appropriate answer is, I'm a ... secretary, student, sculptor or whatever. But 'I'm (only) a housewife' has become a kind of ironic joke since it reflects a truth which our society does not want to see. Housewives may be more in the closet than lesbians these days. Their work has become unnameable: I wiped some noses and bottoms, washed up a few times, did the washing, talked to Doris when I got the mail, went shopping, saw Jill's teacher about her spelling, brought the washing in when it started to spit, started to read the local paper, put the washing out again ...

If women's unpaid work is devalued and made invisible, the same is true of women's paid work. We recognise the pattern in both. We are familiar with the way 'rich wives who don't work', as the article puts it, are seen as an adornment of their husbands, and their work made invisible. But in fact all women who are economically dependent on men, on fathers, husbands, de factos, brothers, sons, are seen as secondary beings in a patriarchal society, their social power and status not autonomous but derived from that of the men with whom they are associated. This is generally true even if these women are in the paid workforce, since most women earn less than men and are therefore economically secondary. There are, of course, a growing number of women who *are* economically independent of men, and many more now understand the desirability of aiming towards such a goal, though they may not be able to achieve it.

But despite the long political struggle on the part of women, especially over the last twenty years, to achieve wage justice, women's overall earnings remain only about two thirds of men's. The devaluing of women's work in the domestic sphere carries over into a devaluing of their work in the public sphere, and this is true not only in relation to financial remuneration but to conditions of work and a proper respect for the dignity of women workers as well.

A working God

Considering the commitment of the Christian churches in Australia to issues of social justice, it is surprising how silent they are on the whole question of work. The Bible, however, has a lot to say, beginning with the first great work, the creation of the universe: 'In the beginning God created the heavens and the earth.'[1] It goes on, 'The earth was without form and void, and darkness was upon the face of the deep; and the Spirit of God was moving over the face of the waters'. Instead of 'moving' another version gives 'brooded over', so the whole combination of darkness and deep and brooded and water carries a memory of the creation myths of the early goddess-worshipping peoples. Marija Gimbutas describes these myths as combining a dark watery context with a story of the world coming from a great egg, and there is often the suggestion of a waterbird around, a female, who might have laid the first egg. After glancing back to this long tradition of female creation stories, the Bible hurries on: 'And God said, "Let there be light"; and there was light'. And so on for six days. God spoke and everything was separated out, formed and ordered. 'And God saw that it was good'. The image is of a supremely powerful, transcendent, beneficent male being, making the universe through instant commands. He is totally other. We are separate from him, part of his ordered, hierarchical creation. This is the image one gets from reading the first creation story in Genesis and from traditional theology.

Feminist theology, woven from many threads in the theological tradition, sees it quite differently. Since God created male and female 'in his own image', every person is creative. That is part of our being. The whole creation is seen as a process in which we, as humans, participate with the divine energy in the continual work of creating and sustaining the universe. When a child is born, for example, it is both God and the mother who create it, give it birth. When children are nurtured, crops planted, people healed, food cooked, clothes made, meetings held, it is a collaboration between God and people in the work of the universe. We are co-creators with God. The earth also contributes to the process by growing the food, providing the air, water, trees, space and so on. And we, like God in Genesis, like the mother with her child or some engineers with their bridge, look on it, assess it, and in most cases we find that 'it is good' − the cake is made, the meeting organised, the sheep shorn, the class taught, the plumbing fixed, the clothes washed and hanging on the line. Making, doing our daily work in some kind of harmony with the energies of others and the universe, is a divine-human act.

The way in which the patriarchal church has separated the religious out from the everyday has, however, led to a deep division between 'God's work' and secular work. A preacher or priest or religious-education teacher is doing 'God's work'. But for the rest of us, well, work is work, and usually rather joyless at that. In the twentieth century the sense of our work as collaborating with God or the energy of the universe has largely been lost although traces of it remain in our occasional organic sense of the real worth of work as creative, renewing us and the world, or when we feel a proper satisfaction at a job well done. But if work has in general lost its sense of intrinsic worth and enjoyment, the enjoyment of rest has also disappeared − in a puritanical or workaholic inability to stop working, or in a desperate pursuit of pleasure. For many people both work and rest have become alienated and joyless.

Here is how Susan Ackley, in 'A Meditation on Diapers'[2], reimagines and revalues work in a feminist context of meaning. Her words are American, but doing the washing is surely the same in any language.

It is two or three days since the last time I did this − fill the washing machine, rinse out the poopy diapers in the tub (hope for no raisins!), then dump the soggy mass in the hot water and soap. I use a wringer washer to save our primitive septic system, so I have a lot of time for contemplation as the process goes on.

So I meditate on diapers. The reasons I use cloth diapers are ecological and economic and spiritual. And it is the last that carry me through the smell and the seemingly blank time spend standing at attention to avoid flooding the bathroom. Because what is happening here, after all, but renewal: behold, I make all things new. Here is heat, and the earthy rubbing of matter on matter, but above all here is water, water freshening, refreshing, bringing these squares of cotton fiber back to what they were before. And so it is with changing the diapers in the first place, dumping them in the pail, wiping off the tiny soiled rear end – refreshing, renewing.

Of course, all the time, from diaper change to diaper change and wash day to wash day, there is more profound change happening – the diapers are softening, becoming more and more absorbant and forgiving, and finally wearing out to rags. And the baby grows. But this small, quotidian access to the sacred mystery of renewal returns wash day after wash day, reminding, guaranteeing that renewal is possible in the universe we belong to.

And this is because the tedious, smelly process of diaper washing reveals what in our universe can be done – the world gives renewal to us as a gift. It is *that sort of universe.*

So I'm not talking about a mere metaphor in which the cleansing of a soiled diaper is analogous to psychological or spiritual renewal. Rather, I'm seeing the universe as a matrix or cauldron or *materia prima*, in which we live and move and out of which we have our being – beyond which there is nothing. And this *materia* mothers forth bodies and consciousness out of an endless richness of tendancies, laws, influences, and possibilities. Diaper washing reveals that renewal is one of these possibilities.

Here is traditional 'woman's work' par excellence, indeed perhaps the most menial of woman's work, and yet it comes to at least the verge of being sacramental. By 'sacramental' here I mean giving bodily access not to an external, transcendent divinity but to the most profound qualities of reality itself. Among these, I believe, are fecundity, renewal, transformation, and the breaking down of structures.

The legacy of Adam and Eve

Susan Ackley brings this 'most menial of woman's work' back from all its alienations to its place as one of the 'events of pleasure and necessity which are at the same time embodiments and reenactments of the deepest cosmic processes'.[3] This reintegration of work with sacred meaning may be possible and life-enhancing at an individual level but we need also to consider the web of relationships which locates our work within the structures of society. Again Genesis as commonly interpreted sets the pattern for the patriarchal structures our society has developed. After Eve and Adam have been tempted by the serpent and have had a bite of the apple, they are driven out of the garden of Eden and God speaks to them:

> To the woman he said,
> 'I will greatly multiply your pain in childbearing;

in pain shall you bring forth children,
yet your desire shall be for your husband,
and he shall rule over you.'

And to Adam he said, . . .
cursed is the ground because of you;
in toil you shall eat of it all the days of your life;
thorns and thistles it shall bring forth to you;
and you shall eat the plants of the field.
In the sweat of your face you shall eat bread
till you return to the ground.[4]

The focus on woman's childbearing role, with man as breadwinner, sets
the scene for the contemporary separation of men's and women's roles and
the corresponding public and private worlds, in a context of male domination and female submission. The words are given great authority by the
patriarchal church and society because they are 'in the Bible'. But when
they are read in context their meaning is quite the reverse. This story is
presenting what happened after Eve and Adam disobeyed God. It is showing
the result of the fall, the broken and sinful relationships from which
Christianity sees Jesus as having come to redeem the world. But although
Genesis is describing a destructive fallen relationship rather than prescribing
a norm, the patriarchal church and, to an extent, society continues to use
this biblical story as divine justification for patriarchal oppression.

This misreading of Genesis contributes heavily to attitudes of both church
and society to work today: seeing work as some kind of punishment; seeing
the male as breadwinner and women as having no role in the economy;
seeing women's role in terms of having children and as not involving any
real 'work'; seeing male earnings as naturally and necessarily more than
women's; and seeing women in a service role to men. The church clings
to this tradition both theologically and socially, using its patriarchal theology
to support and maintain a patriarchal family and state. It is hardly surprising
then that the church, although sensitive to many areas of social injustice,
is almost incapable of taking any initiative in relation to the appalling
discrimination against women in the workforce and the consequent poverty
and socioeconomic powerlessness of women, with all the suffering to women
and children this entails.

Certainly the church plays an important role in caring for socially
disadvantaged women and children, but it is not able to confront or challenge
the sexist structures that cause this disadvantage. Even in its own life it
is notorious for exploiting women as workers, whether they are working
for church institutions, ministers' wives, sister in religious orders, or the

worthy parishioners who do the cleaning, serving, caring jobs for the church or congregation.

There *are* movements for change within the church structures. Women students have started caucusing in theological colleges, some councils have begun to be aware of EEO principles in making new appointments, some ministers' wives are claiming their autonomy, defining their roles independently from their husbands' work. But on the whole these remain brave exceptions.

Women in the paid workforce

Because of the paralysis of the churches and also the sexism of the traditionally male-dominated trade unions, it has been women in the secular world who have initiated and sustained the immense campaign, first to make visible the scale of injustice to women in the area of work, and then to devise and fight for measures to overcome it. The struggle has been long and hard and is far from over.

Let us look at the present situation of women in the paid workforce. The hard-won equal pay decision of 1972 resulted in women who did the same work as men getting equal pay.[5] But a very narrow definition was put on these words, and although further victories have been won, the overall inequality continues. We are far from achieving a situation of economic justice between women and men in Australian society.

Compared with other members of the Organisation for Economic Co-operation and Development (OECD), Australia has an extremely high degree of female segregation in its workforce.[6] Women are concentrated in a narrow range of industries, in the lower-paid services sector of the economy, as well as in lower skill-levels and in a narrow range of skill-specialisations.

Apart from this industrial and occupational segregation, a further reason for women's lower earnings is that many more women than men are in part-time rather than full-time work. In 1988, 78.8% of all part-time employment was undertaken by women, mostly married women. In 1990, adult women's total earnings from full-time work across all occupations were 83% of men's, but when part-time and casual earnings were added, the figures showed that adult women's earnings from full-time and part-time work were only about 65% of men's.[7] Recently in Australia women's employment has been increasing, but most of the new jobs are part-time, even though 72% of unemployed women seeking work want full-time jobs.[8] This trend towards part-time and contract work for women means that even though women's participation in the workforce is increasing, the work conditions are deteriorating.

In a recent paper on the pay equity issue concerned with the devaluing of women's skills, experience and qualifications,[9] Clare Burton said the problem is not just that women are in low-paying occupations, but that such occupations are frequently low-paying because women work in them. Skills and qualities required in female-dominated jobs are often not included in the list of criteria used to determine work value, so that because they have not been acknowledged, they have not been remunerated. For example, 'Work-value assessments might overlook the lifting of heavy patients but not the lifting of heavy objects; they might overlook the amount of responsibility involved in the education of children but not the responsibility for finances and equipment; they may overlook the stressful working conditions of looking after people with serious mental health problems, but not the noise of machinery; they may overlook the clerical and administrative skills of secretaries but not the manual skills of machinery repairmen'.[10] In other words, male bias in the assessment of skills results in unjust decisions about work-value, and therefore about pay.

In Australia, as in other western countries, women in lower socioeconomic classes have always had to work for a living. In the last twenty years a much higher percentage of women, both married and single, have joined the paid workforce and have thus achieved a higher degree of financial independence and autonomy. But overall the structures of employment remain patriarchal: men are overwhelmingly in control and benefit from women's access to and conditions in the workforce. Men are paid more, and are in higher jobs, keeping control and power and defining value. Referring to women's increased economic independence, Lois Bryson points out that the changes 'have been partly in response to women's own demands, but the particular demands that have been achieved have been those which absorb women into the capitalist labour market structures. There has been less success where women's demands challenge these structures,[11] for example in the provision of affordable child-care.

In this fundamental area of paid employment the struggle for justice remains intense: women still work in a narrow range of jobs, mainly in the service sector, their work is undervalued and underpaid, they suffer more unemployment, have intermittent work-patterns, work part-time when they would prefer full-time, and are much more vulnerable to poverty and dependence on the welfare system. Employed women still do most of the domestic work, and so have a double work-load. For Aboriginal women, for women with a disability or for those of non-English-speaking background, these disadvantages are compounded by additional discrimination.[12] The Government's Affirmative Action and Equal Opportunity programs require employers to make certain changes in their employment practices which benefit women and minority groups, but the response of most businesses has been less than enthusiastic. A superannuation scheme appropriate to women's working lives is also proving difficult to devise in any effective way.

Child care remains a huge problem for many women who are or wish to be in paid employment. It is mainly women rather than men who take responsibility for the care of children, and both private and government funded child care places are scarce and expensive. In 1988 only 9.5% of pre-school children were in government-funded child care, and even this funding is under threat from the economic rationalists.

There are as yet very few work-based child care centres in Australia. It is clear business has felt no desire or obligation to change working conditions developed around a male lifestyle to accommodate the different needs of women. However, a recent study published by the Federal Government's Affirmative Action Agency indicates that future labour shortages may make it imperative for business to provide child care and flexible working practices if it is to attract and retain key staff (*SMH*, 27.6.89) Business people are prepared to consider work-based child care when it affects their recruitment capacity, and no doubt their decision is made easier by the Federal Government's offer to subsidise 1000 child care places established by the private sector employers. However, the price of child care continues to rise beyond affordable limits and the Federal Government is now threatening to reduce its commitment to new places, even though studies have shown that overall, child care saves the country money rather than being a drain on resources. The gain from women's contribution to the economy through the work done, the tax paid, and the saving of welfare payments outweighs the cost of child care. But even though easier access to child care would be to the country's advantage as well as beneficial to children and sought by mothers, deepseated misogynist attitudes continue to surface in the entrenched resistance to either providing child care as a right like public schools, or introducing the flexible working conditions that would enable women and men to fulfil their parental responsibilities.

The tradition of dualism

These misogynist practices, which make it almost impossible for most women to combine work and motherhood in a satisfactory way, have a particular form at this time and place in history, but underlying them is the patriarchal tradition which we have just discussed in relation to Genesis. We can trace it back through Christianity and Judaism to the male dominance of the early Yahweh warrior kings, and the dualistic body-denying philosophy of early Greek culture[13]; and beyond that to the violent male-supremacist beliefs and practices brought to Europe by the Indo-European or Kurgan invasions of about 5,000 years ago.[14]

We have seen in the previous chapter how the association of mind, spirit and intelligence with the male, and sensuality, the body and emotion with the female, was not simply a recognition of difference or polarity, as in day and night, but a power relation in which the men claimed power over women, and qualities associated with the male side of the duality were regarded as superior to and more virtuous than the qualities associated with the female.

In a similar way the opposition between private and public spheres, is mapped onto a conception of social, economic and political life as a male domain, and family life and personal relations as a female domain, with women as a group under the control of men as a group in both. The dualisms of race and class intensify those of sex to create a complex pattern of exploitation and oppression affecting relations between nations and races as well as economic and social groups and individuals.

The same split is apparent even in the design of our cities, requiring a rush hour every weekday morning from the feminised dormitory suburbs to the masculinised central business district (CBD). The CBD is where 'work' happens: business, law, politics, medicine, banking, insurance, publishing and so on. It is a world which makes men more visible than women, geared to male patterns in dress and working hours, in its competitiveness and in the hierarchical structures which intensify its stereotyping of men and women into roles of dominance and submission. The suburbs are the 'feminine' world, still revolving round the male, as father and breadwinner, but as his place of leisure and rest rather than 'work'. The 'home' is the centre of family values, personal relationships, love, feeling, caring, the place where fathers and children are nurtured, fed, housed, clothed, loved, the place of 'morality' in contrast to the amoral CBD where the pursuit of profit and self-interest are paramount.

If the public world, the world of production, the masculine world, controls and exploits women's labour for its own advantage, let us now look at the other side of the dualism – the feminine sphere. How does the private world feel to women? Adele Horin, after spending six months in the 'neighbourhood' rather than the workplace, says that 'Time out to live in the neighbourhood is a luxury many dream about', and claims she has 'risen to the challenge of the unstructured life'. Her identity and status and income (reduced to part-time) as a journalist are still intact, but even so she asks: 'And if we could afford it, how long before we felt bored, depressed and brain dead . . . ?' She recognises the dangers, but also the pleasures, and feels 'grateful and privileged for this chance, this flirtation with life outside the workplace'.[15] But she, like others, is 'just passing through; doing a "gentle stretch" one week, back at the word processor the next'. She recognises that 'What we do [at work] becomes not only what we are, but who our friends are.'

Another woman, who is not passing through, defines her work as 'being a mother'. Jane's husband is an engineer and they have two children. Her experience is different from Horin's:

> Being a mother has presented many contradictions to me.
>
> The feeling of guilt because I went back to work. The feeling of guilt because I stayed at home with my children.
>
> The feeling of failure because Sally doesn't sleep through the night or Christine feeds every hour or so.
>
> It is the first time in my life that I'm ultimately and totally responsible for something. For everything else there is usually someone to whom you can offload the burden but with mothering the baby is completely and totally my responsibility – and I do it alone.
>
> Having children condemns me to the periphery of society. There are places I cannot go because of the children:
>
> – shops with no stroller access
> – cinema, theatre
> – public meetings with no child care
> – railway stations with two flights of stairs
>
> I've become isolated from adults except other mothers.
>
> I've become distanced from myself through the 'busyness' of children who give you no time to think and contemplate.
>
> There is no one telling me that I am doing a worthwhile job and that I am competent as a mother.
>
> Jane

Jane's clear statement of guilt, failure, isolation, distance from herself and lack of appreciation will resonate with the experience of many women, many mothers. It was in the mid-sixties that Betty Friedan called attention to this 'problem without a name'. Since then the women's movement has radically changed our awareness of female–male relations. Some men share or 'help with' child care and housework, and many more women than formerly share the breadwinning role. There have been changes in law, in language, in access to education and training. But Jane's letter was written in 1989. It speaks for women still in their 'place' in the home, often isolated and burdened, doing the crucial but invisible work of love. This arrangement reflects power relations so pervasive that everyone is affected by them. Nearly everyone is so strongly socialised into them that to challenge them requires both individually and collectively an act of imagination and courage. Daly calls this a 'qualitative leap' from the 'pit of patriarchal possession' into free space.[16]

This leap is a religious act, in the sense that it is a move from one system of meaning to another. To some people it comes like a sudden explosion, to others it is a process of slow growth into a more whole world. To the whole society it is happening as a deep shift in world view. It grows out of the coming together of women to share experience, and the political understanding and action that develops from that. As I have suggested in an earlier chapter, this radical shift can be thought of as a changing of the gods, a renaming of the divine as women reclaim ourselves.

Renaming work

How do women rename work? It is depressing for women to look at work from a patriarchal viewpoint as we have been doing, because it reminds us of all the divisions and injustices. From a patriarchal point of view, for example, the term 'work' has increasingly been used to mean paid work. It is opposed to rest, leisure, play, pleasure, all of which are often associated with women and home, or women and sex. The actual work women do is devalued and made invisible both in the private domestic sphere and in a parallel way in the public sphere of paid employment.

Seen from a different point of view, the work women do includes much of the basic work of the world. It can be divided into six categories – paid employment, housework, birth, nurturing, voluntary work, and political/spiritual work. First, *paid employment*. A proper valuation of women's work is essential to women's well-being, since economic inequality not only contributes to the disproportionate poverty among women (which affects many children) but also subverts their autonomy or any real mutuality in relationships. However, it is not only in terms of money that a greater value needs to be placed on a more equal participation of women in the paid workforce, since this could also go some way towards promoting cooperative rather than competitive styles of work, a more equal sharing of power and a more just and compassionate consideration for all those at present disadvantaged by aggressive competition for wealth and power.

Second, *housework* – a misleading term to indicate the unpaid work done at home. As a single category it is so reductive as to be false, but the fact that there is no adequate word for it is a sign of its invisibility. As well as housework I mean it to include the unpaid productive work of households and farms, and the unpaid work women do as part of or to support their husband's work. The productive activities of households, still of course largely done by women, are not only unpaid but are left out of the Gross Domestic Product and the national accounts. On a world scale, Marilyn Waring has found that the United Nations' national accounts rule books exclude subsistence farming, the bulk of the world's farming done almost exclusively by women, as well as housework and voluntary community work. Waring comments that this exclusion embodies 'every aspect of the blindness of patriarchy, its arrogance, its lack of perception. It enshrines the invisibility and enslavement of women in the economic process as of little or no importance.'[17] Waring comments, 'If you're invisible in the national accounts, you're absent when public policy is made. If you're not counted in income, you're not seen in outcome.' Both the relatively low pay for women in the workforce, and the lack of any pay for productive work in the home, contribute to the definition of women's work as secondary, and perpetuate women's economic dependence on men.[18] This economic dependence, and often powerlessness, is closely related to women's political powerlessness, both within the family and in the making of public policy. As women are becoming more independent economically, there has been an increase in the number of women in parliament, and a change in sexual politics within the family, but the structural gains have as yet scarcely gone beyond tokenism, and the smallest gain still brings a backlash. A just financial remuneration for women's productive work at home, including child care, would revolutionise both the economy and relations between the sexes, personally and politically. At this stage that seems an impossible fantasy. But women are already breaking the silence about it, and in the meantime, as we work towards a more just recognition of it, the increasing role of women in the paid workforce and of men in the work of the household will have a loosening and humanising effect.

It is worth mentioning here that the ecological cost of much economic activity is also unrecognised. As Waring says, the price in polluted water, destroyed rainforest, degraded and irradiated soil, should be on the deficit side of GDP and appropriate deductions made (*SMH*, 5.4.89). To the patriarchy, women and the land are equally exploitable, though the land, like women, is striking back.

Third, we come to *birth*, the reproduction of the species. It is ironic that what has traditionally been considered a central function and achievement of women, and is even referred to by the word 'labour', is now scarcely thought appropriate to include in a discussion of 'work'. Seen as an event, birth takes only a moment: the baby pops out. And of course mothers are not paid for this 'labour of love' (or at least not until the recent controversial introduction of the practice of surrogacy). Yet even in these days of perhaps too many births, when many countries are trying desperately to reduce their population growth, and also when women are quick to point out that we will not be reduced to the role of baby factories, or have our worth as persons equated with child-bearing, nevertheless, the actual *work* of bearing children remains a crucial part of women's lives, as well as being, obviously, of critical importance to the continuance of the race. Far from being the work of a moment, preparation for childbirth occupies our bodily and social selves for years, and after the event, if we do have a child, our lives are never the same again.

The bodily and emotional processes of menstruation, pregnancy, birth and the nurturing of the young (and of other people) are important in women's lives in a way that they are not for men. In fact some feminist theorists see men's alienation from these processes as a major causal factor in male dominance. In her book *The Politics of Reproduction*, Mary O'Brien sees men's ambivalent relation to sexuality as the basis for their claim to both power and dominance. 'For men, sexuality is the basis of a free appropriative right, a power over women and children and a power over time itself. It is also the basis of the radical uncertainty of that right, of a fundamental alienation from the natural process, and a lack of immediate recognition as progenitor. It is, further, a power sustained in its contradiction by violence, sometimes overt, sometimes covert, in part personal, in part political. The social relations of reproduction are relations of dominance precisely because at the heart of the doctrine of potency lies the intransigent impotency of uncertainty, an impotency which colours and continuously brutalises the social and political relations in which it is expressed.'[19]

Rosemary Ruether links the origin of male domination of women to the cultural assumption of the hierarchy of culture over nature, going back to the male puberty rites which bring male socialisation out of the mother's into the father's sphere and define the process hierarchically. The young male is taught to identify with the male sphere as higher than the female sphere, the place of an earlier, lower self that he has now 'transcended'. 'The domination of women throughout most of human history,' Ruether says, 'has depended on the freeing of males for cultural control by filling women's days with most of the tasks of domestic production and reproduction.' Ruether continues: 'The domination of woman's labour is essential to an understanding of the cultural metaphor of dominated nature as dominated woman. Woman's body — her reproductive processes — becomes owned by men, defined from a male point of view? The reduction of women to silence is an important part of this process: 'The male monopoly on cultural definition makes women the object rather than the subject of that definition . . . Male transcendence is defined as flight from and warfare against the realm of the mother, the realm of body and nature, all that limits and confines rather than being controlled by the human (male)?[20]

For women, however, giving birth and nurturance are central to our personal and social lives and values and, as Jane's story (below) shows, can be a source of real empowerment. Whether particular women choose to have children or not, it is important for us all as women to claim the bodily power and spiritual strength which the capacity to bear and nurture children implies. As in the areas of paid work and housework, women are refusing to submit to male control in our reproductive lives. The struggle centres around many issues — access to safe contraception and abortion, freedom from forced sterilisation, good pre-natal and post-natal health care, and majority participation by women in decision-making about in vitro fertilisation programs, surrogacy and other reproductive issues. Because these issues are related to sexuality, they are seen as part of the private, moral sphere rather than the public, political sphere, so the struggle is somewhat elusive and hard to clarify, but in all these areas men cling to control with an appalling level of violence and tenacity. This reaches the height of absurdity and arrogance in the Catholic Church's attempt to keep control over women's bodies in the hands of a group of celibate men. Compulsory celibacy, and fear of the power women may derive from control over their own sexuality and birth-giving capacities, are, of course, not unrelated.

At the heart of this struggle are questions of bodily integrity, of sexuality, and of women's moral agency. Respect for 'our bodies, ourselves', for the bodily integrity of every person, has been fundamental to the secular women's movement and to feminist theology. It involves a transformation of the body/mind, body/spirit dualisms into an understanding of personhood as wholistic and embodied. Linked with this is an affirmation of sexuality as good, to be celebrated as an aspect of our embodied selves. Unless we are free to make decisions about our own sexuality, our power as self-regulating moral agents does not develop. The state and the church, in controlling women's bodies, deny women's moral agency. Enforced pregnancy and enforced sterilisation are totally unjustifiable violations of women's bodily integrity.

Women's sexual freedom is denied in the dualistic mindset which sees men as initiators and women as sexually passive; in the view which sees only procreative sex as good; in the tendency to see women who deny sex as good and those who are sexually active as whores. Women are as capable of enjoying sex as men, and are redefining sexual pleasure in ways that reject the narrow focus on genital sexuality. To use Beverly Harrison's definition, the feminist insight is that 'sexuality is mutual pleasuring in the context of genuine openness and intimacy'[21] Sex-role patterns which control or limit women's sexuality also limit women's 'ability to achieve a self-defining role in relation to their bodies', and so contribute to inequalities of power.

The struggle to control the birth process is one aspect of women's struggle towards greater autonomy in the area of sexuality and reproduction. Through the establishment of birthing centres, through access to midwives, and through sympathetic support for the mother's active role in the birth, women are reclaiming power. Jane, whose description of her life at home with two small children was quoted above, talks here about the birth of Christine Mary:

> Giving birth to my second daughter was a time of great joy and strength. I was the active driving force. I worked with the pain rather than trying to dull or ignore it. This gave me great strength as I could listen to my body and participate in the birthing process.
>
> Remaining upright and mobile during the labour was imperative. This enabled me to be in control rather than the medical staff. As the time drew near I selected several birthing positions on the floor. Ultimately I gave birth upright, in a squatting position.
>
> Through my endurance I had given birth to my child without medical intervention. I had listened to my body and responded to it. That was the moment of strength.
>
> Jane

This is a long way from the Christian and Jewish view of birth as 'unclean', which, even in the Anglican church until recently, required that women be 'churched' six weeks after the birth before they could fully participate in church services again. A long way too from birth seen as sickness, and therefore needing to take place in hospital, with the male obstetrician as star and the mother not only lying on her back but often anaesthetised and with her legs in stirrups as well. Many women now see the in vitro fertilisation programs as another mode of male domination of the birth process, exploiting women's desire to have a child. The cost to women in terms of time, pain, money and intrusion into the woman's body and bodyself is only now being balanced against the less-than-ten-percent 'success' rate. Again it is the male medical and research scientists who, in the media for example, are seen as the heroes, while the women's 'labour' is ignored.

The fourth kind of work, *nurturing*, is closely related to reproduction and to housework. The immense amount of time and energy and loving care spent by women not only on caring for babies and children but also partners, friends, the elderly, the lonely, the handicapped, is certainly not recognised in the money economy and is scarcely acknowledged anywhere, even by women, though we know it in our bodies and lives. Harrison writes, 'Women's lives literally have been shaped by the power not only to bear life at the biological level but to nurture life, which is a social and cultural power'. She argues that though our culture has come to undervalue nurturance, the ability to give genuine nurture is a formidable power. Insofar as such nurture has been given throughout human history, it has been largely through women's action . . . Because we do not understand love as the power to act-each-other-into-well-being we also do not understand the depth of our power to thwart life and to maim each other.[22] In reducing this power to the status of an aspect of women's passive role rather than seeing it as the active and crucial doing of the work of love and nurture, we are following a dangerous path for ourselves and our society.

Our culture celebrates the individualistic, powerful, invulnerable male who acts from a position of strength and therefore sees others as less powerful, less important, than he. But relationship based on such built-in equality cannot have the back-and-forth flow of mutuality based on receiving as well as giving, caring and being cared for. The masculine repression of feeling cuts off relationship in a way that cripples growth. It is deathly.

The Christian church depends on the daily work of women both to maintain its physical life, through cleaning, looking after keys, serving suppers, etc, and to care for the people by keeping in touch, listening, welcoming newcomers, and so on. But much of this work is not only unpaid but also largely unrecognised. The gospel celebrates love, but the work of love tends to be more important in some cases than others. When men, especially priests, do it, it is called pastoral care. When women do it, if it is noticed at all it is thought of as housework or gossip.

Voluntary work, fifth, is an extension of nurture outside the family into community services. It reveals the dependence of the market economy on an immense amount of unpaid labour. Lorraine Wheeler points out that in Australia the (paid) community services industry, which is larger than the manufacturing industry, is the largest single employer of women and employs far more women than men. Of those who work for pay, most are women (800,000 out of 1.3 million in 1987), and unlike other industry sectors, this industry has an unpaid volunteer workforce twice as large as the number of people it employs for pay. It also relies heavily on unpaid work carried out by paid staff. This could only happen in a female-dominated industry. Men do not and are not expected to work without remuneration in this massive way. The continuing reduction in government community services also adds to the caring work of women, euphemistically called 'the family' – and thereby disappears from view and from the national accounts.

There are advantages for society and for some women in this system of voluntary work. Margaret Bell, Executive Director of the Volunteer Centre of New South Wales, claims that 'volunteerism in the 80s in being recognised through its army of women care-givers as a force in itself which can be mobilised as an agent for social and economic development, and changes can become a means through which women may be empowered to become owners of their own destiny'[23] – but this exploitation of women's willingness to give care goes counter to the drive for women's economic independence[24] and although freely chosen by some, can put women in the position of enforced service. It also provides the government with a huge resource on which it depends to prop up its welfare system and reduce the welfare bill.

These five kinds of work, paid employment, housework, giving birth, nurturing and voluntary work are perhaps best summed up in the following simple statistics:

Women
- represent 52% of the world's population;
- perform 2/3 of the work hours per annum;
- are paid 1/10 of the world's wages;
- own 1/100 of the world's property. [25]

The sixth kind of work, which I would call *political/spiritual work*, is the constant daily work we do to bring ourselves to birth as women, and to participate in celebrating life, ourselves, all that is. It is communal work, and involves 'hearing one another to speech'.[26] It is political in that it involves bringing ourselves and everyone to empowerment in their lives, over against all the structures of domination — of class, race, sexism, heterosexism, imperialism and domination of the environment. People are already engaged in long-term struggles around these issues in the public sphere, which is where politics is supposed to happen. What is new and unsettling to people is that they have become political issues also in the private, supposedly non-political, sphere. Major structural change is crucial — and has not yet happened. But the struggles in the private sphere are undermining the foundations of the public oppressive structures. The major ground is now being contested not in the public sphere but between the public and private, the male and female, spheres. At the centre of the political struggle are issues of economic independence and sexual autonomy which are crucial to women's empowerment, issues such as family violence, child care and child support, the valuation of women's domestic and paid work, abortion, sex education, the controversies around in vitro fertilisation and child maintenance. What has been the invisible private pain of women is now being translated into political strategies and action as women's experience is voiced and heard.

The patriarchal church is in an awkward position in regard to the public/ private split. On the one hand it finds itself on the private side, its power associated more with the 'morality' of the home and the family, and the churches in the middle class suburbs, than with the 'real' world of work and politics. When Archbishop Runcie in the United Kingdom recently took a position on the war with Argentina which was at odds with the Prime Minister's view, she quickly tried to put him back in his place in the private sphere, outside the world of politics and war.

Yet to the extent that the major religions have been patriarchal, they, or certainly the clergy, have identified themselves with the male side of all the dualisms. The church hierarchy has largely aligned itself with the public male power-structures, and its own misogyny and fear of sexuality have had a strong influence in sacralising the sexism of public policy and

morality in the secular world. Feminist theology is challenging the patriarchal values which the hierarchy idolatrously sees as the foundations of
Christianity. Women, placed by the church on the underside of all the
binary oppositions, are rejecting the whole dualistic way of thinking, not
in order to be on top ourselves, but in order to transform both sides into
an integrated whole. In claiming our own power, we are challenging the
devaluation of women and the feminine, and reasserting our own worth
and dignity and that of other oppressed groups.

The way to do this, since men are as deaf as the grave to women's claims,
can only be through political struggle. As Rosemary Ruether pointed out
years ago, anger and a pride are now theological virtues for women.[27] We
are right to be angry at a church which, for example, would grant full human
rights to a tiny zygote or embryo but not to a fully mature woman; which
has canonised a woman for remaining with a husband who regularly bashed
her; which celebrates the incarnation but is afraid of bodies and sexuality,
and prevents students from learning the facts of sexuality, reproduction
and contraception; which never supports women's struggle for pay equity;
and which is fixated on the image of God as Father and excludes women
from the image of God. The harm the church does by modelling male
dominance in its imaging of God, its sexist doctrines, structures and
language, and its misogynist ethics, permeates western culture. Until the
church is transformed in all these aspects of its life, its sexism will continue
as a malign force.

The recovery of wholeness and health in church and society cannot
happen only from the resurrection of women and of 'feminine' values, with
a proper recognition and valuation of women's work in production and
reproduction. Men also must act to heal alienations by relinquishing their
claims to superiority and their destructive habits of domination and violence.
It is a Jungian insight that wholeness comes from identifying with your
shadow side. Instead of projecting emotionality, sexual anxiety, inferiority
and uncleanness onto women, men have to own their own mortality and
imperfection, their vulnerability and, in Christian terms, their fallenness.
Healing the dualistic splits in our church and society may seem an impos-
sibly idealistic and cosmic task. Nevertheless it is not impossible to make
a beginning in all the areas related to women's work, child-care and reproductive responsibility already mentioned.

Within the church and in the public mind, ordination has become a
focal point around which all the conflicts of power, doctrine and feeling
swirl. Some men and churches seem unaware of their arrogant reduction
of 'the image of God' to a male image. Equating themselves with the divine
image, they are outraged at impure women claiming dignity and worth

as persons also made 'in the image of God', and acting on that claim. It is a deep resistance, drawing on thousands of years of patriarchy, but as Elisabeth Schüssler Fiorenza shows, it is quite contrary to the Christian gospel, to Jesus' teaching and practice, which includes every person in the new community and promotes the discipleship of equals.[28] Rosemary Ruether points out that the conservatives are right to see that the ordination of women 'threatens the entire psychodynamics by which the God–human, the soul–body, the clergy–lay, and finally the church–world relationships have been imaged in terms of sexual hierarchicalism.' The revolution represented by the ordination of women in significant numbers threatens the foundations of a symbolic structure which sacralises not only these sexist divisions but also those of race and class, which operate out of the same implicit elevation of the 'head' people over the 'body' people. But this is precisely why the ordination of women is necessary, so that the church can recover its role as the representative of a liberated humanity. 'The gospel of the church', Ruether maintains, 'must again come to be recognised as the social mandate of history, not the means of setting up a new regime of domination or, on the other hand, of withdrawing into a private world of individual salvation.'[29]

While the church continues to refuse to ordain women, or to allow only token numbers, it remains captive to patriarchal thinking which is damaging to women and to the church itself. Women see the church as hypocritical when it proclaims 'salvation for all' but models sexism in its ordination practices, its employment patterns and salary scales, its continuing attempts to control women's reproductive lives, all totally against its own gospel. Even the ordination of women will not be significant unless the women are strong enough, in numbers and in determination, to overthrow the church's idolatry of the male.

Much of women's work of celebration therefore takes place outside the church. The etymological meaning of the word liturgy is sometimes given as 'the work of the people', but almost all the liturgy we now experience in church and synagogue is far from being the work of women, and is quite cut off from the work women do. In this area as in others there is a strange reversal going on.

The church I belong to is the Uniting Church in Australia, formed from the coming together in 1977 of the Presbyterian, Methodist and Congregational churches. My local church came into the Uniting Church from the Congregational tradition, which has been ordaining women since 1932. Although we respect the new forms and structures of the Uniting Church, I feel that in our local church authority and power are still centred in the local congregation rather than the wider synods and assemblies, or in what might be called the Uniting Church hierarchy. The pews are arranged in the round, the minister wears ordinary street clothes, members of the congregation, women as much as men, participate in the services in many ways including doing the Bible readings and the intercessory prayers. We celebrate the Spirit among us. I experience the congregation as a loving community, which I feel is a rare privilege. Nevertheless we struggle with the usual gaps – between those who like the old hymns and those who prefer contemporary words and music; those who want traditional church language and preaching and those who want to be more exploratory and create new forms out of contemporary experience; those who respond to the traditional male images of God and those of us who can no longer bear the accumulated weight of them.

One morning when I was feeling rather fragile I went to church and was disappointed to find the service was being taken by a visiting minister whom I experienced as traditionalist and pietistic, caught up in a sentimentalised fatherly gospel. It was a communion service and when he said the words 'This is my blood, shed for you' I felt a sudden rage – at him and at all the men who perform this rite, who have done so down the centuries and who still control and dominate it. Our church does have women ministers, but the forms of the sacraments are still almost entirely composed by men and enacted by male celebrants. My sudden fury came from this ineffectual man identifying with the male Jesus' shedding of blood and proclaiming that it was done for me, when I knew it was my mother who at my birth shed blood for me, and that it is my women friends who listen to me and support me in the long slog of the real bearing of one another's pain. It was the arrogance built into the church's structure that presents as a solo male act something which in the lived world is mostly done by women. And of course it was a woman after the service who asked me how I was and gave me her shoulder when I burst into tears.

We are so used to these strange reversals in the church's life and teachings that we hardly notice them. We know it is women who give birth, so how is it that religiously Eve is born from Adam? In daily life it is usually women who buy the groceries and cook and serve the meals, so why in the church is it mostly the male clergy who dispense the bread and wine? At birth the breaking of the waters is the first wetting of our heads as we enter life, and yet men take over the baptismal rite of our 'religious' birth with water on our heads again. The every-day work of women in giving birth, feeding and nurturing, so little recognised or valued in our church and culture, is precisely what *is* valued when in its symbolic form, it is performed as a religious rite by men.

There is something strange going on when the religious ritual feeding, performed by men, is given higher value that the actual daily work of feeding, done largely by women. I think it is one of the lingering vestiges of the way the male-centred tribes and culture (and the religions such as Buddhism, Judaism, Christianity and Islam which express it) took over 5,000 years ago from the earlier, long-established Goddess-worshipping societies. The celebration of birth, life, food, sexuality, nature, in the ancient Goddess-worshipping societies around the Mediterranean was violently put down by the followers of Yahweh. Birth, food preparation, sexuality and closeness to nature remain associated with the female, but are now devalued and to some extent have gone underground in our culture. But in their religious version they still form the centre of the rituals of the patriarchal church. The ancient myths were changed to become male centred, as we see for example in the tree of life becoming the Christian cross, and in the Adam and Eve myth where instead of Eve's birth-giving being celebrated, what is now central is Adam's authority over her. In art the strong and beautiful female figures were replaced by sad statues of Mary, no longer looking out at the world with curiosity and self-possession but gazing soulfully at the baby boy on her knee. Male priests have appropriated religiously the trappings of ancient female power – the cassocks and robes which imitate women's dress, and the sacraments of baptism and communion in which men do symbolically what women do in daily life. As well as being a male takeover of women's daily work, these rituals point to a drastic split between sacred and profane. Instead of the life-giving spirit present in the whole of life, we have a sacred spiritual Godly domain connected with the church and mediated to us through male priests and bishops and a profane world which they preach to and visit and give pastoral care to.

A sense of celebration is rising again among women in our generation, but the patriarchal church remains largely closed to it. Women know that the wine of the spirit is present in daily life, in encounters between people, in political movements, in nature, in joy and sorrow, in birth and death. It is not mainly in some sacred space set apart. A church which excludes us from the image of the divine, from its language and its decision-making councils, which excludes our sexuality and exploits our work, is hardly a place where women can freely celebrate life in its fullness.

No wonder such groups as Women-church are springing up where women are simply going outside the male claim to authority and orthodoxy, and are developing new liturgies celebrating all the aspects of life – birth and death, marriage, menopause, divorce, birthdays, spring, winter, summer, and so on. It is, after all, women who usually organise children's birthdays,

Christmas dinners, family celebrations, even office parties. We can even, as we get older, celebrate what we might call the work of diminishment, of letting go.

It is when we understand life as celebration that we can think of and experience our work as a dance, a dance which incorporates ecstasy, love, enjoyment. If women's work or sexuality or reproductive freedom is controlled by men and devalued, if women's bodies are devalued and made into objects by being under the control of men, the dance disappears, creativity disappears. And it disappears for men as well as for women. Mechtild of Magdeburg wrote in the thirteenth century that:

> if the body should lose its power
> men and women
> would become
>
> unfruitful.[30]

This brings us back to the Genesis story of the fall, which placed work on one side (male) and babies on the other (female). In renaming work from women's point of view we have been undermining that opposition, showing that work is involved on *both* sides of the dualism, and needs to be valued in both, whether it is done by women or men. Home is also a workplace, and the workplace is also a home, a place for nurture and good relationships and the proper recognition of each person. As these patterns are affirmed and strengthened, and justice sought, the destructive oppositions are destroyed and wholeness becomes more possible both in individuals and in society.

In all six areas above where women are renaming work and fighting for its proper valuation, these rigid divisions are breaking down. Women will continue to struggle for a more just system of remuneration, a more humane and caring workplace, and a more equal sharing of power and responsibility at 'home' and at 'work'. But it is time the patriarchal church came to its senses and joined in. As Edna Ryan and Anne Conlon said, 'There is no benign power which will dispense equality – the realisation will come from active participation.'[31]

This chapter began in the centre of great alienations, because it is impossible in today's world to speak of women's work without finding oneself immediately caught up in the terrible alienations between female and male, private and public, body and mind. It is certainly a question of justice that we have been dealing with, but it is also a question of restoring joy to the experience of work. By moving into and affirming the darker side of each dualism it is possible to transform both sides into a new wholeness, a new mutuality, and the alienated world becomes again a garden where we can all dig and plant and share the fruit.

M.T.

Notes

1   Genesis 1:1
2   Susan Ackley, 'A Meditation on Diapers' in *Woman of Power*, Issue 12, Winter 1989, Cambridge, Ma., p.13.
3   *Ibid*, p.14.
4   Genesis 3: 16–19.
5   For a history of the equal pay struggle in Australia, see Edna Ryan and Anne Conlon's chapter, 'The Elusive Equal Pay, 1951–1974' in *Gentle Invaders*, Thomas Nelson, Melbourne, 1975, pp.145–75.
6   Women's Bureau, *Women's Work, Women's Pay*, Department of Employment, Education and Training, Canberra, 1988.
7   New South Wales Women's Co-ordination Unit, *Women's Policy Statement*, Parramatta, 1990, p.6.
8   Women's Bureau, *op.cit.*

9 Clare Burton, 'Pay Equity in Australia', unpublished paper of a talk to mark the fourth anniversary of the Sex Discrimination Act, Sydney, 1988.
10 *Ibid.*, p.7.
11 Lois Bryson, *The Proletarianisation of Women: Gender Justice in Australia*, Social Justice, Vol.16, No.3, 1989, pp.87–102.
12 New South Wales Women's Co-ordination Unit, *op.cit.*, pp.2–6.
13 Rosemary Radford Ruether, 'Motherearth and the Megamachine: A Theology of Liberation in a Feminine, Somatic and Ecological Perspective', in C. Christ and J.Plaskow, eds, *Womanspirit Rising*, Harper and Row, New York, 1979, pp.43–52.
14 Marija Gimbutas, *The Goddesses and Gods of Old Europe*, Thames & Hudson, London, 1982, p.9, and Merlin Stone, *Paradise Papers: The Suppression of Women's Rites*, Virago, London, 1977, pp.78–118.
15 *Sydney Morning Herald*, 8 July 1989.
16 Mary Daly, *Gyn/Ecology*, Beacon Press, Boston, 1978, p.2.
17 Quoted by Yvonne Preston, *Sydney Morning Herald*, 5 April 1989.
18 Susan Yeandle, *Women's Working Lives: Patterns and Strategies*, Tavistock Publications, London, 1984, p.38.
19 Mary O'Brien, *The Politics of Reproduction*, Routledge and Kegan Paul, London, 1983, p.191.
20 Rosemary Radford Ruether, *Sexism and God-Talk*, Beacon Press, Boston, 1983, pp.73–75.
21 Beverly Wildung Harrison, *Making the Connections: Essays in Feminist Social Ethics*, Beacon Press, Boston, 1985, p.87.
22 *Ibid.*, p.11.
23 Margaret Bell, *Volunteers as Care Providers*, Paper from the Conference on the Future of Women's Services, Sydney University, 1988, p.2.
24 Bell herself points out that she opposes 'any return to the humiliations of Victorian philanthropy, whereby some people become the passive recipients of other people's "good works"'. She says, 'Women as volunteers in the 90s will remain in the forefront of action for social change and development', and goes on to claim for volunteers 'the right to appropriate recognition and training in what they do.'
25 Quoted by Bell, *op.cit.*, p.2.
26 Nelle Morton, *The Journey is Home*, Beacon Press, Boston, 1985, p.99.
27 Rosemary Radford Ruether, 'Sexism and the Theology of Liberation: Nature, Fall and Salvation as Seen from the Experience of Women', in *The Christian Century*, December 1973.
28 Elisabeth Schüssler Fiorenza, *In Memory of Her*, Crossroad, New York, 1983, *passim*.
29 Rosemary Radford Ruether, *New Woman, New Earth: Sexist Ideologies and Human Liberation*, Dove Communications, Melbourne, 1975, pp.82–83.
30 Sue Woodruff, *Meditations with Mechtild of Magdeburg*, Bear & Company, Santa Fe, 1982, p.96.
31 Edna Ryan and Anne Conlon, *Gentle Invaders*, Thomas Nelson, Melbourne, 1975, p.175.

CHAPTER FOUR

Refusing to be victims

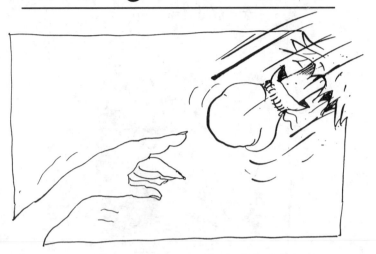

Humans live surrounded by violence, a violence Christianity accommodates and promotes. This is a stark statement. That we live in violence is a truism. That Christianity accommodates and promotes violence is also a truism for some, but for others it will need to be demonstrated.

In this chapter, I shall present evidence that Christianity, victimising women, promotes and models violence in its rituals, scriptures and theology, in its administrative structures and legislation, as well as in its traditions and history.

Violence is not all that Christianity models, of course: it also models peace, justice and love. Christian symbols and traditions, imaging a liberating relation with ourselves, with others, with nature and with divinity, can free us and speak to us of life. In Christian communities we sometimes experience this life. This positive aspect of Christianity remains an assumption of the present chapter.

What Christians do not readily admit is that Christianity conforms to and supports the injustice of other institutions in that it too is based on a hierarchy of domination and subordination, it too models, often unconsciously, a structure of violence. A key example is its misogyny appearing both in the subtle form of exalting and idealising women and the blatant one of denigrating and ignoring them. There is no contradiction between these. Exaltation of women is intimately connected with, even conceptually necessary for their denigration. These are simply different manifestations of a continuum along which Christianity has constructed womankind.

There is, then, a need to revolutionise the Christian symbol system and the misogynous structures it maintains. Simply rectifying symbols and structures that denigrate and omit women will not suffice, even if this were possible. Womankind, mankind, gendered humanity need to be conceptualised in new ways. While acknowledging the need, I do not undertake so grand a task here. I simply focus on the underside, on women as victims whether by exaltation or denigration, on Christianity allowing and promoting this victimisation, and, most importantly, on women's refusing to be victims.[1] Articulating women's experience of violence, analysing symbols and structures that promote it, and exploring ways of living peacefully and justly: these are life-giving measures empowering us all.

When violence is mentioned, certain words and images come to mind: rape, murder, abortion, incest, wife-beating, child-beating, pornography, crime, drugs, war, and perhaps politics, big business, advertising and sport. Violence runs through, dominates even, both private and public worlds. Looking at our daily newspapers, we are overwhelmed by examples of violence on our front doorsteps as well as in foreign lands: wars and rumours of wars, rape and rumours of rape. And the Christian churches speak out against violence often enough. Why then am I proposing that Christianity is partly responsible for a violent world?

Plotting the stories of women

In response to this question I begin with stories of women victims and survivors of violence. The first is about a woman whose life has been publicly endorsed by the Roman Catholic church. I present it to suggest that violence against women is not confined to single, numerous instances, but is endemic in contemporary society, and that all systems, religious, legal, political, economic and cultural, generally support and maintain each other in oppressing women. A system of misogynous violence is institutionalised through the apparently innocuous actions of church and state.

The Madagascan woman saint

The following extract is taken from a report published in *The Sydney Morning Herald* quoting from *The Los Angeles Times*:

> **Madagascar, Sunday:** Pope John Paul II beatified a 19th century Madagascan woman today at a mass for half a million people and called her faith and loyalty to a difficult husband a model for women.[2]

After reporting that the Madagascan President and four leaders of the Opposition attended the mass, that the Christian Church Council had offered to mediate between Government and Opposition following riots which left six people dead, and that the Pope's Secretary of State would meet Opposition leaders, the newspaper item goes on to say that:

> . . . the crowd, many barefoot, broke into wild cheering when the pontiff proclaimed Rasoamanarivo a 'blessed' of the Church and unveiled a large painting of her . . . The Pope said she maintained her 'beautiful womanly qualities' despite the persecution of Catholics and her marriage to a member of the royal household whose drunkenness and infidelity caused her much pain. Earlier, the Pope warned Malagasy youth, who in the past fortnight have taken part in lethal political riots, to 'reject violence, lies and scorn'.[3]

The interweaving of religious and political concerns and the dangerous complementarity between them are here quite apparent. Without discussing the particularities of either this woman's life story or the political tensions in Madagascar, we can still note a destructive connection between religious and political spheres in the way the incident is reported here. On the one hand, the woman is beatified for her 'beautiful womanly qualities', meaning no doubt her gentleness, humility and meekness in the face of an oppressive monarchy and an unfaithful, drunken husband, while, on the other, the youth are reprimanded for taking part in political riots and for resorting to 'violence, lies and scorn'. The woman, as a symbol of obedient and enduring submission, has become an object lesson for the people of Madagascar, particularly the youth. Both the affirmation of the woman and the reprimand directed to the youth implicitly condone and support the prevailing patriarchal arrangements.

Canonising Women

The beatification of this Madagascan woman is a political act: the spiritual, enacted in a public forum, is always political. The enduring woman is held up by both church and state as a model to other women and to wayward youth. Here the different systems, religious and political, can be seen as maintaining current hierarchies, the right order, as they would believe, of society.

We are not talking here about the frequency of violence against women, though statistics in this area are alarming;[4] but rather about *understanding connections*, those between this woman's story and the ideology of misogynous violence in which we all live.

The Madagascan woman does not tell her own story, so we cannot tell whether she agrees or disagrees with the way her story is told. From this media report we only know that church and state have appropriated her story, turning her into a symbol of long-suffering fidelity and constructing her life as one of faithful service to a persecuting husband and church. Thus presented, her story supports rather than subverts the present unjust arrangements and serves patriarchal ends. Feminist women do not condemn her for this. We do condemn, however, the transforming of flesh and blood woman into a symbol of endurance and passivity, a truly enervating image for today's women. Not only in her own lifetime, but in the very memory of that life, this woman, via political and religious institutions as reported in the press, is a victim of patriarchal history. It is essential that we condemn, not the flesh-and-blood woman, but the symbol she has become, lest we too should become its victims. Constructing symbols or images in order to manipulate groups of people, image-making as it is called in the political arena, is a most violent abuse of institutional power indulged in by the church, as well as by other patriarchal institutions.[5] Deconstructing harmful images, like that of the saintly and long-suffering wife, is the only life-giving response.

The cash-register wife and the marriage ritual

Some women may distance themselves from that story saying that they are never likely to be beatified, nor would they want to be, and that they are a long way removed from a 19th century Madagascan noblewoman. But we can all, in some ways, identify with women who suffer violence. If we do not experience this kind of suffering ourselves, we can recognise it in women we meet, in the eyes of women in the street. There is a hidden publicness about family violence. Frequently recognised, it is rarely named. We have all seen what Kate Llewellyn here describes.[6]

> She is too far gone
> to do more than register
> we are smiling
> under the water where she drowns deeply
> at her cash register pushing the keys
> leading only to mistakes and punishment
>
> her husband is shouting
> something abusive in Greek
> I knew when I saw her and that beaten way
> we didn't need language
> to say what was going on
> let's face it
> a violent man beats regularly

> if he shouts like this now
> what else does he do?
> our money hurries to the rescue
> it'll buy respite but nothing more
> people are so thick
> one woman keeps asking for the right change
> while he shouts at his wife
> who is quietly going to pieces
> at the register
>
> when the animal sees the knife its eyes go like hers
> nothing can save you sister
> nothing
>
> language isn't appropriate
> money is only useful
> smiles grease his sores a bit
> brutality and panic
> are up against the wall sister
> nothing can save you sister
> nothing

Like the poet, we can stand with this woman and name her pain. We can reflect on the way the church commends a woman for staying with a difficult husband and enduring the good fight, on the way the law, like the neighbours, will not want to interfere.[7] We know, as this woman knows in her gut, that should she do the unthinkable, should she hit back, separate and divorce, the law may restrain her and the state fail to provide adequate means of support, while the church will most certainly forbid her all further sexual relations. Voices naming her suffering, encouraging her to act on her own behalf cannot penetrate the structures walling her in. A sister's look, a sister's words, cannot reach beyond these walls of private violence and public control and indifference.

These violated women could be any of us. Patriarchal structures allow it to be so. My critique of violence is focused, not just on the men violating these particular women, but more especially on the structures and institutions betraying all women. *Individual* lawyers and politicians, priests and ministers, both male and female, may well help a woman leave a violent husband, just as *individual* women may, against all odds, leave the institution of a violent marriage. We all know of such instances. But such individuals are often working against structures and rules, against the very code of their institutions, so that should their subversive activity become public they will be officially reprimanded by these same institutions.

To determine what any institution stands for we look not to individuals, but to public examples, to the rules and statutes, to the methods of internal organisation, to the face the institution presents to the world. In the case of the Roman Catholic church, for example, we look to its Code of Canon Law, to its interpretations of scriptures, to its doctrines, myths and symbols, to its official statements and administrative structures, to the people it chooses to canonise and its reasons for canonising them. We look also to the tensions existing in each of these aspects, for the church, like most institutions, is neither wholly good nor wholly evil: as noted initially, the church promotes peace as well as violence. For the purpose of this chapter though, I am delineating only its tendencies to violence, tendencies already seen at work in the beatification of the abused Madagascan woman. We can detect them again in another, related structure of the church, in the official marriage ritual. Here the ground rules are laid for a tradition of violence against women and children.

Everyone is familiar with a traditional church wedding. The virginal white bride, always the centrepiece, arrives at the church when priest, guests and bridegroom are all assembled. On her father's arm, she proceeds slowly up the church aisle, her way defined between blocks of wedding guests. At the foot of the altar, her father delivers her to the waiting groom, and the priest, presiding from the altar steps, conducts the ceremony. At his prompting, the couple exchange vows and rings. The deed done, the priest retires behind the altar and the bride, on her husband's arm, makes the return journey towards the back of the church and the daily domestic world. From a bird's eye view it is quite apparent that the priest, representing the church, conducts a ceremony in which a woman changes hands from old male to young male, an exchange witnessed and applauded by a congregation of people.

All present have well-defined roles, and the bride, the sole veiled, white-clad figure, is the pivot. From beginning to end, the ceremony follows her actions: all eyes are on her. The *words* of the ceremony, too, focus on her. The official Roman Catholic Mass for the bridegroom and bride, for example, the one celebrated until the mid-1960s, included a Nuptial Blessing addressed by the presiding priest to the couple. To say that three-quarters of this blessing focuses on the bride does not adequately express the imbalance. I quote it in full.

O God, by Thy mighty power Thou didst make all things out of nothing. First, Thou didst set the beginnings of the universe in order. Then, Thou didst make man in Thy image, and didst appoint woman to be his inseparable helpmate. Thus Thou didst make woman's body from the flesh of man, thereby teaching that what Thou has been pleased to institute from one principle might never lawfully be put asunder. O God, Thou hast sanctified marriage by a mystery so excellent that in the marriage union thou didst foreshadow the union of Christ and the Church. O God, thou dost join woman to man, and Thou dost endow that fellowship with a blessing which was not taken away in punishment for original sin nor by the sentence of the flood. Look in thy mercy upon this Thy handmaid, about to be joined in wedlock, who entreats Thee to protect and strengthen her. Let the yoke of marriage to her be one of love and peace. Faithful and chaste, let her marry in Christ. Let her ever follow the model of holy women: let her be dear to her husband like Rachel; wise like Rebecca; long lived and faithful like Sara. Let the author of sin work none of his evil deeds within her; let her keep the Faith and the Commandments. Let her be true to one wedlock and shun all sinful embraces; let her strengthen weakness by stern discipline. Let her be grave in demeanour, honourable for her modesty, learned in heavenly doctrine, fruitful in children. Let her life be good and innocent. Let her come finally to the rest of the blessed in the kingdom of heaven. May they both see their children's children unto the third and fourth generation, thus attaining the old age which they desire. Through the same Jesus Christ . . . Amen.[8]

Thus ends abruptly the lengthy Nuptial Blessing *for the couple*. Just when we expect the groom to be officially exhorted in a way comparable to the bride, the blessing switches to the plural and ends with a desire for the couple's long life together. In the eyes of the church, the *couple* will be blessed if the *bride* fulfils her role, one of being faithful, chaste, disciplined, grave, honourable, modest, fruitful, good and innocent. Bride and groom are both ceremoniously told what is expected of a wife: he can expect her to be this way for him. By implying that the good of the couple and the success of the marriage rests solely with the woman, this ritual encodes a blatant inequality meriting the title, not of a blessing, but of a curse. For all its high moral statements, the ritual violates the selfhood of women, imposing an unnecessary and unjust burden and condemning them to subservience and to the possibility of violent abuse. To return to Raso-amanarivo, the church has canonised this Madagascan noblewoman precisely because she is perceived, rightly or wrongly, as having taken to heart the message of this marriage ritual.

Readers may be raising the objection that it is unfair to draw conclusions from this pre-Vatican II blessing, one no longer used by the church today. We cannot, however, truthfully distance ourselves in this way. This blessing, used throughout the Roman Catholic world until the mid-to-late 1960s, was actually bestowed on a significant number of contemporary Australian couples, those now married for twenty years and more. Many of these churched couples have actively sought to relate to each other and to bring up their children in accordance with the ground rules laid down by this blessing. Moreover, the blessing was not an isolated event. It was a sign of the patriarchal mind of both church and society, an integral part of a sexist marriage liturgy, a sexist church, and a sexist world. That the blessing is no longer bestowed does not mean its ill effects have suddenly ceased.

On the contrary, the stories of abused women told already in this chapter indicate that the unjust structures endorsed by this blessing still prevail. Right at the beginning, the injustice is succinctly coded: 'Thou didst make man in Thy image, and didst appoint woman to be his inseparable helpmate'. Man is made in the image of divinity so there is no need to exhort him to goodness. Woman, by contrast, is made, not in God's image, but to be man's *inseparable* helpmate; she alone must be exhorted to virtuous service. 'Inseparable' tolls the death knell for woman. And the knell tolls again and again when she is told that she was made from the flesh of man, and that the marriage union is a mystery so excellent that God here foreshadowed the union of Christ and the Church. Taking on such transcendent significance, the marriage union becomes truly indissoluable. As it was in the beginning, is now, and ever shall be, the right order of things demands that the man and woman God has joined together shall on no authority be put asunder. There are no exceptions. In the face of such an injunction from God, Christ, Church, Society and Husband, how can a lone woman possibly leave an abusing man? And the church, in concert with society generally, still issues the same injunction. The recent beatification of the abused Madagascan woman stated it precisely. Stay faithfully united to your husband, for this union reflects the love between Christ and the Church. Always obey the authority vested in the church, the state, and especially in your husband. And above all, no matter what the cost, endure, and your endurance will be ratified on earth and rewarded in heaven. Little wonder, then, that the abused woman will stay yoked to her husband's cash register; and all the more wonder that some truly extraordinary women can, after many tears, finally make their escape.

The granddaughter

In the context of family violence, one more story needs to be told, the story of incest, the most hidden, violent abuse. Here is another violated woman, another indelible memory. Using the pseudonym Anne Johns, this woman puts words around the unnameable.

> I am about four years old, staying at my grandparents' house. My grandfather, my mother's father, is sleeping on the verandah. He always does that and my grandmother locks the front door to keep him out. I asked her if she has made sure that it is locked and she assures me that she has. The room I slept in is opposite the front door. I have become afraid of this room. It is very dark and, apart from my bed, it is full of old furniture pieces which make black holes and cast strange shadows. There is mosquito netting over my bed and my blankets are tucked in tightly. I see the lock on the front door glinting in some shaft of gratuitous light. It is moving. I realise that the door cannot have been locked after all. Maybe it never is. Someone is tugging at the mosquito net at the foot of my bed, then the blankets are being pulled out. I remember nothing more until all the lights go on. There seems to be some dreadful drama. I lie rigid, close my eyes and pretend to be asleep. Someone's shadow interrupts the light as they peer in at me: 'She's gone back to sleep', they say. And all is quiet.
>
> My mother told me that she hated her father, that he bullied and threatened her as a child and often came home drunk and thrashed her.[9]

The above story, like many stories of violence, allows no easy identification of men as aggressors and women as victims. The web of violence is more complex. Women, being part of a patriarchal culture and having a patriarchal heritage, practise violence. In this story, the grandfather's act of violence towards the child is preceded by his wife's act of violence towards him, locking him out, forcing him onto the verandah, the very edge of the family home.[10] A further act of violence, probably an unconscious one, leaves the small granddaughter, the most vulnerable member of the family, in the room opposite the front door. What precise circumstances led to these arrangements, the story does not say. It does say though that the grandfather was given to acts of violence and we can surmise that he was banished because of earlier incidents. The cycle is more complex still, however, for the above episode appears in the context of a story recounting the writer's own experience of violence at the hands of her *mother*. So the legacy of violence is bequeathed from father to daughter who in turn becomes a mother abusing her own daughter. Across three generations the story unfolds and could possibly unfold further if not for the limitations of memory.

Women often collude in the violence. This is not to blame the victim, for often women have little choice but to lie rigid, close their eyes and pretend to be asleep, utterly reduced. Avoidance, silence, rigidity, because incest is too painful to recall, too forbidden to name. Pretence of some propriety is preferable. And as I have shown, the church colludes. In saying that a woman belongs to a man, that she is his to protect and care for, to have and hold, and that as helpmate she must so behave that he will want to do his duty by her, the church effectively structures an inequality into the marriage which is damaging to both parties, even where the man is benevolent. At best, 'to have and hold' means to protect and keep innocent, to guard and defend, and at worst, it means to abuse and dominate, to manipulate and undermine. Either way, the marriage relationship, as currently *structured* by church and society, does not signify mutuality and equality. In such a structure, the father's task is to protect children in relation to the outside world and the mother's is to nurture them in the private, domestic world. This so-called complementarity of roles with regard to children does not signify equality any more than does the relation between husband and wife. Boy children and girl children, witnessing no equality in the relation between their parents quickly learn to dominate and to submit respectively. Married couples and families who *do* succeed in living out the ideals of mutuality and equality in some measure, do so largely in spite of and not because of society's norms and the church's teachings.

These three stories – the Madagascan saint, the cash-register wife, and the granddaughter – all speak a familiar pattern of domestic violence. They are only three stories amongst millions, three stories representing the tradition of violence into which we are all born. These are relatively dramatic stories, common enough, but each memorable in its own way. What I have not yet mentioned here are the extremely subtle forms of violence that cannot be perceived in the way a beating or a molesting can. This subtle violence takes myriad forms. Consider, for example, the partial witholding of what is necessary for life, the witholding of money, of conversation, of companionship, of sexual intimacy, of education, of transport, of help with house or children. This form of abuse can be so subtle that visitors to a home, even those on extended stays, may not perceive it. While it is true that men as well as women can suffer from this kind of witholding behaviour, it is also true that women, where confined in the private domain, are more vulnerable and more likely to suffer subtle forms of abuse. Too often the family home can become an emotional, and even a physical cage. Behind a facade of respectability women can be trapped in structures made by social institutions, including the church.

In recounting specific instances of violence, I have kept returning to the role of the church in accommodating and promoting violence. There is nothing gratuitous in making this connection. While these are not specifically church stories (except for the Madagascan saint), they are all stories of domination and submission, an hierarchical structure, which the church not only models in its own organisation but also promotes in other institutions, especially the family. To examine more closely the ways in which Christianity has helped shape a culture permeated with violence, we need to consider its scriptures, theology and history. This is, of course, an enormous task. Here I simply introduce some recent thinking of feminist scholars in the context of a few examples of violence occurring in the public arena.

Plotting the stories of Christianity

The violence of the Bible

The Bible itself contributes to the violation of women in Western culture, despite or perhaps because of its widespread recognition as a sacred text. Through myths, rituals and laws that are demonstrably violent towards women, the Bible provides the foundation for a totally misogynous culture. Both Hebrew and Christian scriptures were written by men, for men, and in the interests of men. In other words, these scriptures are thoroughly androcentric and patriarchal. This violence towards women is coded in the biblical texts in a number of ways: women are dominated by men and subsumed under them by being omitted or ignored; they are abused and denigrated; or they are removed from the human realm by being exalted and idealised. These violations against womankind occur in the texts themselves as well as in translations and interpretations of the texts.

As a Christian I grew up believing that the Bible revealed a God who is good and loving, and a way of life that could save and liberate humankind. Revealing to humankind not only God but its own possibilities, the Bible was beyond all question a life-promoting text – the basis of all that was good in Western culture. Today, warned by feminist scholars, a strain of caution has entered my approach. One biblical scholar, a Christian, advises that the Bible should carry a warning for women: 'Caution! Could be dangerous to your health and survival.'[11] This healthy suspicion towards the Bible is supported by an increasingly vast and compelling body of scholarship. Since the end of the last century and particularly in the past twenty years, an enormous amount of feminist energy has been devoted to exposing how the Bible reflects a hatred towards women, the kind of hatred manifested in the above stories. Although only an inkling can be given here of what this work has produced, much of the source material is both readable and easily obtained.

The stories of violence recounted above find their counterparts in both Hebrew and Christian scriptures. Typically, these ancient stories, like most stories in our present culture, are told from the perspective of the dominant male. One scholar of the Hebrew scriptures, Phyllis Trible, has retold some of these stories from the viewpoint of the violated woman.[12] Noting the almost universal indifference of the biblical text to the plight of women victims, Trible retells terrifying tales, while inviting the reader to attend to the underside and to interpret the story against the narrative's own plot and its male protagonists. In this way, women are strengthened to name and then to face the ancient and ever-present monster of patriarchal violence.

The biblical rape of the unnamed woman

Trible retells, for example, the story from Judges 19 of the unnamed woman who is raped and murdered, a story most of us will be unaware of because the tradition, like the scriptures themselves, has been largely silent in its regard.[13] This story tells of a certain Levite living in the remote parts of Ephraim whose concubine, becoming angry with him, left him and returned to her father's house in Bethlehem of Judah. The Levite, accompanied by a servant, goes after his concubine in order 'to speak kindly to her and bring her back' (19:3).[14] Finding his concubine at her father's house, the Levite is pressed by his father-in-law to stay, so he and his servant tarry in Judah for five days, eating, drinking and making merry. Eventually, they and the concubine set out for Ephraim and home. By nightfall, however, they are still far from home having reached only Gibeah, a city of the Benjaminites. Here they sit in the city's open square waiting because no man takes them into his house to spend the night (19:15). At last an old man, himself from Ephraim, invites them to his home where, just as they are 'making their hearts merry', some 'men of the city, base fellows' beat on the door demanding the Levite be released so 'that we may know him' (19:22). The old man goes out to them and defends his guest, saying,

> No, my brethren, do not act so wickedly; seeing that this man has come into my house, do not do this vile thing. Behold here are my virgin daughter and his concubine; let me bring them out now. Ravish them and do with them what seems good to you; but against this man do not do so vile a thing (19:23)

But the 'base fellows' will not listen to the old man, so the Levite:

> . . . seized his concubine and put her out to them; and they knew her and abused her all night until the morning. And as the dawn began to break, they let her go (19:25).

The next morning as he was preparing to depart, the Levite found his concubine at the threshold of the old man's house. He said to her, 'Arise, and let us be going' (19:28). When there was no answer he put her onto an ass and went away to his own home in Ephraim. There,

> . . . he took a knife, and laying hold of his concubine, he divided her, limb from limb, into twelve pieces, and sent her throughout all the territory of Israel (19:29).

How can one respond to a story of such terror, horrifying even when recounted so summarily? One way is to dismiss both the events themselves and this way of recounting them as ancient barbaric acts quite removed in time and place from the refined sensibilities of late twentieth century Christian culture. This refusal to remember is one of the ways we women protect ourselves from a woman-hating culture, for it is too painful and too frightening to attend to such hatred. But we cannot truthfully do this, for similar events occur regularly in our own times. Anyone can recall them. Listen to these recent statements of hatred quoted by the feminist scholar, Jane Caputi:

> I am down on whores and I shan't quit ripping them until I do get buckled . . .
> Jack the Ripper

> It wasn't fuckin' wrong. Why is it wrong to get rid of some fuckin' cunts.
> Kenneth Bianchi, the 'Hillside Strangler'

> The women I killed were filth, bastard prostitutes who were just standing around littering the streets. I was just cleaning the place up a bit.
> Peter Sutcliffe, the 'Yorkshire Ripper' [15]

In a patriarchal culture, these men are not aliens. They express, in the most violent form possible, a misogyny intrinsic to this culture. They represent the extreme end of a continuum of women-hating attitudes that includes exalting and idealising, ignoring and excluding, and, finally, abusing and ritually murdering. As representatives of an ancient and deeply rooted male tradition, these men, like the ancient murderers of the unnamed concubine, are engaged in male ritual, one that has primitive religious associations. The noted scholar of religion, Mircea Eliade, says it succinctly:

> *One becomes truly a man only by conforming to the teaching of the myths, that is by imitating the gods* . . . in *illo tempore* the god had slain the marine monster and dismembered its body in order to create the cosmos. Man repeats this blood sacrifice, sometimes even with human victims.[16]

In a patriarchal culture, woman is monster. Patriarchal tribes, from the ancient tribes of Israel to the present day, are founded on the dismemberment of monstrous women.

How can women, perceived as monsters, respond? One way is to rename the monster, this time identifying it correctly as the very silencing, exclusion and idealisation of women engendered by patriarchy. Trible does precisely this by retelling the ancient biblical story from the point of view of the victimised woman, the woman without name or voice.[17] In her retelling, the perpetrators of the crime and the indifference of the text towards the victim are exposed, so that this grievously wronged woman begins to find again the voice and name stolen from her so long ago. It is impossible to reproduce here Trible's detailed exegetical work, but a few examples will indicate the process of her empathetic reading, a process that could be adopted for all such stories, ancient and modern.

The story begins with the woman's actions when, becoming angry with the Levite, she leaves him and returns to her father's house. These actions – and the story does not comment on their rightness or wrongness – precipitate all the following events in which the woman becomes objectified as 'property, object, tool and literary device'.[18] Reading and retelling from the woman's perspective, Trible does not allow this total reduction of person to thing to go unremarked. Without putting words into the woman's mouth, she still meticulously notes the way the male protagonists, the Levite, the woman's father, the old host and the base Benjamites, as well as the literary text itself, all ignore, exclude and abuse the woman, reducing her to the status of object.

The story continues benignly as the Levite, prompted by the independent actions of the woman, states his intention of going after her 'to speak to her heart, to bring her back' (19:3).[19] Not once in the course of the story, however, as Trible constantly reminds us, does the Levite act on this apparently innocent and worthy intention. Having found the woman at her father's house, he fails to communicate with her in any way, let alone 'speak to her heart'. Instead, as the story says, 'the two men sat and ate and drank together'(19:6) over the next five days. The woman, daughter of one man and concubine of the other, is explicitly excluded from this male ritual. Having brought the men together, she disappears, and only reappears when the Levite decides to depart for home.

Similarly, at Gibeah in the house of the old man, the woman is excluded from the feasting, and only reappears as a convenient male possession when the base fellows of the city interrupt the male carousing. Having lingered over the instances of male companionship, the story now speedily and with apparent indifference recounts the Levite's act of betrayal and the subsequent events of the night. Being under threat, the Levite, the very man who had pursued his concubine in order to speak to her heart and to bring her back, seizes her and pushes her outside beyond the protection of the house and into the hand of the base men. 'And they raped her and tortured her all night until the morning. They let her go as the dawn came up'(19:25).[20] Without comment on these events, the story hurries on: 'The woman came at daybreak and fell down at the doorway of the house of the man where her master was until light'(19:26).[21] As Trible notes, 'for the first time since the beginning of the story, the lone female is the subject of active verbs, though she is no longer a subject with power to act'.[22]

With the arrival of morning the Levite acts quickly, resolved to return home, a resolve that is barely interrupted by the discovery of his raped and tortured concubine 'fallen at the doorway of the house her hands upon the threshold'(19:27).[23] When the Levite commands her, 'Arise and let us be going' (19:28).[24], she makes no reply so he puts her on the ass and returns home, as the story matter-of-factly tells us. The Levite's words of command are the only words addressed to the woman in the entire story, words certainly not addressed to her heart as was his initial intention. In this context they have become the callous words of a murderer. Whether the woman was found dead or alive, the story does not say. From the Levite's point of view it hardly matters, for he intends to use her body as a sign of the way the Benjamites have wronged him and, by extension, all the men of Israel. When he enters his house he takes the knife and dismembers the woman sending her limbs throughout all the territory of Israel. The divine hand, having once intervened on behalf of Abraham's son, Isaac, does not stay this knife. Can we infer from this that the male God, Yahweh, approves the Levite's action? Certainly the biblical text itself, by failing to speak on the woman's behalf, infers that this unnamed concubine is disposable, her body destined to be symbol and object lesson in a patriarchal male world.

Translating the silences and ruptures in the text, Trible thus notes how the story is violent towards women in both content and form. Alone in a male world, the concubine is used and abused not only by the protagonists within the story itself, but by the very failure of the narrator to register any concern for her plight or any condemnation of the murderous Levite and the old man. Told from the point of view of the Levite, the story reserves condemnation for the men of Gibeah, not on account of their having raped and tortured a woman but because they have offended a member of the tribe of Israel by abusing his property. So the narrator of the story, by his very silence, betrays misogyny. Trible also draws attention to the silence of the rest of the scriptures in regard to this woman. Only twice do brief references to the story occur with the prophet Hosea warning the people of Israel that they will be punished for 'they have deeply corrupted themselves as in the days of Gibeah'.(Hos. 9:9, 10:9) For the rest, there is silence. From ancient Israel to early Christianity, the canonical tradition fails to remember this afflicted woman. Finally, Trible recommends that we modern readers do remember her, clearly naming the wrong done to her, and mourning the manner of her life and death. Drawing on the biblical tradition itself, Trible vividly commemorates her:

> . . . she is no more than the oxen that Saul will later cut in pieces and send throughout all the territory of Israel as a call to war (1 Sam 11:7). Her body has been broken and given to many. Lesser power has no woman than this that her life is laid down by a man.[25]

Thus ritually remembered and mourned by women today, this ancient woman's suffering and death need not be in vain.

The violence of the tradition

Trible is one of many scholars now producing critical feminist readings of biblical texts. Their work, along with the question of women's ordination and related changes in church order, commonly provoke violent opposition. This is because it is rightly seen as threatening the very foundations of the patriarchal symbol system. The omission and denigration of women, along with their idealisation and exaltation, in the West's foundational text, the edifice of systematically sexist theology built on this text, and the continuing widespread exclusion of women from the priesthood are all fundamental to a misogynous self-understanding on the part of both men and women, a self-understanding which justifies current patriarchal arrangements in every facet of Western society. This self-understanding and its concomitant cultural arrangements are still widely regarded as natural, so that their inherent violence to women remains largely invisible. Any attempt to uncover the misogyny and ultimately dislodge it meets massive and sometimes violent opposition from both men and women.

The Woman's Bible

Consider the example of *The Woman's Bible* (1895 and 1898), a work that in many ways marks the beginnings of the modern feminist struggle in the area of religion.[26] Elizabeth Cady Stanton and seven other women, including the noted scholar Matilda Joslyn Gage, produced this work in the form of a scientific commentary on all the biblical passages dealing with women. The first appearance of the work provoked violent opposition, as violent as any greeting current feminist biblical scholarship. And then strangely, or perhaps naturally, given a patriarchal world, the work virtually disappeared for sixty years and had to be rediscovered by today's scholars. Currently, *The Woman's Bible* is widely read because, although its exegetical methods are no longer acceptable, the arguments presented by Cady Stanton for the necessity of such a work are still relevant. From a century ago the words of these women demonstrate both the inherent violence of the biblical text towards women and the violent opposition to the uncovering of this misogyny.

Essentially Cady Stanton argued that the Bible is androcentric, not just in its interpretations and translations, but in the *texts themselves*, a conclusion now widely accepted. In this she differed significantly from other feminist scholars and political activists of her day who argued that androcentrism belonged, not so much to the Bible itself, as to translations and interpretations by patriarchal scholars. Sarah Moore Grimke said, for example, that she had:

entered her protest aginst the false translations of some passages by the MEN who did that work, and against the perverted interpretations of the MEN who undertook to write commentaries thereon. I am inclined to think when we are admitted to the honour of studying Greek and Hebrew, we shall produce some various readings of the Bible, a little different from those we have now.[27]

Today, now that women have been 'admitted to the honour of studying Greek and Hebrew' and with nearly thirty years of feminist biblical scholarship behind us, we know that Grimke was right, but that her critique did not go far enough. Cady Stanton knew this at the time. While she shared Grimke's suspicions, she also perceived the problem as more radical than that of mistranslations and wrong interpretations, asserting that the *Bible itself* sought to keep women within a 'divinely ordained sphere', an unacceptable sphere for any self-respecting woman:

> The Bible teaches that woman brought sin and death into the world, that she was arraigned before the judgment seat of Heaven, tried, condemned and sentenced. Marriage for her was to be a condition of bondage, maternity a period of suffering and anguish, and in silence and subjection, she was to play the role of a dependent on man's bounty for all her material wants, and for all the information she might desire on the vital questions of the hour, she was commanded to ask her husband at home.[28]

Elements of this critique sound not unlike my own deconstruction of the stories presented in the first part of this chapter. In direct opposition to these misogynous biblical teachings, Cady Stanton argued that 'self-development is a higher duty than self-sacrifice and should be a woman's motto henceforward'.[29]

The publication of *The Woman's Bible* provoked violent opposition for a number of reasons. On the one hand, it was opposed by feminist women fighting for the right to vote, women who thought it impolitic to attack the Bible at that time, and on the other, by the clergy who considered the work detrimental to the natural order in both church and state. With clarity of thought and a wit that still delights, Cady Stanton handled opponents. To a clergyman describing *The Woman's Bible* as 'the work of women and the devil', she replied,

> This is a grave mistake. His Satanic Majesty was not to join the Revising Committee which consists of women alone. Moreover, he has been so busy of late years attending Synods, General Assemblies and Conferences to prevent the recognition of women delegates, that he has no time to study the languages and 'higher criticism'.[30]

And to those, including many in the women's suffrage movement, who thought it 'not *politic* to rouse religious opposition', she had this to say:

> This much-lauded policy is but another word for *cowardice*. How can women's position be changed from that of a subordinate to an equal without opposition ...? For so far-reaching and momentous a reform as her complete independence, an entire revolution in all existing institutions is inevitable.[31]

Fiery words from a perceptive 83-year-old living at the end of the last century. Ninety years later her words are still a rallying cry for a revolution that's barely begun.

Today many respected biblical scholars agree in general with Cady Stanton's position that the Bible is patriarchal and androcentric, though the degree to which this is the case is debated. Whatever about the degree of correctness in Cady Stanton's position and the adequacy of the biblical scholarship employed in *The Woman's Bible*, there can be no doubt that Cady Stanton was right in her assessment of the political significance of this undertaking. She judged, correctly, that exposing the inherent andro-centrism of the Bible was a significant political act, and that as such it would provoke violent opposition. She judged women's lives to be deeply affected by the Bible, women being the main practitioners of religion, and men, particularly the clergy, using the Bible as a weapon to control women. She also judged that the oppression of women in one institution, in this case the church, supported and maintained oppression in all other institu-tions. Both her insights and the violence with which they were suppressed still have something to say to those involved in the same struggle today.

Exclusion: women priests and women soldiers

Another telling example of Christianity's violence towards women is our widespread exclusion from the office of ordained priest. Although women are now accepted, albeit with varying degrees of willingness, in almost every profession and institution, we are still frequently excluded from the role of priest or minister. Something can be learned by looking at this example in the light of an analysis of women's exclusion from the role of combat soldier. Why are women so widely perceived as unfit to be a priest or a combat soldier? Why are these such strongly guarded male preserves? These questions are particularly relevant for the present discussion, war being an example of violence on the most comprehensive scale, and contemporary women's ordination being the focus of a most acrimonious public debate both within and beyond church institutions.

First, the role of women in war. What rationale can be provided for the specific ways in which women are included in and excluded from the arena of war? One rationale for the exclusion of women from combat positions is that provided by General Robert H. Barrow, commander of the US marines, a rationale cited and analysed by Genevieve Lloyd in her article, 'Selfhood, War and Masculinity'. Barrow asserts that:

> War is a man's work. Biological convergence on the battlefield would not only be dissatisfying in terms of what women could do, but it would be an enormous psychological distraction for the male, who wants to think that he's fighting for that woman somewhere behind, not up there in the same foxhole with him. It tramples the male ego. When you get right down to it, you have to protect the manliness of war.[32]

Lloyd's analysis shows that Barrow's rationale for excluding women has instinctively touched on a profound truth, namely that the entire symbol system of the West, a system built on what man 'wants to think', is put into disarray by the presence of female combat soldiers. Drawing on examples from Western philosophical tradition, Lloyd shows that only by transcending woman can man become a fully-fledged citizen, and that nowhere does he achieve this status more surely and more sublimely than in the field of war. If woman enters this male preserve, then man, by her very presence, is deprived of his identity or, in Barrow's words, the male ego is trampled.

War is an initiation ceremony for the adult male, one in which the female, by definition, cannot play a leading role. Sometimes this is stated quite explicitly. Listen to Phillip Caputo reflecting on the significance of his platoon's first 'fire-fight' in Vietnam:

> As I moved from one man to the next, I became aware of a subtle difference among them, and I might not have noticed it if I had not known them so intimately. They had taken part in their first action though a minor one that had lasted only ninety minutes. But their company had killed during those ninety minutes; they had seen violent death for the first time and something of the cruelty combat arouses in men. Before the fire-fight, those marines fit both definitions of the word *infantry*, which means either 'a body of soldiers equipped for service on foot', or 'infants, boys, youths collectively'. The difference was that the second definition could no longer be applied to them. Having received that primary sacrament of war, baptism of fire, their boyhoods were behind them. We didn't say to ourselves, we've been under fire, we've shed blood, now we're men. We were simply aware, in a way we could not express, that something significant had happened to us.[33]

Boys leave their boyhood behind by killing or at the very least by witnessing the violent spilling of blood. What is not said here, and what is said quite explicitly in Barrow's statement, is that leaving one's boyhood behind entails leaving behind the world of children and *of women*. Women are not mentioned in Caputo's statement, for the maleness of the ritual is simply taken for granted. Female combat soldiers are unthinkable. Given this male-centred context, it does not even seem odd that the second definition of infantry, a word that is usually common gender, should explicitly exclude female children, infantry being 'infants, boys, youths collectively'. In this typical picture of war women are not part of the scenario except implicitly. Woman is simply assumed as the transcended other.

Caputo's statement is also typical in that the rhetoric of war calls on God, or religion, to sanctify carnage. From time immemorial, the male warrior God has fought on both sides, for each and every war is, from the perspective of those doing the fighting, a just war. 'Gott mit uns' can be translated into any human language, past or present. God is always on 'our side'. War and religion accommodate and justify each other in such a way that the language of religion belongs comfortably on the battleline and the language of war sounds at home in the churches. Combat soldiers partake in the 'primary sacrament of war, baptism of fire', and those praying in the pews are soldiers for Christ, marching bravely on. Typically, this mutual contamination enhances each activity, making it appear noble and sublime. In this manner, the repulsive grisliness of war is purified and spiritualised by being referred to as 'sacrament', and the ethereal spiritualism of religion is grounded and dramatised by being referred to as battle.

This traffic between the language of war and the language of religion does not always enhance one or other activity, for occasionally a crass statement names the unmentionable and turns commonly accepted values inside out. The following statement from a young soldier does precisely this:

> I had a sense of power. A sense of destruction . . . in the Nam you realised you had the power to take a life. You had the power to rape a woman and nobody could say nothing to you. That godlike feeling you had was in the field. It was like I was god. I could take a life. I could screw a woman.[34]

Here the worst aspects of war and religion and the contamination between them are on display. War, like religion, is about infinite male power. This feeling of power can only be expressed adequately by the language of religion. In war everything and everybody are at the disposal of the victorious combat soldier. Anything is sanctioned, for the all-powerful soldier is God. Woman is included in the drama as a sign of this power, as the booty or prize with which the conquerors can do as they please. Being merely the property of the enemy, she is even less protected by codes of war, even less worthy of respect than the enemy themselves.

This statement of the young soldier naively expresses what must always remain unsaid in General Barrow's view of women's place in war. Women cannot be active in war because that would preclude them from functioning symbolically as that which the male must transcend, as pawns in a male game. Combat soldiers become men by a double transcendence: they transcend their own women by protecting them (as implied in Barrow's words) and they transcend the enemy by debasing the enemy's women (as made clear by the young soldier's words). Here the intimate link between protection and debasement becomes apparent, as the *same men* will protect one lot of women and children because it is their duty, and will, with relish, debase another lot because it is their right. Whether exalted or denigrated, women are objectified as the other, as something less than human in this male ritual. The noble side of this equation, that expressed by General Barrow, is heard frequently enough: war is a manly activity in which soldiers risk and lose their lives to protect the liberty and safety of their own women and children. The corollary of this, and one not frequently expressed, at least publicly, is that the women and children of the enemy are fair game, part of the reward for risking one's life, the booty of victory.

One final question about women and war needs to be addressed. How and why do women collude in this male game? Why do so many women – mothers, wives, lovers, daughters – willingly send 'their' men to war? As a brief response, I suggest that women, like men, have internalised the prevailing symbolic structure. In this system woman has her rightful place, one in which many of us have become comfortable, not only because of the safety of familiarity but also because of the numerous pay-offs. Against all evidence to the contrary, women have internalised the claim that they are especially vulnerable and fragile and need to be protected. This protection, always enacted in public, can range from what are termed tiny courtesies like opening doors for a woman to major life choices like going to war to fight for her continued safety.

Doubtless this display appeals to the demanding and frightened child lurking in all of us. In addition, however, and at a deeper level, the symbol system keeps women subservient by calling those women heroines who can produce such manly men. In this system, women find their full worth according to the value of the men with whom they are associated. Since this is the principal, and perhaps the only way in which women can experience themselves as valued, it becomes imperative that women, for the sake of their own identity, produce and be associated with manly men. To be truly a woman, the female must display her own need for protection and, if need be, must send her man out, even to war, to protect the purity and fragility of womankind. Transcending her own needs, she allows herself to be transcended in this way. This is her true role and glory.

This outlook, symbolically underwritten by Christian churches, is harmful not only for women but also for men. It actually encourages violence. Briefly, women *appear* more vulnerable and fragile than men because we are preyed upon in ways that men are not. As constructed by this system, women, or at least virtuous women, need to be protected by men against other men. It might seem from this that there are good men who are manly and bad men who are unmanly, but the symbol system does not structure man in this way. The system divides, not man from man, but woman from woman. In the arena of war, there are 'our women' and 'their women'. In the arena of everyday life, there are virtuous women who are mothers and virgins, and women of easy virtue, whores and prostitutes. Male debasement of 'their women', and of whores and prostitutes, is the necessary and unacknowledged underside of male protection of women considered virtuous. In both cases, the same male imperative operates, dictating that our women must be protected and their women debased. The identity of the fully fledged male citizen, as of the Christian gentlemen, erects itself on this division.

In the context of this analysis of women's role in war, some of the murkiness surrounding the question of women's ordination to the priesthood disappears, or at least the main sources of the murk can be identified. Both opponents and supporters of the ordination of women judge correctly and perhaps unconsciously the significance of this move. Ordaining women priests, like allowing women combat soldiers, puts in disarray prevailing key symbols. The priest celebrating at the altar, offering the sacrifice, is as necessarily male, according to the structure of the current Western symbol system, as is the combat soldier up there in the foxhole. The significance of both positions, the source of their power, lies precisely in their transcendence of the sphere of nature, the arena of womankind. If it were normal for women to preside at the altar and on the battlefield, then two of the most hallowed male domains would have been breached. This in turn would jostle other symbols of domination and subordination, perhaps to the jeopardy of the whole system.

Exclusion of women from the priesthood parallels and complements exclusion of women from the battlefield. If women were combat soldiers, men would have nothing to fight for, so it is necessary that they remain at home in the domestic sphere unsullied by war, pure and close to nature. Men fight precisely to protect, and to transcend, this sphere. Similarly, if women were priests, men would have no one to represent before God, so it is necessary that women remain in the pews, contaminated and sinful, representatives of fallen nature waiting to be redeemed. Priests are ordained to intervene on behalf of, and also to transcend, this sinful humanity. In the game of clerical religion, as in the game of war, women are pawns. Rather than fully participating in our own right in a self-determining manner, we are largely acted upon. Put plainly, at their best patriarchal structures connive in promoting the physical and spiritual dependence of women, and at their worst they do nothing to prevent women's physical and spiritual debasement. In any event, patriarchal structures work against the well-being of women.

Both soldier and priest represent their people, a soldier to the enemy and a priest to God. To a patriarchal mind, the only fitting representative of any tribe or nation is a male, for a woman simply does not have the necessary human status to speak or act on behalf of the people. In this respect, the symbolic value of priest and soldier are parallel. But the symbolic significance of the priest is more complex and even more essentially male than that of the soldier, for not only does the priest represent the people in the eyes of God, he also represents God in the eyes of the people. This two-way representation, God to the people and the people to God, must, according to patriarchal logic, be filled by a male. Consider this statement from Lucy Beckett, an opponent of women's ordination:

> . . . the whole of creation since the beginning has been generative and relational. God is father and son; Mary, his daughter, his mother, his sister, represents us all, men and women, the material (maternal) upon which he fathers whatever in us is good. While the priest is sacramentally representing God, his maleness is that ordinary but deeply resonant fact without which the feminine receptivity and fertility of all the rest of us, men and women, cannot be made real. God 'calling the lapsed soul' in and through the sacraments, acting on his patient faithful, must be represented for all of us by a male priesthood, just as the rest of us, both men and women, are at these most serious, most attentive, most open and most hidden meeting-points with him, most perfectly represented by a woman. In the context of this living and, to most Catholic men and women, profoundly fair and profoundly appropriate tradition, the demand for the ordination of women comes as a keenly felt shock.[35]

Pervading this statement is the domination–subordination model which leads to a complete lack of mutuality between male and female. Creation has always been generative and relational, says Beckett, but who's been doing the generating, and who initiating relations? No mutuality here, for it has always been the male principle, divine or human. God is father and son and this divine maleness implies activity: God acting on humanity, fathering forth goodness, calling lapsed souls. In this schema, the priest, sacramentally representing God, is authorised to continue these activities on behalf of humanity, an authority vested in him on account of his maleness. The attribute of maleness, beyond all others, resonates godliness.

On the other and decidedly inferior side of the coin is femaleness, the principle operating in Mary and in all men and women in relation to God. Beckett's concept of human femaleness, of essential femininity, is materiality upon which the male God acts. This feminine materiality is open, receptive, fertile, perhaps lapsed but still serious, attentive, secret, waiting and faithful. All humanity, male and female, should, in Beckett's view, adopt this feminine stance before a male God. This means women cannot be priests because their very femaleness resonates the receptivity of humanity, not a fitting symbol for divinity, and men can be priests because their very maleness resonates the activity of God.

This patriarchal logic is not satisfactory even on its own terms. If Beckett were consistent she would have to agree that if women cannot resonate the activity of godliness because of their femaleness, then men cannot resonate the receptivity of humanity because of their maleness. Logically, you cannot have it both ways. Precluding women from being priests on account of their femaleness or their lack of masculinity, means precluding men from being lapsed souls and sinners, recipients of God's gracious activity, on account of their maleness. Beckett and much of the Christian tradition construct *men* in such a way that they can easily pass back and forth between the symbols of masculinity and femininity, gaining the benefits and avoiding the disadvantages of both. So men can be priests, their maleness representing the activity of God's gracious goodness, and they can also be human sinners with a feminine openness and receptivity to the activity of this male God. *Women,* on the other hand, are constructed in such a way that they have only the latter possibility open to them, they can only be lapsed souls, they cannot be priests. In this theology, men, despite their maleness, have symbolic versatility, and women, because of their femaleness, do not.

This analysis shows that the Catholic tradition, far from being 'profoundly fair and profoundly appropriate', clearly favours men and disadvantages women. Why then does the demand for the ordination of women come 'as a keenly felt shock'? What is shocking about changing an inherently unfair and violent system?

Having women priests, like having women combat soldiers, does shock because it profoundly upsets current symbolic arrangements, not only in the circumscribed areas of war and religion, but throughout society. Such a change does not simply turn the symbols upside down, it alters the relations between them, creating chaos in the symbolic world. The widespread acceptance of women priests and women soldiers would require a profoundly altered self-understanding in both men and women and there is not the will for such far-reaching changes. We 'live, and move, and have our being' in a coherent symbolic world which we do not generally attempt to analyse, and which in fact never can be analysed except in terms of its own symbols. By and large, symbols are internalised unconsciously. Critical analysis disturbs this symbolic world bringing possibilities to consciousness. Is it possible, for example, that the majority of women find combat distasteful because it is constructed as an inherently masculine activity? In other words, does the symbolic construction of femininity shape women in ways of which they are largely unaware? It is also possible that the majority of men find the practice of religion distasteful, at least in ritualised form, because it is constructed (except for the activity of the priest) as an inherently feminine activity? I suggest that the symbols of masculinity and femininity do shape, in ways of which we are largely unaware, our perceptions of certain activities, and only by analysing the symbols, gaining some awareness of their shaping power, can their hold on us be reduced.

While it is clear that symbolic constructions do have an impact on the violent world in which we live, it is not clear how these constructions can be altered in order to reduce violence. Feminists generally adopt one of two broad positions with regard to the inclusion/exclusion of women in traditionally male roles such as soldier and priest: the first is that women should be free to take up all male roles; and the second that women, having their own sphere equal or superior to men's, should not on any account adopt such roles. The first position advocates sexual equality, the second sexual differences. These two basic positions are mediated by a third which holds that women taking up male roles will transform them by functioning within them in more traditionally feminine ways. In this view, women are equal to men and every human endeavour should be open to them, and they are also different from men, having peculiarly female ways of doing things.

These two basic positions can readily be identified in current debates on both women soldiers and women priests. Those advocating sexual equality argue that women must be free to be soldiers or priests, for such pursuits define human self-identity so that to exclude women *qua* women is to diminish womankind (and humankind). Many feminists advocating this position acknowledge having problems with certain tendencies in traditional male roles, namely with the militarism, jingoism, and lack of respect for the other to which the combat soldier is prone and with the triumphalism, clericalism and superiority over the other which frequently beset the priest. Some feminists assert that if sufficient numbers of women were to become soldiers or priests, then these roles would necessarily change, becoming less prone to specific destructive tendencies. If equal numbers of women as men were soldiers and priests, say these feminists, then not only these two roles, but womankind and even humanity itself would be conceptualised differently.[36]

The second basic position is constituted by feminists who advocate sexual difference. According to this thinking, women should never be soldiers or priests, for these roles are intrinsically tainted with patriarchal values, and women have their own non-patriarchal ways of being and acting. In this scheme it is impossible to have a femininst soldier or a feminist priest and it is hoped that, as more men become feminist, these destructive, essentially masculine roles will die out. Women who become soldiers or priests are simply perpetuating patriarchy. This is true, say these feminists, even of those women who hope to change the meaning of combat soldier or the meaning of priest, for such intrinsically patriarchal roles cannot be redeemed. For the sake of clarifying the position, I have here lumped together soldier and priest, although thcy do not, of course, necessarily belong together. Some feminists, seeing one role as inherently violent and patriarchal but not the other, may support women in the role of priest but not in that of soldier or vice versa.

Each of these positions carries its own dangers and limitations. Women who become priests or soldiers can easily be absorbed into the clerical or military world, gradually losing consciousness of the specific ideology working on them. Such women, having successfully transcended their own femaleness, are regarded as honorary men in a patriarchal world. It seems likely that their femaleness is somehow ignored, represeed and 'forgotten'. It is telling that images which do not easily allow for repression of femaleness, images such as that of the pregnant priest or the pregnant soldier, evoke especially violent opposition. In these instances, femaleness cannot so easily be covered over and 'forgotten', which means such women cannot so easily be transformed into honorary men. So the question remains whether women becoming soldiers and priests can transform the roles or whether, on account of the structures, they will inevitably be transformed and patriarchalised by them.

The second basic position, that of avoiding roles perceived as inherently masculine, has its own limitations. Feminists opting for this position want traditional feminine roles to be valued in their own right. In their view, the symbol of femininity, while being equal or perhaps superior to masculinity, is essentially different from it. The problem with this position is that 'femininity' is contained symbolically and practically in precisely such a way that the present unjust arrangements instead of being challenged are tacitly maintained. In the western tradition masculinity is constructed as dominant, powerful and relevant in the public domain and femininity as subordinate, powerless and largely irrelevant in the public domain. By not taking on traditional masculine roles, such as priest and soldier, do we as women simply maintain this dualistic structure and so remain, despite our own feminist rhetoric, generally subordinate, powerless and irrelevant, if not in our own eyes, at least in the eyes of a patriarchal society? How can women, working from the inferior position, challenge the current unjust relations between masculinity and femininity as they are constructed?

This discussion of priest and soldier has brought together roles usually kept apart and spheres defined as religious on the one hand and secular on the other. My brief analysis reveals that clerical and military institutions support and maintain each other, violating women whether by exaltation or debasement. They both work in a patriarchal way. As Barrow and Beckett state so succinctly, the manliness of war and the maleness of the priesthood must be protected. Nor is this pattern restricted to military and clerical worlds alone. It is repeated in muted forms in well-nigh all institutions of the West. When you come right down to it, what must be protected is male leadership enacted as male domination and female subordination, the familiar pattern appearing in the individual stories recounted in the first part of this chapter.

The choice of the pregnant woman

My final example of ways in which Christianity enacts and promotes violence against women concerns the church's absolute opposition to abortion. This is a key example, for Christian misogyny appears in its most violent forms in the area of female sexuality.

Christian churches taking an anti-abortion stand make frequent reference to the 'sanctity of life', often speaking as though they alone hold all the high moral ground. Describing themselves as 'pro-life', these churches infer that anyone who does not adopt their position is automatically anti-life. This inference is a lie. Those who advocate a woman's right to choose an abortion, that is those who adopt a 'pro-choice' position, may be very well grounded indeed in respect for the sanctity of life. The issue at the heart of the abortion debate is not respect for life, for no one is arguing against such respect. The point at issue is *whose life* is to receive ultimate respect, whose life is to be finally preferred. The abortion debate is about competition between lives, and it is so volatile because most humans, at bottom, do not want to choose between lives.

There is then no high moral ground in the area of abortion because, whichever way we go, there are undesirable consequences. For or against abortion, both positions *can be* immoral. In the context of the present discussion however, I will explore only the particular immorality of the Christian church's anti-abortion stance, the particular misogyny behind many 'sanctity of life' arguments. In this area as in others already explored, a relation appears between idealisation of the woman (this time the mother figure) and her debasement, between lofty rhetoric and misogynous practices.

Church (or state), legislating absolutely against abortion, acts immorally because it fails to acknowledge that women are capable of making moral decisions, that women are morally competent. Legislation outlawing abortion takes away the possibility of choice and so reduces women to the status of objects. Lurking beneath this reduction is the unarticulated belief that women are merely receptacles in which the foetus must grow. This belief, based on two thousand years of faulty theology and physiology, has been internalised by men and women alike. *If* the pregnant woman were only a receptacle in which the foetus could grow, then the fulsome rhetoric concerning the rights of the foetus and the complete silence concerning the needs of the pregnant woman might be explained and even justified. But the pregnant woman is not simply a receptacle and it is immoral to treat her so. She is, potentially at least, free, responsible, adult and female, as capable of full humanity as any male. To allow her the possibility of deciding to have or not have an abortion is to honour female humanity. Not to allow this possibility is to withold from women the status of being fully adult and human.

Here then are some moral questions for a misogynous church.[37] What has the church done to reduce the number of abortions due to contraceptive failure, due to ignorance, and due to rape? The church's track record in each of these areas is poor. First, the church, the Catholic church in particular, on account of its active opposition to the use of contraception and its related failure to support the education of men and women in safe contraceptive practices has surely contributed to the number of abortions due to contraceptive failure. Second, by romanticising sexuality and presenting a warped view of it frequently described as ladylike, the church has contributed to the number of abortions due to ignorance. Third, Christian scriptures and theology, by objectifying woman through a dual process of idealising and denigrating, have legitimated patriarchal violence against flesh-and-blood women, a violence which finds its classic expression in rape. Maintaining a symbol system which subordinates women, the church has contributed, consciously or not, to the number of abortions due to rape.

These are three instances in which the church, with due regard for the sanctity of life, could act in order to lessen the number of abortions. It could give up opposing contraception; it could give up idealising and spiritualising sexuality; and it could critique its own theology and structures, acknowledging the symbolic and actual denigration of women. Put positively, the church could teach and theologise safe contraception practices, exploring the respect and love for oneself, for the other, and for what is named holy in the responsible use of contraception. It could engage in an open, public, full-blooded exploration of the many expressions and meanings of sexuality, encouraging women and men to take delight in their bodies and their own well-being. And it could restructure church practices in such a way that they signalled the full human status of womankind. All these steps would reduce significantly the number of abortions, but to undertake them the church would require a revolution in its own self-understanding. If its anti-abortion stance stemmed from a genuine concern for life and not, as I suspect, primarily from misogyny, then the church would move willingly into such a revolution.

This suspicion concerning the source of the church's anti-abortion stand is well-founded. Here is just one observation to support it. Traditionally, Christianity has advocated two types of morality: the morality of the absolutely desirable and the morality of the relatively possible.[38] When it is a question of a woman's issue, such as abortion, the church will argue every time for the morality of the absolutely desirable: there are to be no abortions, for, in the best of all possible worlds, this is absolutely desirable. When it is a question of a man's issue such as war, however, the church will argue for the morality of the relatively possible: there are occasions, regrettably, when wars must be fought. Just wars, says the church, but no just abortions.

Another sign that the church's anti-abortion stand is grounded in misogyny is the false priority given to this issue. Concern for the human foetus is important, but it is not the only or even the first concern. The first concern in the contemporary misogynous world is for every female already born. So the church's primary concern should be to create institutions, symbol systems and theologies which explicitly and implicitly honour the full humanity of women, as well as of men. When there are no women in refuges seeking asylum from assault in the home, when there are no longer females forced to make a living by prostitution, when women are no longer abused and raped, then perhaps the question of abortion can have priority. Then too, of course, the need for abortions will be greatly reduced.

The current widespread practice of abortion is due, not to woman's hatred of the foetus, but to man's hatred and fear of woman. The widespread opposition to woman's right to make a choice about abortion is due, not to concern about the foetus, but to hatred towards woman. In other words, the need for abortion will be largely reduced, when man's hatred of woman ceases. These claims, running counter to many well-known arguments of anti-abortion groups, might at first sound extraordinary, and yet they are almost self-evident, there being so much evidence of male hatred for women, some of it recorded in this chapter, and there being so little evidence of women's special hatred of the very young or for men's special care of them. In fact, any comparison of women's and men's practices of nurturing shows exactly the opposite, that women-as-a-group exhibit a far greater degree of concern and care for the young than men-as-a-group do. Not only does the foetus grow within the woman's body, but she is often solely or primarily responsible for the care of the very young and for the long hard task of child rearing.

In this context, the church's absolute prohibition of abortion is basically unjust and misogynous. Under the respectable guise of concern for the sanctity of life, the church has neglected the sanctity of every existing adult woman's life, thus creating and perpetuating a pattern of violence that runs right through institutions, symbol systems and all aspects of daily life. When the church changes its attitude to women, when it stops being anti-female, it will finally become a truly moral institution. Until then, despite its life-loving rhetoric, the Christian church largely lacks credibility.

Conclusion

This chapter has displayed connections between disparate incidents of violence towards women *and* specific church structures and theologies maintaining this violence by debasing and idealising women. Many other examples could have been chosen, for not only are there myriads of individual incidents, but there are numerous *types* of violence practised towards women, too numerous even for mention in this short discussion. Drawing on a large body of feminist scholarship, this chapter has briefly outlined some of the patterns in Christianity's practice of patriarchal violence. My choice of examples has been almost arbitrary since misogynous violence in a Western Christian society is all-pervasive, structured into relations with the self, with the other, with nature, and with the divine. Significantly, material for discussion and analysis does not have to be sought. It is at hand wherever and whenever we choose to look.

Important areas have been omitted from the discussion, areas such as race and class relations, the threat of nuclear war, abuse of animals and the environment, the dictates of economic rationalism, and the daily assault by the mass media. Each of these could well be claimed as *the* crucial issue of our times, and each is in some way connected with violence towards women. Feminist scholarship, gradually deconstructing the harmful ideology of domination and subordination, is uncovering many of the connections.

This ideology, named patriarchy, takes a complex and coherent form. Always a dominant will is imposed without due regard for the true needs or well-being of the other or indeed of the self. This dominant will, whether benevolent or not, is, from God the Father down, predominantly male. This is not to say that women do not dominate or that women do not practise violence.[39] It is to say that the pyramid of power is itself male and that women find their place on this pyramid according to the status of the man to whom they 'belong'.[40] Whatever about the violence or the virtue practised by individual women and men, the prevailing ideology in the West is structured as male, and in a world of human males and females and of sexed and non-sexed nature, this hierarchical arrangement is inherently deceitful, violent and unjust.

Christianity, by constantly arranging people and things in order of so-called divine preference and by failing to celebrate the similarities and differences among them, simply reinforces this violent arrangement. That there are, and always have been, Christian voices challenging this patriarchal hierarchy, does not remove the scandal, for such voices have not prevailed. Historically, patriarchy has won and these counter-voices have lost. Unless these voices prevail, however, and unless men refuse to victimise and women to be victims, we will all lose. We will lose the life of the world.

E.W.

Notes

1 This expression, which also forms the title of this chapter, comes from the lips of Margaret Atwood's unnamed protagonist in her novel, *Surfacing* (Simon & Schuster, New York, 1972): 'This, above all, to refuse to be a victim . . . give up the old belief that I am powerless'(p.222).
2 *The Sydney Morning Herald*, 1 May 1989.
3 *Ibid.*

4 In 1987–88, 11,000 women and children used women's refuges in New South Wales. In the same period, twice that number were turned away for lack of space. 'Research conducted by the NSW Bureau of Crime Statistics and Research has shown that over 42% of all homicides occur within the family. Spouse killings account for almost one in four of all homicides, and most of these (75%) involve husbands killing wives. . . . as many as one in three married women may be subjected to domestic violence at some stage'. *NSW Women's Policy Statement*, NSW Women's Co-ordination Unit, March 1990, p.47. See also *Report 1985–1988*, NSW Domestic Violence Committee, Women's Co-ordination Unit, November 1989.

5 Compare with Hannah Arendt's statement that, though lying is nothing new in politics, 'Image-making as global policy is indeed something new in the huge arsenal of human follies . . .' ('Home to Roost', *The New York Review of Books*, 26 June 1975, pp.3–6, quoted by Mary Schaldenbrand in *Studies in the Philosophy of Paul Ricoeur*, Charles E. Reagan, ed., Ohio University Press, Athens, Ohio, 1979, p.80, note 1.

6 'Lunch' in Kate Llewellyn, *Trader Kate and the Elephants*, Friendly Street Poets, Adelaide, 1982 , p.39.

7 Every state in Australia now has legislation to protect women and children from violence in the home. New South Wales led the way in obtaining this legislation. Through the work of the Women's Co-ordination Unit of the NSW Premier's Department changes were made to the Crimes (Domestic Violence) Amendment Act in 1982, 1983 and 1988 to protect women and children specifically. Unfortunately, with a change of government, the name of the Act was changed in 1989 to Crimes (Apprehended Violence) Amendment Act, increasing the likelihood that violence against women and children in the home will again become a hidden crime. Even the term, '*domestic* violence', does not adequately name the crime of assault by men against women and children in the home, but since 'domestic' is usually associated with women and children it certainly names the crime more clearly than does the non-generic term, 'apprehended'.

8 *Saint Joseph Daily Missal: The Official Prayers of the Catholic Church for the Celebration of Daily Mass*, Catholic Book Publishing Company, New York, 1950, pp.1173–4.

9 Anne Johns, 'Images of God', *Eremos Newsletter*, Eremos Institute, 189 Church St, Newtown NSW 2042, No.20, August 1987, p.13.

10 Locking her husband out of the home may not have been an act of violence on the part of this woman, but an act of self-affirmation and defence. The story does not tell us which it is. The point remains that women do sometimes act violently against men.

11 Elisabeth Schüssler Fiorenza, 'The Will to Choose or Reject: Continuing Our Critical Work' in Letty Russell, ed., *Feminist Interpretation of the Bible*, Basil Blackwell, Oxford, 1985, p.130. In Schüssler Fiorenza's work, a hermeneutics of suspicion is accompanied by a hermeneutics of consent. She shows how the Bible can be resource for women's struggle for liberation despite its being so thoroughly patriarchal and androcentric.

12   Phyllis Trible, *Texts of Terror: Literary-Feminist Readings of Biblical Narratives*, Fortress Press, Philadelphia, 1984.
13   *Ibid.*, chapter 3, 'An Unnamed Woman: The Extravagance of Violence', pp.65–91.
14   Unless otherwise indicated, all biblical quotations are from the Revised Standard Version.
15   Jane Caputi, *The Age of Sex Crime*, The Women's Press, London, 1987, p.33.
16   *Ibid.*, p.9, with Jane Caputi's emphasis.
17   Trible, *op.cit.*, pp.65–91.
18   *Ibid.*, p.80.
19   Trible's translation.
20   Trible's translation.
21   Trible's translation.
22   Trible, *op.cit.*, p.77.
23   Trible's translation.
24   Trible's translation.
25   Trible, *op.cit.*, p.81.
26   Elizabeth Cady Stanton and the Revising Committee, eds, *The Woman's Bible*, European Publishing, New York, reprinted 1978 (6th printing), Coalition Task Force on Women and Religion, Seattle, USA.
27   Schüssler Fiorenza, *op.cit.*, p.11.
28   Dale Spender *Women of Ideas (and what men have done to them)*, Ark Paperbacks, 1983, p.291.
29   *Ibid.*, pp.293–4.
30   Schüssler Fiorenza, *op.cit.*, p.8.
31   Spender, *op.cit.*, p.293.
32   Genevieve Lloyd, 'Selfhood, War and Masculinity' in *Feminist Challenges: Social and Political Theory*, Carole Pateman and Elizabeth Gross, eds, Allen & Unwin, Sydney, 1986, p.64.
33   Sam Keen, *Faces of the Enemy: Reflections of the Hostile Imagination*, Harper & Row, San Francisco, 1986, p.130.
34   Caputi, *op.cit.*, p.10.
35   Lucy Beckett, 'The Essential Feminine' in *The Tablet*, 28 October 1989, p.1243.
36   See, for example, Sara Ruddick 'Pacifying the Forces: Drafting Women in the Interests of Peace', in *Signs*, Spring 1983, Volume 8, No.3.
37   Beverly Wildung Harrison covers similar ground in 'Theology and Morality of Procreative Choice', *Making the Connections*, Carol S. Robb, ed., Beacon Press, Boston, 1985.
38   Paul Ricoeur, 'The Problem of the Foundation of Moral Philosophy', in *Philosophy Today*, 22, 1978, p.190.
39   A body of feminist scholarship is devoted to the particular violence practised by women towards themselves, towards children, towards other women, towards men, and towards nature. Women-as-a-group exercise the kinds of violence practised by many oppressed peoples: violence towards the peer group, in this case other

women, violence towards inferior groups, in this case children, and violence towards
the self in relation to the dominant group, in this case lack of respect for the self
in relation to men. In her numerous books, Alice Miller, for example, develops
the thesis that violence in society can be traced to conventional child rearing and
education. She argues that many children adapt from birth and even before birth
to the needs and desires of their parents or early carers (usually the mother) and
lose touch with their own needs, desires and potential. See Alice Miller, *The Drama
of Being a Child*, Virago Press, London, 1988 (first published in German, 1979).
Christianity, as one of the main institutions supporting conventional child rearing
practices, is implicitly critiqued by Alice Miller's thesis.

40   Elisabeth Schüssler Fiorenza, *Bread Not Stone*, Beacon Press, Boston, 1984,
p.xiv.

CHAPTER FIVE

Women together

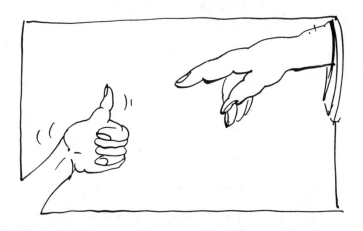

This chapter imagines the world in an uncommon way, it imagines women loving women, women being together and identifying with each other. By saying 'imagine', I do not imply that this world does not exist; I mean simply to acknowledge that this world is not frequently attended to, being overshadowed by ideologies of male bonding and of male-female romance.

This female world has a quality of its own. Female relations can be regarded as a particular revelation of life. Here I attend to this neglected world in a number of ways. Principally, I analyse how patriarchal institutions, especially Christianity, have worked against positive relations among women. I also consider how female relations have survived and flourished in spite of these institutions. Before this analysis, however, I will recall a few poetic images evoking the peculiar quality of positive relations among women.

Diverse images name female connections. Ones that occur frequently are singing and listening as in Valery Wilde's poem, 'Singing the Uncurling Woman'[1]:

> While you wait curled
> listen
> move slow
> slow and listen to your grandmother's grandmother sing
> sing the earth warm
> sing its core to rippling
> sing the melting of the rock.

> listen
> and listen to the hiss
> when she licks the earth
> moulds its shape
> with her tongue rounding edges
> lets the clay soak
> at the corners of her mouth.
> listen
> and listen as she sucks mud
> hard against her palate
> pressing the shape of her word
> into the sod.
> listen
> listen while you uncurl
> then start to turn slow spirals
> along the line that connects.

Addressed to women, the poem is about and for women. There is something primal about this listening-singing activity, this slow, spiralling reverberation. There is a sense of going back to the beginning when the world was made, when the word was formed, and when the word and the world were female. Singer and potter both, this primal mother licks and sucks, shaping word and world to her form. Hearing the word and recognising the shape, women uncurl and connect.

The images of singing and listening occur in many poems. The female 'I' in Louise Crisp's 'Evocation'[2] names singing as the way of salvation for women: 'I sing and sing her/ the only thing I can do/ that may save us'. It is the oldest Goddess that she is singing, 'in the guise of Hekate/ source of women words of power'. Singing the female self, she exorcises the silence of an isolating domestic world. Another example is Gwen Harwood's poem, 'An Impromptu for Ann Jennings'[3], which begins: 'Sing, memory, sing those seasons in the freezing/ suburb of Ferntree'. Recalling her own seasons of pain, her memory sings its way back, via friendship, to the 'roots of dreams', to the knowledge that as women 'we are our own'. Paradoxically, this going back shows a way forward, 'a way through the boulders by listening' as Crisp says in her 'High Country Hiking Song'.[4] With 'hearing intense for direction', women discover their own way. 'My sister's singing is swinging us on', chants the hiking song 'dedicated to Ros'.

The energy and connectedness evoked by listening and singing appear again in the images of women's bodies. Pervading many women's poems is a sense of relaxing into our own bodies and claiming ourselves just as we are. These celebrations of female bodiliness link women with each other and with nature as we reclaim the look-feel of this body from the inside. A good example is Kate Llewellyn's poem, 'Breasts',[5] a low-key celebration of those most noticed and neglected parts of a woman's body. Women enjoy the homeliness of Llewellyn's images, the naturalness of the language, and the taken-for-granted quality of her descriptions:

> there is a dark blue river vein here
> straggling down taking its time
> to the little pale strawberry
> picked too soon and left too long
> in the punnet in a warm shop.

Llewellyn gets it right. Without idolising or trivialising, she honours all women's breasts by describing in intimate detail the geography of one breast. It is as though Llewellyn has let the reader in on a secret, a quite ordinary and delightful secret. It is not that she's giving secrets away, for only women can have actual body-knowledge of what she is talking about. As to men who peer and stare, 'what they don't know is the breast stares straight back/ interested as a reporter'. It is women alone who know how the breast (explores) the inside curve of my elbow', or '(pries) hanging over fences' or makes a point of 'always getting there first'. This kind of assured playfulness arises from inside knowledge shared with a whole people. A poem like 'Breasts' comes out of and contributes to a strong female tradition, bonding women at an intimate level. Here women are subjects, *together* naming ourselves and the world.

Recalling these images of female bonding breaks an androcentric tradition which destructively conceptualises humanity as if men's relations with women and mens' relations with each other were always pivotal. Female relations are rarely attended to in their own right. But women *do* respect themselves and each other as friends, sisters, lovers, colleagues, mothers and daughters, aunts and nieces, women do bond. Frequently, women–women relations are central.

In this chapter I explore some of the historical and cultural expressions of female bonding. I am concerned with two questions: is female bonding in any way fostered by the theologies and structures of Christianity? and how has Christianity hindered the flourishing of female relations? The lack of symmetry in these questions betrays my own belief that Christianity has been harmful to positive relations among women. Given the evidence of the earlier chapters, it is fair to assume that women have bonded in spite of Christianity, but it is doubtful that relations among women have strengthened because of it.

Towards a theology of female friendship

To love the neighbour as the self

In the Christian tradition, Jesus' two commandments to love God and to love our neighbour as ourselves are seen as foundational. These commandments are actually borrowed from the older Hebrew scriptures.[6] Even omitting historical questions about the original contexts in which these commands were said and written, they are not easy to interpret. To the scriptural question 'Who is my neighbour?',[7] we can add the equally significant questions, Who is God? and Who is my self?

In a patriarchal world, God is always male and my neighbour and my self, even in the case of women, are always male-identified. However as feminists we can and should read Jesus' command as an injunction to women to love themselves and other women, along with men. Elisabeth Schüssler Fiorenza give it as one of the basic principles of interpretation that we presume women are addressed and referred to unless they are explicitly excluded, for to interpret otherwise is to collude with an androcentric world view.[8] While the Christian tradition has often interpreted Jesus' words as primarily for men, a women-excluding interpretation cannot be justified. Interpreting the command inclusively *is* in keeping with all the evidence of Jesus' respect for women. And even if Jesus or the individual or community recording these words did exclude women, the words themselves allow an inclusive intrepretation.

The second of these two commandments enjoins us to love our neighbour in the same way as we love ourselves: 'Thou shalt love thy neighbour as thyself'. When the command is taken to specify women as both subjects and objects of neighbourly love, i.e. 'you women are to love other women (and men) as you love your own female selves', the effect is startling. Making a point of addressing women specifically the commandment sounds unfamiliar. This is because Christian theologies have so subordinated, excluded and alienated women, that it can sound odd when they are restored to the centre. Interpreted inclusively, this second commandment says that women are to love and care, not just for men and children as the tradition emphasises, but for other women. Women are women's neighbours.

Equally, the commandment's presupposition that women are to love and care for themselves runs counter to the dominant construction of reality in the West. This encourages women to meet the needs of men and children, and men to meet their own needs.[9] Or stated more negatively, the tradition discourages women from meeting their own needs, just as it discourages men from meeting the needs of women and children. In fostering self-sacrificial attitudes in women and a preoccupying egoism in men, Christianity is damaging to both, as well as being unfaithful to its own origins.

Concern for others to the exclusion or detriment of the self, and concern with the self to the exclusion of others, tend to be female and male sins respectively. Not that women are never egoistic and men never destructively altruistic, but the dominant structures entice women and men to sin in these gender-specific ways.[10] Significantly, the Christian command, like the Hebrew command before it, actually focuses on love of neighbour and takes love of self for granted. Yet, as far as women are concerned, love of self cannot be taken for granted, given the effects of thousands of years of Hebrew and Christian patriarchal traditions. Women are far more in need of being enjoined to attend to the self than to attend to the neighbour. In a patriarchal world, this apparently neutral command is actually androcentric in its emphasis.

A possible feminist interpretation of Jesus' second commandment suggests that one must at the same time and in the same manner love one's neighbour and oneself, with the emphasis being on the female neighbour and the female self since these have been neglected by the tradition. A feminist interpretation takes into account the needs and desires of both self and other so that both are respected and enhanced and neither suffers detriment.

Christianity in practice has failed to foster a simultaneous love of self and other, causing conflict within the self, among women, among men, and between women and men. Women contribute to healing these conflicts by loving themselves and other women, and by expressing this love in a public symbolic form. It is essential that a tradition of female bonding be widely acknowledged and celebrated so that it can contribute to the health of individual women and transform androcentric social structures. Bonding between women has always existed in some contexts and in the last two waves of the feminist movement has become more publicly celebrated. But unfortunately it is still only an undercurrent to the dominant Western tradition and is widely seen as being in destructive competition with it.

Three types of mythology

Humanity needs three types of mythology: one that is female-centred, one that is male-centred, and one in which mutuality between male and female is adequately represented.[11] To date, Christian mythology has not provided an adequate base for the conceptualisation of these three gender-related mythologies. Indeed, it is a matter for debate whether Christianity has within itself the resources necessary for conceptualising gendered humanity in a comprehensive and adequate way. Whatever may be its inherent capabilities, Christianity has always, in practice, concentrated on a male-centred mythology. This is often destructive in itself because it tends to exalt images of dominance, and it is always destructive in relation to both a female-centred mythology and one representing male-female mutuality because it attempts to usurp their rightful place.

THE TRINITY

Even a cursory survey of Christianity betrays the predominance of male-centred mythology and hierarchical male-female mythology, as well as the lack of a female-centred mythology.[12] In the heavenly realm Christianity has emphasised the male–male relation between God the Father and God the Son, and the male–female relation between Christ and the Holy Spirit or between the risen Christ and Mary assumed into heaven. In this transcendent realm no celebration of the female–female exists. Similarly, in the traffic between heaven and earth, male–male and male–female relations are emphasised. The faithful are sons of the heavenly Father, for example, and the Church is the Bride of Christ. And in the immanent earthly domain, female–female relations are again largely excluded. Either male–male or male–female relations characterise the college of cardinals, the relation between a bishop and his priests, or that between a priest and his people. In every instance, the essential maleness of the church hierarchy ensures the exclusion of female-centred relations. The one possible exception is the communities of nuns in the Roman Catholic and Anglican churches, but this is a poor example, since these communities are still largely controlled by male ecclesial structures.

It can easily be seen that not only are female–female relations largely excluded from Christianity, but the male–male and male–female relations are generally lacking in mutuality. Domination and subordination characterise most relations so that the foundational myths and fundamental structures of Christianity generally model an androcentric and hierarchical worldview. But a revolution is under way.

This explosion of female energy is epitomised in Ntozake Shange's passionate declaration of love, 'i found god in myself and i loved her/i loved her fiercely'. This declaration of self-love and God-love was first proclaimed during the Broadway performance of Shange's highly-acclaimed musical, 'for colored girls who have considered suicide when the rainbow is enuf.[13] Leaving aside the command to love one's (male) neighbour as one's (male) self, Shange takes up the neglected part of the Christian tradition, the concern for a female self and for God in a female image. This healing avowal has been repeated many times as women have recognised the divine in themselves and in each other, the God-like aspect of being female and the female aspect of God.

From this brief introduction it is apparent that the search for a theology of female bonding entails both an appropriation and critique of the Christian tradition. On the positive side, there are feminist impulses within Christianity, the injunction to love the (female) neighbour as the (female) self being one of them. Feminist scholars are exploring the possibilities of these impulses which can heal and nourish the community. Whether these feminist impulses are essential or peripheral to the origins of Christianity is largely a matter of conjecture, scholarly and otherwise.

Leaving aside the question of origins, it is also certain that in the later and current practice of Christianity any feminist impulses have been excluded or forced to the periphery. Hence the need to critique the tradition. Being shaped as much by what we reject as by what we appropriate, women need this life-enhancing work of critiquing the tradition. So I turn to Women-church, an example of a community of self-affirming women, and consider the ways in which Christianity has hindered and promoted this community. This work of critique and appropriation contributes to a theology of female bonding.

Women together: Women-church

Women-church is a large, public and very active community of women and men found in many countries of the Western world. It is currently engaged in two related tasks: discovering and creating both a female-centred mythology and a mythology representing male–female mutuality. Women-church also provides a place where women and men can practise the social and political implications of these mythologies. Encouraging female bonding and defying patriarchy, Women-church is a strategy. I here explore its effectiveness by recounting a few specific stories thus grounding my comments on this world-wide phenomenon in the experience of a local group.

A local group

The Women-church group to which I belong consists of about 80 women with about 25 attending the bi-monthly meetings.[14] We meet for nourishment, support, affection, challenge and information: legitimate needs, not adequately met in a patriarchal church. We are women-centred and aim to contribute to the discovery and creation of a female mythology and praxis. We aim to be non-hierarchical, non-competitive and non-authoritarian, in our internal structures and dealing with other groups. In positive terms, we aim to conduct all our activities in a way that honours the divine in our female selves.

We do not, of course, always succeed in these aims. We acknowledge we are sometimes patriarchal. We know we easily slip back into the accustomed man-made and especially church-made ways of being, that we become either dominant or subordinate, destroying ourselves and others in the process. Nevertheless, Women-church provides a space where we can be conscious of our own patriarchal attitudes and analyse them, a space in which we can outwit prevailing patriarchal customs and play with women-centred possibilities. Stories, rituals, casual language, political actions, all affirm us as women.

The experience of affirming and being affirmed as women, an uncommon experience in a patriarchal world, is not simply confined to the brief time feminist women are together. Women carry the experience with them and, fortified by it, are better able to be self-affirming and female-identified in daily dealings with patriarchal institutions. Not only the experience of female affirmation, but the memory of the experience is healing and strengthening. As a woman from a similar group expressed it, 'the finest thing about (this) group is that *it sits in our minds* when we are apart, as a place and time where women can be honest with each other, can share some deeply felt angers, fears, dreams'.[15] What 'sits in our minds' and hearts, matters enormously. If there is no women-centred mythology there, no conceptualisation of women at the centre, and precious little of this can be gleaned from Christianity, then women are undone, and men along with us.

A ritual dedicating a girl child to the Goddess

What exactly do I mean by female-centred mythology as practised by Women-church? Here, as an example, is part of a ritual celebrated in May 1989 by our local group, a ritual dedicating a girl child to the Goddess.[16] The ritual begins with the mother, Kath, welcoming all present, and then telling her baby daughter, Cara, the story of selecting her name.

A few weeks before you were born, I had several dreams. In the first dream I was visited by a white leopard. I knew this was the Goddess visiting me and I had a feeling she was giving me a message regarding your identity. Following this, I had two dreams about lions and then I set about finding your name.

Cara is derived from Kore, an ancient name for the Goddess. The Greek and Latin roots for the name mean 'heart', hence the connection with the lion, lion-heart. Courage and strength are your special qualities given to you by the Goddess. In Gaelic, Cara is Cairdean, a term used for maternal blood relationships between women. The Goddess Kore is known as 'the heart of the world'.

Brady is the name of your maternal ancestors from Mallow in County Cork in Ireland. When your grandmother Prue and I were travelling in Ireland in 1983, we came to Mallow to search for the tombs of the Brady family in the Protestant cemetery. We finally found the gravestone of Kingsmill Brady and his nine descendents in the ruins of the old Protestant cemetery, cracked and broken and overgrown with weeds and long grass.

It was from this family that the first Brady woman came to Australia last century. It was also in this cemetery some months before that a young girl found herself one night, desperate and forsaken by family and friends, church and community, in the throes of labour with her child. Her baby was born on a cold, windy night and she cut the umbilical cord with a pair of old scissors. Both mother and child were found dead in the morning, victims of a cruel and heartless church and state, that refuses women both abortion and support for their children. Finding the Brady tombstone will always in my mind be linked with this woman and her child. I thank the Goddess for a healthy baby, for a girl-child and for a caring and supportive family and friendship network. This young woman and her baby whose lives were so uselessly wasted rest now within the loving arms of the Goddess, her blood having returned to the earth and to the Goddess. May we always remember your love for us Mother. May the tree of life always sustain and nurture us.

It is possible to dismiss the significance of this story saying it is but one mother and child, one odd group on the fringe of mainstream society. Look, though, at the wider implications. This is a naming story and naming is a highly significant act, a power which, according to Mary Daly, women have had stolen from them. In calling on her own authority *to name* her child, this mother defies dominant patriarchal ideology in a number of ways. She *listens* to a peculiarly female tradition, both personal and cultural. She engages in an all-female conversation *speaking* to her daughter in the presence of women, including the child's grandmothers. She *remembers* the sufferings and achievements of her own foremothers, thus drawing on the wisdom of the female community. These acts of listening, speaking, remembering, strengthen the existing community: we know we are not alone, that there are women before us, women coming after us, and women beside us. In going counter to androcentric customs of naming these actions subvert the traditions of male dominance that we have internalised.

Subversive, too, is the naming of divinity in female terms. The dedication of this girl child takes place in a community of women conscious of the sacred imaged as Goddess, Kore, Mother, Sister. Listen to some of the blessings that women bestow on this girl child, blessings acknowledging that the divine and the human female reveal and honour each other.

> Welcome Cara to the wonderful world!
> The Goddess says to you, Cara,
>
> Fly, dove-winged one,
> and soar in all things
> beyond yourself.
> And when you are tired and weary,
> return to the flood again.
>
> I the Goddess am your playmate!
> I will lead the child in you
> in wonderful ways
> for I have chosen you.
>
> adapted from Mechtild of Magdeburg (1210–1280)[17]

And the final blessing:

> Holy Wisdom, Our Mother, Our Sister, Our Lover,
> You who nurture, befriend, and love passionately
> This girl child,
> Teach us your wise and daring ways,

Ways that we have not yet recognised and do not yet know.
May we be open to these ways.
May we learn what this blessed girl child has to teach.
In the name of Holy Wisdom and of Kore
May Cara be blessed.[18]

Questions of ritual

Women hunger for communities in which such female-centred rituals can be celebrated, rituals concerned with becoming pregnant and not becoming pregnant, with mothering and abortion, with desertion and divorce, with menstruation and menopause. A patriarchal church and society have not ritually recognised these female experiences in any adequate way. Instead, they have frequently co-opted them. As women become aware of this co-optation and of the corresponding loss of a female mythology, there is a move away from patriarchal rituals. Listen to the agonising questions of a mother who realises the harm done by such rituals. This poem by Margaret Curtis speaks powerfully of a mother's relation with the institution and with her child.[19]

> You struggle
> cry in your sleep
> amongst late summer leaves.
> > Cry for a bath
> > cry for play
> > cry to be fed
> > bath water relieves the frustrations
> > of your body
> > warm soapy floating
> > slippery soft in my hands.
> > Sing me your little love song.
> > Your infant's joy
> > glistens in
> > a forest mystic's eyes
> > I fear their purity their
> > no memory of pain.
> > For a tingling instant
> > we can share
> > our pre-existence despite
> > old blood and urine stains.
> > > Your tiny fists beat
> > > > exultant
> > > > > with the power

to raise yourself
up against my
breast.
Are you awake?

One day soon you will be
  clothed in water
    wrung from warm arms
into the stinging air
  held under by
a man of the cloth
  spoken about or over
not to . . .
so brief
so comfortless scrubbed insideout
with God the Father
when the Spirit
has never been anywhere else more content.

Get 'em young, they say
and you've got 'em for life.
You can't take this water off!

As a man
will you walk on water
feet washing
taking baths of self doubt
ever thirsty?

Will you sicken
at the sight of a collar
smell of the cloth
folds of priest skin
will you remember why
I enact a kind of theft
of your free will
to satisfy my own
will you curse me
when you understand
how you parting water
makes a difference
to a few dead.

What right
you'll demand
did I have to claim
to initiate
you in the ways of wearing
water!

Your head shaking
drops like Yod flames
dance unchecked
on the shoulders of men
and women you kiss
shells on legs
correct gestures
correct lives being shed
suffer
chronic dehydration
fish scale people
forcing me to choose
between isolation and betrayal.
I stay, a fog wintering under desert.
Without amphibious rebels
   like me
   we would soon be wading dust.

You have shared
your bath with me
soaked me to the bone
dripping
my hands cup your head
I ache to say those words
  what are the words
    the special easy
      quick words that will
        shape water about you forever . . .

Is there nothing I can give you
  more than life?

  all I say is
  live
  live

You open your eyes.

A baptism fit for a girl

The questions, put so eloquently in this poem, are asked by many women and a few men. 'What do people do when the set text for a sacramental celebration is not an authentic celebration of their faith?'[20] One response is to dedicate a girl child to the Goddess. Another is to adapt the church liturgy so it includes females. This latter option was taken by the parents of a baby girl, Miriam Patricia. These parents approached Colleen O'Reilly and Walter McEntee who 'set about writing a text which honoured our

Christian tradition of infant baptism on the basis of promises made, which was sound theologically and which placed Miriam in her rightful place as the focus of the celebration, not an aberration from the male norm (included in brackets)'.[21] In accordance with the parents' wishes, everything about this ceremony reflected the mutuality of male and female. Colleen O'Reilly describes their intentions this way:

> Walter McEntee and I conducted the baptism together. We both vested in albs and he wore a stole. By alternating we imaged in the way we led the baptism the equality of women with men which we believe to be fundamental to the gospel. The text, 'In Christ there is neither Jew nor Greek, neither slave nor free, neither male nor female', is thought to have been an early baptismal formula of the church. [This] liturgy is an attempt to recover that ancient insight which so rarely surfaces in the patriarchal church.[22]

Significantly, every aspect of a traditional baptism featured in this revised ritual: the reading of scripture, the affirmation of faith, the promises, the pouring of the water, the signing of the cross, the anointing with oil, the clothing with a white garment, the blessings. Contrary to a traditional ceremony, however, the language and actions of this baptism affirmed femaleness, as well as maleness. By mining the female images *within the scriptures* and not excluding the male images, the ritual remained faithful to the Christian tradition and at the same time honoured the child's female self. Consider the opening statement of the ritual, a celebration of the name chosen for this child:

> Miriam, prophetess and sister of Moses and Aaron, led the women of Israel in song and dance after the crossing of the sea. Her song is the oldest fragment of our Scriptures. Her role as a leader of the Exodus has always been remembered by God's people. (Exodus 15:20; Micah 6:4).[23]

Consider also the way this ritual images God:

> We believe in God
> Source of all life
> Source of all love
> Creator with us
> our past and future
> mother and father of all that's to be. [24]

The focus is female because the child is female, but, unlike the ritual dedicating a girl child to the Goddess, all reference to maleness has not been removed from the ritual. This adapted baptism simply modifies the maleness of the ritual; it does not delete it. Conducted by a man and woman and imaging divinity in male and female terms, this ritual seeks to represent the full power of womankind alongside the full power of mankind.

Tensions within Women-church: two mythologies

These three examples, the dedication to the Goddess, the questioning poem, and the adapted baptism, all evoke the spirit of Women-church, all witness to the strength of female bonding and to the power of the female tradition. Certainly, they are different expressions of that tradition and different responses to the problem of a patriarchal church, but they are not contradictory. They are appropriate expressions and responses, each in a tensive relation with the other, each taking its place on the same continuum of meaning. Placed side by side, they indicate tensions within Women-church, signalling a range of positions embraced by this community.

These tensions exist because Women-church is simultaneously involved in two related tasks: in the discovery and creation of both a *female-centred* mythology and a mythology representing *male–female mutuality*. It is also engaged in fostering the praxis engendered by such mythologies. The dedication to the Goddess contributes more to a female mythology, while the adapted baptismal ritual contributes more to a mythology of mutuality. The poem, entitled 'The Mother God Question', moves between the two.

Not everyone interprets these tensions positively. Elisabeth Schüssler Fiorenza, whose work of the last decade has explored the significance of Women-church,[25] names quite differently the phenomenon described above. Instead of seeing a creative tension within the movement, she sees *two* movements emerging, both called Women-church, one devoted to a struggle against patriarchal institutions and the other involved in an Exodus movement away from these institutions.[26] While she supports communities engaged in struggle, she is critical of those involved in Exodus seeing this movement as largely irrelevant, elitist and self-indulgent. Struggle, not Exodus, she says, is a name for Hope.[27]

Let us consider briefly this critique of Exodus communities, a critique directed mainly towards the Women-church movement in the USA. Schüssler Fiorenza believes that any Exodus movement distracts from the main task of Women-church which is to live out a vision of freedom, not on the boundaries of or outside the patriarchal church, but *at its centre*.[28] In her view, Women-church seeks, not to live in a dialectical relation with the church, but to be at its centre in such a way that the patriarchal power operating there is gradually replaced by a liberating power. She judges it as politically unwise for women to be so concerned with their own spiritual well-being that they fail to fight against a church that excludes and subordinates them. She warns that Women-church is in danger of becoming a 'spiritual service station' or a 'liberated zone', an isolated community that comforts its own members by concentrating on their spiritual needs, but is so removed from the everyday needs of most women and men that it is largely irrelevant.[29] In her judgment, this kind of Women-church simply repeats the mistakes of a patriarchal church, except that, unlike the latter, it is devoted to the spiritual needs of a minority of *women*, not men. She sees this kind of Women-church as providing a parallel to the home as a place of refuge from the concerns of the world,[30] an arrangement that signals the privatisation (and feminisation) of religion. She is critical, then, of a Women-church that is nothing more than a safe place where women can be self-absorbed, reassuring to those involved but removed from the world and ineffective in terms of widespread change.

Certainly the symbols of Exodus and struggle do suggest, correctly, that there are tensions within Women-church. But both symbols link Women-church inexorably with patriarchal church, by always imagining women as either exiting from this church or struggling with it. This link, binding women to an eternal protest, is disempowering. Is it possible to find less constraining symbols that evoke the range of positions within Women-church? I believe it is. The symbols of being *at home* and being *at the front*, for example, while being less grand than Exodus and struggle, better reflect mutuality and their meaning is centred, not in a patriarchal church, but in the self-identity of women themselves. Here are two concrete examples.

In 1989 a group of about 400, mostly women and a few men, gathered one weekend in an idyllic spot on the eastern seaboard of Australia for a national feminist theology conference.[31] During the entire weekend, lectures, discussions, rituals, meetings, entertainment and meals affirmed women. All present celebrated the spirituality of women. No voice objected to this celebration, for we were all believers there. Being in a place and time where we were freer to express our women-selves, we were *at home*. Not entirely at home, of course, and not entirely free, for patriarchal attitudes went with us and there were struggles. But we did experience an unusual degree of freedom. It was not that we were in exodus from a patriarchal church. It was rather that we were, to some degree, in exodus from patriarchy. We were in a place where women-identified women could still be church.

At the conclusion of this weekend, a number of conference participants went from the seaside place to the city centre for a procession through the streets to the doors of the Anglican cathedral.[32] Here, immediately before the opening ceremony for a General Synod which was to debate the ordination of women, a group of women and men participated in a televised ritual celebrating womanlife and lamenting both the exclusion of women from the priesthood in local Anglican churches and the exclusion of women from full participation in Christian churches generally. The time and place of this ritual and its public character made it a highly political act. Those participating were undoubtedly *at the front*, celebrating divinity in female symbols and engaged in a public struggle with the patriarchal church.

Mediating two mythologies

The first activity, the conference by the sea where femaleness could be freely celebrated, was an experience of being at home. The second, where women and men celebrated the divine in female form and protested against the institutional exclusion of women at the very doorstep of patriarchal church, was an experience of being at the front. Enacted by many of the same people, these two events were closely related. Representing two ways of being church, they both express and nurture women's power.

The examples quoted earlier can also be interpreted in the light of the same symbols. The ritual dedicating a girl child to the Goddess is closer to the symbol of being at home and the revised baptismal ritual closer to that of being at the front. I say only 'closer to' because the dedication ritual also *implies* a struggle against the initiation of children into an androcentric tradition, and the inclusive baptismal ritual, while evoking protest and confrontation, also *implies* being at home in an order which bypasses androcentric rules. Implying each other, the symbols of being at home and at the front belong together.

We can detect the same interaction within all the tensions evident in Women-church. Consider the tensions between God language and Goddess language, between Bible-based ritual and experience-based ritual, between fighting for ordination and seeing no need for ordained ministers, between politics and spirituality, between political activity directed at the church alone and political activity directed at 'secular' institutions, between groups for women and men and groups for women only. In each case, the first term is closer to a patriarchal church. This means that some women choose to celebrate and lament in a place that a patriarchal church claims for itself, while others choose to remove themselves from the space claimed by the institution. This difference between self-identified women is not fundamental, however, for whatever the choice, the primary focus of Women-church remains the celebration of womanlife. At base, these women are united.

Individual groups, as well as Women-church as a whole, move between these symbols of being at home and being at the front, both symbols having spiritual and political significance. No one group will always and everywhere opt for one symbol over the other, even though most groups will prefer to identify primarily with one or other. In practice, each group will meet different needs at different times. Sometimes a group will celebrate femaleness in a way that directly challenges the institution, at other times the challenge is indirect. In both instances the energy is centred, not in the institution, but in the group of women itself.

The tension between being at home and being at the front, or between Exodus and struggle, recalls what I have described as a tension between female-centred mythology and a mythology of male–female mutuality. Some Women-church communities contribute to a female-centred mythology and praxis by choosing, in the hallowed tradition of an Exodus movement, to leave patriarchal churches in order to celebrate new women-centred ways of being church; others contribute to a mythology and praxis of male–female mutuality by choosing to stay within patriarchal churches and celebrate women-centred ways of being within their precincts. In practice, as I have said, most groups and individuals oscillate. I see these tensions as necessary and creative. I do not think one mythology is to be valued in absolute terms over the other. I do not think one is more radical or more essentially feminist than the other. Excluded and neglected by Christianity and western culture generally, both mythologies are desperately needed and both can work for the well being of women, and ultimately of men.

I have analysed the tensions within Women-church in some detail because they bring to light the necessity for bonding between women; they bring out the strength and potential weakness, not only of Women-church, but of the women's movement as a whole. In other contexts also feminist women choose sometimes to move away from a patriarchal institution in order to create their own space outside it, and sometimes to stay and struggle against the institution thereby creating their own space within it. The choice made does not matter. The strength of the movement lies in the bonding between women essential for the creation of their own space. Discovering and creating a female-centred mythology or a mythology representing male–female mutuality and living out the implications of this mythology, women employ different strategies to the same end. That end is the affirmation of the female self. What matters is that women choose their particular strategy primarily because they value themselves and other women, that they recognise and unambiguously celebrate femaleness and lament its repression, and that they recognise the divine in themselves. This is the heart of Women-church, indeed the heart of the women's movement.

The danger for Women-church, its temptation to weakness, is to empha-
sise, not the bonding and friendship between women, not the specificity
of femaleness, but the patriarchal church that women are struggling against
or exiting from. Patriarchal institutions seek such an emphasis. Assisted
by the androcentric bias of language itself, all patriarchal institutions
constantly seek to remain paradigmatic. It is impossible, therefore, to ignore
them completely and extraordinarily difficult not to conform to them.
Women who concentrate *all* their attention on a patriarchal church, even
when disagreeing with it, simply reinforce this paradigmatic status. To
divide over the choice of struggling against such a church or departing
from it is to allow this church, yet again, to set the agenda for women.

A definition of Women-church: self-identified women and women-identified men

The term 'Women-church' was probably coined by Schüssler Fiorenza and
it initially took hold in North America and Europe during the last
decade.[33] In discussing the meaning of 'Women-church', Schüssler
Fiorenza returns to the Greek notion of *ekklesia* which she understands
as 'the public assembly of free citizens who gather in order to determine
their own and their children's communal, political and spiritual well
being'.[34] Essential to this notion of assembly is the right to choose what
serves one's own well being and that of one's community. So the term *ekklesia*
specifically endorses notions of communal freedom, choice and self-
determination.

Historically, though, the Greek assembly excluded women because they
were not admitted to full citizenship of the state.[35] To this day the modern
ekklesia or church excludes women (and also most men) from participating
fully in decisions concerning their own spiritual well-being and that of
their children. Adopting the term *'ekklesia* of women' or 'Women-church',
Schüssler Fiorenza seeks, not the exclusion of men, but the inclusion of
women. She seeks to empower women and make them visible. As she says,
'Women are church, we women always have been church, we women always
will be church'.[36]

Members of Women-church are 'self-identified women' and 'women-
identified men'.[37] These rather odd sounding terms mean *women* who
affirm themselves as women and who make choices based on women's needs
and desires, and *men* who support women in such a choice. These women
and men act contrary to prevailing customs and contrary to the interests
of patriarchy. To return to the terms of my earlier discussion, these 'self-
identified women' choose to love their female neighbours as they love their

own female selves, and these 'women-identified men' choose to love their female neighbours in the same way as they love their own male selves.

'Self-identified women' refuse to find their identity solely in relation to men, they refuse to be the 'others' of the culture, a derivative of some male norm.[38] Instead, 'self-identified women' bond with each other, finding their primary identity in relation to their female selves and to other women. This does not signify a hatred for men or an avoidance of relationships with them. It does signify, though, refusing to be man-made, that is refusing to comply with patriarchally-endorsed female subordination. It means claiming the right to name ourselves female and human with a history, symbol-system and culture which is peculiar to us. It means celebrating the specificity of femaleness.

For their part, 'women-identified men' recognise the justice of the claims of 'self-identified women' and support them in every way possible.[39] They recognise and protest against the gender-based oppression of women, while refusing to reap advantages from their own dominant status as men. Belonging generically to the group of oppressors, men can still distance themselves from patriarchal ways of behaving, they can identify with women, the oppressed group. Such identification will, of necessity, change their own self-understanding so that, in the course of acknowledging the specificity of femaleness, 'women-identified men' will come to celebrate the specificity of their own maleness in a non-patriarchal way. In this way, feminist men contribute to the discovery and creation of a liberating male mythology, one that represents mutuality rather than domination and subordination.[40]

Historical examples of Women-church communities

Have such groups of women and men ever existed? Do they exist today? They have and they do. Although the memory of them is constantly repressed, feminist scholarship continues to uncover knowledge of these women and men. The philosopher Janice Raymond speaks of the need for a 'genealogy' of 'loose women',[41] by which she means a record of women who were not completely identified with and submerged in hetero-relations, the very same women that Schüssler Fiorenza describes as 'self-identified'. Such a genealogy already exists and is constantly being added to, though many, on account of the dominant androcentric culture, still remain ignorant of it. In the arts and sciences, in politics and education, in all fields of human endeavour, feminists are currently re-membering 'self-identified' or 'loose' women, thereby discovering a broad-based, female-centred mythology. Here is one example of this re-membering work, a key one in the present context.

An enormous amount of feminist scholarship shows that numbers of 'self-identified women' were present at the very beginnings of Christianity, at the time of Jesus and in the century after his death. One classic work of re-membering these women is Schüssler Fiorenza's *In Memory of Her*.[42] This work presents evidence suggesting that the wandering groups centred around Jesus were female and male, and that, contrary to the patriarchal customs of the day, these groups were egalitarian, practising what Schüssler Fiorenza calls a 'discipleship of equals'.[43] She also shows that women frequently headed the house churches that spread through the city and country areas of the Hellenistic world during the first and second centuries.[44] Presenting models of both female leadership and of male–female mutuality, these original Christian communities threatened the patriarchal family structure forming the basis of the Greco-Roman society of the day. Women, whether Jew or Gentile, slave or free, were able, by joining Christianity, to break out of the different cultural bonds restricting them. In practice then, early Christianity was a subversive movement, proclaiming the equality of women and men, of slaves and free, of Gentiles and Jews. So subversive was it that Christian missions were being accused, right up to the end of the second century, of destroying patriarchal households. This accusation gradually disappeared, however, as Christianity adapted to the prevailing ideology, modelled itself on the same structure, and ceased to challenge it.

Schüssler Fiorenza shows how this process of adapting and modifying is at work in the Christian scriptures themselves. The Household Codes of Colossians and Ephesians, for example, prescribe that wives be subject to their husbands, slaves to their masters, and sons to their fathers, three patriarchal prescriptions endorsing the household arrangements of the day and leaving no room at all for 'self-identified women' and 'women-identified men'.[45] Enforcing a model of domination and submission, these codes are a sign, according to Schüssler Fiorenza, that the transforming impetus of the early Jesus movement was gradually eroded in the first and second centuries. Mainstream Christianity gradually ceased to challenge patriarchy and finally succumbed to it. Historically, patriarchal structures have won out.

So Schüssler Fiorenza's theological and historical reconstruction of the origins of Christianity suggests that, although the patriarchal structures of contemporary Christian churches can be traced back to the first couple of centuries of Christianity, these structures are not faithful to the egalitarian spirit of the early Jesus movement. Her work traces the way these patriarchal structures gradually took over Christianity, and repressed any egalitarian impulses by proclaiming them heretical. This struggle between groups is quite apparent in the Christian scriptures themselves. Women-church, then, insofar as it is a non-hierarchical community practising a 'discipleship of equals' can identify with the earliest traditions of the Jesus movement. Celebrating the bonding of self-identified women and women-identified men, this community can indeed trace its roots to the origins of Christianity itself.[46]

The work of remembering is an act of solidarity with women. By recalling women's sufferings under patriarchy and their victories against it, we are linked with two large communities, with women of the past and with women today. In her scholarly work, Schüssler Fiorenza sees herself as accountable to both these communities. She believes that women of the past, suffering under patriarchy, must not be forgotten, for we have a debt to these women, a debt which we honour by remembering them. She also believes that feminists are accountable to women today. As feminist theologian and biblical scholar, she believes that her own principal responsibility is to the community of women, and that her responsibility to academy and church comes only second. Women, she says, are her people.[47]

Although Schüssler Fiorenza links the spirit of modern Women-church with the origins of Christianity, it must not be thought that this community has sprung up unheralded in the late twentieth century western world, as some faithful re-incarnation of the early Jesus movement. Non-hierarchical Christian communities, manifestations of what I have here described as Women-church, have existed during the intervening two thousand years, as many scholars have shown. These communities represent an unorthodox and largely hidden tradition. Rosemary Radford Ruether's work, *Women-Church*, for example, plots the course of these 'Spirit-filled communities'.[48] With remarkable economy, Ruether shows how a number of these historical communities have lived in a tensive relation with ecclesial institutions. And she is not alone in her view that the feminist community of Women-church is heir to a long Christian tradition.

Women-church: what's in a name?

Is Women-church so inclusive as to lack identity? Is it so universalist that it adopts a kind of all-encompassing catholicism allowing no opposition? I think not. Currently Women-church comprises such a proliferation of groups and most of them are so wary of dogmatisms that the danger of a new orthodoxy hardly exists. Still, differences need to be acknowledged.

While a multitude of feminist communities have sprung up, these groups vary greatly in their self-understanding, in their rituals and symbols, and in their relations with each other and with denominational churches. Some groups, for example, are based in or on the edge of large denominational churches and are widely known for initiating public action, the Movement for the Ordination of Women (MOW) and Women and the Australian Church (WATAC) being two such groups in Australia.[49] Other feminist groups avoid any affiliation, no matter how loose, with institutional churches.[50] Varying widely in their relations to churches, groups may see themselves as 'disassociated insiders' or as 'associated outsiders' or even as 'disassociated outsiders'.[51] Groups vary too in their use of symbols, with some restricting themselves to Christian symbols, and others being open to whatever symbols present themselves. Groups also vary in their commitments to spiritual and political activities. So, while remaining inclusive, feminist groups develop a variety of identities from which they individually gain strength and which contribute much to the wider movement.

Many of these groups would not want to be described as 'Women-church' seeing 'church' as synonymous with patriarchy or seeing 'Women-church' as exclusive of men. Without ignoring this distaste for the term and without imposing a name, we can still recognise the collective energy shared and generated by all women-identified communities. A multitude of feminist communities *do* share an identity, despite their differences. They all, for example, reject the injustice of patriarchal religion and challenge androcentric ecclesial structures, they all recognise themselves as having spiritual needs, and they all affirm the revelation of the divine in womankind. These likenesses create a bond, engendering the kind of energy evoked in this chapter. Belonging to particular groups, women will give this energy a variety of names, and that does not matter. What does matter is that women, trusting the depth and breadth of this tradition of feminist spirituality, become self-identified.

Obstacles and strategies

In describing Women-church, I have touched several obstacles and strategies in connection with female bonding. Indeed, Women-church itself can be seen as a strategy for nurturing relations among women, while the patriarchal church can be seen as a formidable obstacle to female bonding. Not that the division is as neat as this. Obstacles to friendship invade Women-church and the influence of Women-church itself can be found at the core of patriarchal church. This two-way traffic was implied in my description of Women-church. Here I focus more explicitly on what hinders and fosters female friendship.

I consider the lack of a woman-centred mythology and praxis to be the central obstacle to female bonding. The Western tradition has created a mythology which constructs woman as being solely for man and never constructs man as being solely for woman in a reciprocal way. Woman is fantasised as ideal object for the male. Those women who will not or cannot conform to this patriarchal ideal find themselves denigrated and placed in opposition to other women.[52] This tradition has failed to construct woman as being for herself, as human in her own right. So women face the unpalatable choice of being wanted as idealised object of the male or not wanted at all. Rarely if ever does this mythology offer women the option of being self-determining subjects.

Androcentric structures divide women into myriad categories.[53] To take some examples: women are single or married, lesbian or heterosexual, religious or lay, ordained or not ordained, young or old, black or white, attached to rich men or poor men, mothers or maidens, beautiful or plain. These oppositions define according to their relations and potential relations with men. All categories have to do with controlling women, particularly with controlling their powers to procreate and to exercise authority. All categories are designed to indicate which women are available to satisfy the sexual desires of men, as well as which women are safe because, for physical or cultural reasons, they are considered unavailable.

The example of the nunwoman-laywoman divide

The same divisions are generally promoted by Christianity which adopts the same structures as other institutions. It too divides women from each other. A prime example is the division between nunwomen and laywomen in the Catholic church and that between ordained and non-ordained women in several Protestant denominations. Focusing on the nunwomen-laywomen division, we can detect a pattern which operates throughout the entire process of dividing women into categories.

Patriarchal mythology implicitly promotes destructive feelings between these two categories of women. Nunwomen are encouraged, for example, to envy married women their sexual experience, male companionship, children and possessions and laywomen are encouraged to begrudge nuns their seclusion, independence, financial security and opportunities for education. The rift can widen as each side declares that it does not in fact possess these perceived advantages or that they are being vastly overrated. Instructed by a patriarchal mythology promoting competition and manipulation, women on both sides of this divide can feel envious of and threatened by the other.

At the base of this mistrust is the church's creation of a hierarchy evident in the very terms 'religious' and 'lay'. By consistently regarding nunwomen as of higher status than laywomen and bestowing on them certain religious advantages, the church has effectively alienated these groups from each other. A residue of resentment remains in some married women because they were taught at a very early age that a vocation to the religious sisterhood was always a higher calling than that to the married state.[54] Today, when this recruiting technique has lost most of its clout, religious sisters can feel resentment, perceiving themselves as having lost status in relation to laywomen. All these resentments effectively disadvantage women, working only in the interests of a patriarchal church and society and placing women, both religious and lay, potentially at least, at the service of men. Resenting their sisters and unable to see a patriarchal church as the problem, women are divided and lose themselves.

This harmful division can be combatted by several related strategies, all of which are currently underway. I begin with the example of nunwomen. These women are faced with the huge task of freeing themselves from the stranglehold of a patriarchal church which tries to control their lives down to the last detail of dress and daily behaviour. Many orders of religious sisters as well as many individuals are currently liberating themselves from this stranglehold and practising the self-determination necessary for full humanity.[55] In claiming their adult personhood, these women inevitably experience the wrath of a vengeful institution and have consequently been compared to 'battered women', a shocking and apt metaphor:

> An important fact unknown to many within the church is that superiors of relgous orders in the United States are, in many cases, battered women in the church. The form of violence is not as blatant as it is in some marriages, but the physical and mental anguish is strikingly similar. The parallels to domestic violence are unmistakable; the reasons for the silence are identical. But the silence must be broken so all in the church can participate in the ministry of justice, reconciliation and conversion.[56]

Speaking out is here rightly seen as an indispensable strategy in combatting violence, but it is, unfortunately, a difficult one for nuns to put into practice. Like all oppressed peoples, nuns do not readily have the wherewithall to protest. Having been conditioned by both social and theological mythologies to remain humble and hidden, they do not easily make public proclamations of self-affirmation. Having been taught to regard themselves as members of a church family in which the father figure has the ultimate authority, they can experience powerful feelings of disloyalty when they defy this authority. In sum, having been encouraged to internalise a secondary status, they can easily feel guilty when they claim the authority of their own experience. In a multitude of ways, nuns have been conditioned to maintain a patriarchal status quo.

In the case of nuns, patriarchal conditioning takes a very potent form, but actually this conditioning is no different in kind from that endured by all women. The training of nuns is simply an intensified form of the training to which women as a group are subjected. Whether to bishop, to husband or to bureaucratic institution, women are taught to submit. This commonality in the experience of women is implicitly recognised in the use of the 'battered woman' image. In crossing the divide between nunwoman and laywoman, the image acknowledges that *all women* are 'battered' by patriarchy, albeit in different ways and degrees. Such an acknowledgement enables women to bond across male-defined categories in order to name and protest against the battering. Speaking together, women become powerful.

While speaking against patriarchal violence is a necessary strategy, it is not of itself sufficient. Instances of speaking out, of protesting, are too easily suppressed unless they grow out of a strong female tradition, a tradition which is only discovered when women attend to each other. So

speaking against patriarchy must always be accompanied by an equally
passionate speaking *to* women, particularly to women separated by manmade
categories. This supporting of each other across categories, this very defiance
of the categories, helps women to survive the onslaughts provoked by their
protests against patriarchy and to become more fully self-identified. So
nunwomen, for example, protesting against patriarchy, need the support
of self-identified laywomen as well as of their own religious sisters.

This bonding across categories does not signify that there are no
differences between women or that all women will necessarily understand
and relate well with each other. To think that would be to sentimentalise
and trivialise female relations. What female bonding does signify, though,
is that women can disregard these categories so that friendships can develop
across them and that they need not be restricted by them. Women-church
is one of a number of forums in which this can happen. In a feminist forum
like Women-church it is, in many respects, irrelevant whether women are
single or married, nunwomen or laywomen, lesbian or straight, ordained
or not ordained, young or old. Not that it is unimportant in all respects,
of course, for these descriptions do indicate significant aspects of an identity,
but the identity is not circumscribed by the description as it is in a
patriarchal world.

In what respects are these descriptions or categories relevant and in what
irrelevant? Consider the case of nuns again. The description of religious
sisterhood is relevant in that this is one of the forums in which the struggle
against patriarchy is being waged, a forum in which feminist women are
finding their own self-identity. In this forum, women's struggles and
achievements take a form different from that of laywomen. There *is* a nuns'
story, both within each individual congregation and between them.[57]
This story, currently being reclaimed by feminist writers and artists, deserves
to be heard not only by religious sisters themselves but also by laywomen.
Belonging to the larger story of all self-identified women, the nuns' story,
publicly proclaimed, can empower us all.

So the specificity of religious sisterhood should not, in the interests of
female bonding or for any other reason, be suppressed. Nuns have adopted
a particular way of life different from that of laywomen, a way of life involving inherent advantages and disadvantages in the struggle to become self-
identified women. Affirming religious sisterhood does not imply, however,
that nuns are superior to or isolated from lay women. Self-identification
as women means that nuns and lay women are both able to recognise their
common struggle against patriarchy and their common celebration of
femaleness, while not denying the aspects peculiar to each of them.

So, to heal the split between them, nunwomen and laywomen face three common tasks or strategies, which, when accomplished, will foster bonding with each other. For nuns, the first task is to make public the ways in which they experience oppression at the hands of patriarchal institutions including the church, not just in general, but in specific instances. Protest is essential for well-being. Should nuns keep silent through fear or misplaced loyalty, then they will almost certainly direct their anger towards other women, rather than towards the institution deserving it. As is well known, the likelihood of engaging in horizontal violence increases in proportion to the degree to which we submit to being silenced. So to speak against oppression is a way of speaking *for* the self, an act of self love.

In concert with this speaking out against patriarchy, nunwomen need to speak and listen to themselves. Like laywomen, nuns have a particular history, mythology and praxis from which they can draw nourishment. This woman-defined mythology strengthens the bonds between nuns and empowers them to protest against patriarchy. Vital to this task of bonding between nuns is the reconstruction of the origins of women's religious orders, the creation of a women-centred history. Many of these histories have been told solely from the perspective of an androcentric church, a perspective which has, incredibly, subordinated nunwomen in their own stories, and put bishops and priests as well as the odd wealthy layman at centre stage.[58] As feminist historians reconstruct these stories, the pioneer women of religious orders move from the margins to the centre where they belong. Contemporary nuns, nourished by the feminist impulses within their own histories, become self-identified and can truly celebrate the specificity of religious sisterhood.

The third task for nuns is to speak and listen to laywomen so that their own struggles and victories are seen as parallel to that of their lay sisters. Laywomen, like nuns, have a history of being both victims and agents in a patriarchal church, a history currently being reclaimed.[59] By listening to each other's stories, nunwomen and laywomen can detect the same pattern of domination and subordination and the same feminist impulses. They can also support and learn from each other, recognising certain woman-centered advantages inherent in each way of life. Far from vying with each other for the attention of an androcentric church, these two groups can join forces to denounce the exclusion of women and contribute to a female mythology and praxis. They can recognise that they are both part of the universal story of women's oppression and liberation.

The same three strategies or tasks are relevant for all women confined by limiting categories. Lesbians or blacks or old women, for example, begin to free themselves by speaking publicly against the particular form of oppression they suffer. At the same time by listening to women in their own group they can take strength from the sense of sharing a particular form of women-centred identity. Learning that others have dealt with the same kinds of oppression in self-affirming ways, women in similar situations are led to bond with each other. The third strategy and probably the most difficult is for women in each category to speak and listen to women in the androcentrically defined opposing category, so that lesbian and heterosexual women, black and white, old and young can each identify the ways they are played off against each other in the interests of male-dominated institutions. Recognising that they suffer not opposing but parallel oppressions, these women can bond. No longer divided into antithetical categories and subsumed under a male humanity, women can conceive of themselves as a group living in solidarity with each other as a people.

Relating with men

The myriad categories dividing women from each other are actually based on the way patriarchy perceives women's relations with men. Unfortunately, women often internalise this patriarchal perception, which means that they overesteem their relations with men and devalue their relations with women. The classic example is that of the young woman who will forego relations with women friends for the sake of any man.[60] Characteristically, her life is spent waiting, waiting to be asked to dance, to go out, to get married, waiting for the moment when her male is finished surfing or fiddling with his car or attending university. Such a young woman acts out her internalised secondary status, for she does not regard herself or any other woman as highly as she regards men. Although she may have had many women friends, these are unconsciously regarded as mere preparations for the one significant relation of her life, the one with the right man. Once this man appears, her female friends are dropped, having been substitutes for the real thing. This preference for men can become a lifelong pattern where a woman relates principally to her husband and her husband's male friends and colleagues. In this situation, female contact is valued, not for itself, but only insofar as it enables the woman to serve her husband and children. The woman has become male-identified just as patriarchy ordains it.

This is a familar and distressing picture of loss of self. In old theological terms, it is a picture of loss of soul. Yet the church says nothing. On the contrary, by its structures, rituals and theologies it promotes such a loss. In all manner of ways, the church signals that women are less significant than men and that there are no authentic relations between women.

Consider a few obvious and apparently trivial examples. At a very early age, boys in the Catholic church learn that they may serve at mass and girls learn that they may not. At the same time, these children are learning that the mass is the most sacred of all rituals. In the same church, men and women constantly witness the presiding of men at the altar and the predominance of women in the pews. This arrangement typifies all work within the church, which, as in the wider society, is gender-based with male work being considered more significant. So, preaching, educating adults, looking after finances, putting up buildings are examples of men's work, and providing food, taking Sunday school, minding children, decorating the altar, cleaning church premises fall to the lot of women.[61] This gender arrangement characterises almost all church institutions, be they administrative, educational, pastoral or spiritual. By and large, men lead and women are led, men decide and women are the objects of their decisions.

The only way for women to break out of this confining arrangement is to foster relations between themselves, relations based on their own needs and desires and not on those of men and children. Women have to seek out these relationships, often in the face of opposition from family and work colleagues who usually fear and resent and therefore trivialise female friendships. In fact, women face not only local instances of opposition, but the foundational structures of an androcentric society. Family and work patterns commonly leave no room for the kind of woman–woman contact that is not directly devoted to maintaining an androcentric society. Women find themselves expected to maintain personal links in a patriarchal family, church and workplace, a demanding and underesteemed role that often takes all the energy available for relating. Since women-centred relations are regarded as unnatural by an androcentric church and society, women will have to seek them out: they will never be provided as a matter of course.

Having internalised patriarchal expectations, many women experience guilt when they do begin to make room for their own concerns. This means that women sometimes compromise, not being able, even for a short time, to be entirely woman-centred. This tendency is apparent, for example, in the inability of many women, even those with some awareness of patriarchy, to exclude men from feminist meetings and conferences. To them, it seems neither right nor just, neither politic nor sufficiently important to create a women-only forum. This is truly extraordinary. Many of these women have spent their entire lives devoted to the well-being of men and children. That they should feel uneasy about having a women's conference devoted entirely to women's concerns shows the degree to which patriarchy has invaded the female psyche. Such an unease signals little identification with the female self. Above all, it signals a grave impediment to female bonding.

It is imperative that women have space given over entirely to their own concerns. For some women this space constitutes a way of life as they find in women their main emotional, physical, sexual, spiritual and intellectual stimulation and support. These women-centred women contribute much to a liberating mythology and praxis for all women. For other women, this space is a moment of life, a moment in which they taste the kind of stimulation and support that can only come from another self-identified woman. It is not that there are two categories of feminist women, one necessarily more radical than the other; it is rather that women find themselves along a continuum of women-centredness, and that feminist women vary in the ways their self-identification finds expression.

The main point is that all women need some space, no matter how small, which is entirely woman-centred. Without this space women cannot be self-identified, cannot find out who they are in relation to themselves and each other. This relating as female is the core of a revelation from which men are necessarily excluded, because men, no matter how feminist, cannot reveal women to themselves as female. To include men in *all* feminist gatherings is to deny ourselves the chance of this particular revelation, to deny one mode of the selving of the female self. To allow only women in some feminist gatherings is to provide a unique opportunity for the female self to appear, to play, and to take delight in finding herself. Such a revelation remains significant beyond the brief moment of a women-only event. Having recognised her female self, a woman cannot easily be negated by the patriarchal structures of everyday life. Self-identified women know how to love and choose the female self.

Relating with ourselves

Often women bond because they are sister sufferers. They know what it is like to be left alone with small children, to be paid less than men for the same work, to be given all the trivial jobs, to be poor, to be raped, to be excluded from ordination, to be married to a violent husband. Women gather in groups with others who have experienced the same form of patriarchal oppression. This bonding is essential if women are to survive. No lone woman can constantly and effectively protect herself from abuse: ultimately, she will be reduced by it. So listening to each others' sufferings, hearing each other into speech, women strengthen and comfort each other.

One of the dangers inherent in this process of bonding, however, is that women become stuck in the victim role. Suffering may provide common ground for bonding, it can bring women together, but what keeps them together must be more than suffering. If the feminist movement is only a sisterhood of suffering, if women find their principal meaning in being victims, then they will have no will to change patriarchal structures. Constantly repeating 'litanies of patriarchal sins without ever doing anything about them',[62] women only keep themselves and others in a familiar and masochistically comfortable role, one that is inherently passive. Called 'victimism',[63] this tendency takes a particularly destructive form when women direct violence against those women who *do* begin to move away from their victim status. Having become 'victim(s) by vocation',[64] such women thwart change in themselves and others, frequently claiming to speak with the only pure voice.[65] Unconsciously, such women reduce female bonding to ghetto status, repeating the dogmatism of patriarchy and perpetuating patriarchal attitudes to women.

Along with the temptation to remain the eternal victim goes the temptation to mother and be mothered. Women who have suffered much at the hands of men can easily succumb to the false consolation of being mothered, but this is not what abused women need. Healing occurs through acknowledgement of our adult female selves, through recognition from our peers. Abused women need nurture from sisters, not mothers. Since women have been universally infantilised by patriarchy, there is a danger that we in turn will infantilise other women. Playing the familiar role, women are tempted to reduce other women and themselves to children. They are tempted to sentimentalise female friendship, believing that women have some innate mothering ability. This is damaging both to those doing the mothering and those mothered. The mother–child relation, tending towards hierarchy, is not a fitting symbol for the women's movement. By contrast, the egalitarian symbol of sisterhood can much more effectively enable women to move away from the victim role.

Symbols do matter. What we attend to matters. Women remain victims by attending only to symbols which picture us as victims. On the other hand, we women can recognise ourselves as agents of history by attending to the relatively uncommon symbols which picture us this way. This requires a deliberate choice on the part of women. We need to refuse to give all our attention to the symbols that denigrate and exclude us, and to attend to those that celebrate our free agency. It is not enough for feminist women to spend all their energies formulating a critique of patriarchal symbols; we need also to celebrate our own powers and to nourish ourselves in the female tradition. Celebration gives rise to a different kind of bonding from that of a shared critique – one that is centred on the positive aspects of self rather than on the negative aspects of the other. Friendship among women is based, not on shared suffering, but on mutual delight.

I end this cursory survey of obstacles to female friendship with a mention of envy and envy-avoidance,[66] both common enough in women's groups but with the latter probably the more prevalent. Envy-avoidance means, in biblical terms, putting our light under a bushel. We do this hiding away of ourselves for any number of reasons, but a common one is that we cannot bear the envy, imagined or real, that we fear the exposure of our own light will arouse. This hiding away can mean remaining subordinate because we fear the criticism any strong expression of self may evoke. Trained under patriarchy to keep their light under a bushel, women are particularly prone to envy-avoidance. It can be seen operating in groups where women are constantly reluctant to lead or to undertake other tasks of which they are capable lest they appear to dominate. Envy-avoidance destroys female bonding and the female self just as effectively as does envy itself. Envy takes many forms but one of the most common is that of suppressing and denying the gifts of others in the interests of uniformity and collectivism and to the ultimate destruction of a group. The imposition of a false egalitariansim can simply be a refusal to acknowledge the particular giftedness of groups and individuals, a disguised form of envy.

Both envy and envy-avoidance are overcome by exercising and taking delight in women's powers and gifts, one's own and those of others. This means deciding to act and encouraging others to act, it means refusing to suppress creative energy, or to be manipulated by negative feelings. All women need, at least on some occasions, to be high-profile within their own groups, to be at the centre. If we are never noticed or noticeable, it seems likely we are falling prey to envy or envy-avoidance, and we are thereby contributing to the rule of patriarchy. Within the women's movement itself, it is quite possible to conform to the patriarchal stereotype of the submissive female so that, far from being self-identified, one remains principally other-identified. To avoid this loss of self, each feminist woman needs to forgo the temptations of envy and envy avoidance. It is only by expressing her own unique self that each one contributes to the strength of womankind, to the ability of women as a group to say 'we' in relation to ourselves.

Conclusion

The above obstacles and strategies can set us thinking.[67] Female bonding *is* worthy of our attention. If we do not know, for example, what is meant by the feminist dictum, 'no woman is free until every woman is free', then we need to ponder the meaning of 'we' and 'us' in relation to women.[68] We need to notice that not all women live all of their lives dispersed among males, and that some women gather, not as mothers and wives, but as themselves in groups devoted to their own needs and desires. Developing a broad sense of sisterhood and a particular sense of friendship, we discover that many women find enormous satisfaction in being female and in relating to females. Some women can truly say, 'Blessed be the Goddess who has made me a woman'.[69] Pondering all this, we are more likely to experience female friendship and to act in women-identified ways.

This brief chapter has touched only lightly on numerous aspects of female relations and significant aspects have been omitted. I have suggested, for example, that we women need to discover and create a female-centred mythology,[70] one in which we are not subordinate to males but in which we are our own centred selves. I have barely hinted, though, at the massive work of reclamation already under way in this area. Women are discovering images of female strength in artefacts from prehistory; they're discovering the passion of the mediaeval mystics; the practical wisdom of the Beguines; the cunning of witches; the strength of women–women relations in every time and place.[71] They are discovering too the image of the Goddess who defies all neat dogmatic formulae and empowers women today, the Goddess appearing in a multitude of forms, or is it a multitude of Goddesses, from ancient Sumeria, Canaan, Egypt, Greece and Celtic lands.[72] Abused, trivialised and neglected throughout most of recorded history, this divinity imaged in female form has somehow survived.

This mythology or, if you prefer, conceptualisation of femaleness is explored and celebrated in works of history, fiction and psychology, in all the arts. If the human hero has a thousand faces,[73] then half of them at least are female, and all feminist women know this deep in their bones, despite what a patriarchal tradition tells us. This knowledge bonds women, creating sisterhood, and creating within sisterhood the most intimate of friendships. Women are and always have been our own best friends.

E.W.

Notes

1 Louise Crisp and Valery Wilde, *In the Half-Light,* Friendly Street Poets, Adelaide, p.69.

2 *Ibid.*, p.28.

3 Gwen Harwood, *Selected Poems,* Angus & Robertson, Sydney, 1988, pp.76–77.

4 Louise Crisp and Valery Wilde, *op.cit.*, pp.20–21.

5 Susan Hampton and Kate Llewellyn, eds., *The Penguin Book of Australian Women Poets,* Penguin Books, Melbourne, 1986, pp.158–9.

6 In the Hebrew scriptures see Leviticus 19:17–18 and in the Christian scriptures see Matthew 5:43–44; 19:19; 22:37–39; Luke 12:30–31; Romans 13:9; Galatians 5:14.

7 Luke 10:29 *ff.*

8 Elisabeth Schüssler Fiorenza *In Memory of Her: a Feminist Theological Reconstruction of Christian Origins,* Crossroad, New York, 1984, pp.43–48 on 'Androcentric translations and interpretations'.

9 While men are encouraged to meet their own needs in a way women are not, this encouragement is limited to those needs which conform to a patriarchal definition. So men, too, are discouraged from meeting many basic needs: those, for example, which a patriarchal tradition considers unmanly.

10 Some classic feminist texts have named the ways in which women are encouraged to sin. See Carol Gilligan, *In a Different Voice: Psychological Theory and Women's Development,* Harvard University Press, Cambridge, Mass. 1982, and Beverly Wildung Harrison, *Making the Connections,* Carol S. Robb, ed., Beacon Press, Boston, 1985. See also my discussion in 'The Issue of Blood'.

11 Humanity also needs other types of mythologies such as those representing human relations with animals and with nature, but these, though related, are not the focus of the present chapter.

12 Julia Kristeva has drawn attention to this lack in a number of works. See Elizabeth Grosz's treatment of Kristeva's work, *Sexual Subversions,* Allen & Unwin, Sydney, 1989, especially pp.82–85. In the section entitled 'Holy Mothers', for example Grosz says of Kristeva, 'Her point is that there is an unrepresented residue in maternity which has not been adequately taken up in religious discourse, a residue that refuses to conform, as Christianity requires, to a masculine, oedipal, phallic order' (p.84). Christian symbolism does not adequately represent the 'active possibilities' of women.

13 Ntosake Shange, *for colored girls who have considered suicide when the rainbow is enuf,* Macmillan, New York, 1977.

14 This group based in Sydney Australia began in April 1985. It adopted the name 'Women-church' as a way of identifying with women in Europe and the USA. Sometimes this name causes confusion, however, as it is not clear whether it is referring to the small local group or the world-wide movement. While the local group is open, it does not have a high public profile as it is most concerned with supporting and educating its own members. The group did, however, publish a 'Protest Creed' in *The Sydney Morning Herald* (22 November 1986) at the time of the visit to Australia of Pope John Paul II, an activity that provoked some media coverage. The group also publishes *Women-Church: An Australian Journal of Feminist Studies in Religion* which has a relatively large readership.

15 *Women-Church*, No.4, GPO Box 2134, Sydney, NSW 2001, Australia. p.7, with my emphasis.

16 Kath McPhillips, 'A Dedication of a Girl Child to the Goddess' *Women-Church*, No.5, pp.18–19.

17 *Ibid.*, This is Marie Tulip's adaptation.

18 Kath McPhillips, *op.cit.*

19 Margaret Curtis, 'The Mother God Question', *Women-Church*, No.5, p.21.

20 Colleen O'Reilly Stewart and Walter McEntee 'A Baptism Fit For a Girl' *Women-Church*, No.1, pp.18–20.

21 *Ibid.*, pp.18–19.

22 *Ibid.*, p.19.

23 *Ibid.*

24 *Ibid.*, p.20. Part of an 'Affirmation of Faith' by Dorothy McMahon from *Out of the Darkness: paths to inclusive worship*, Australian Council of Churches, 379 Kent St, Sydney, NSW 2001, Australia.

25 Given the breadth of Elisabeth Schüssler Fiorenza's understanding of the notion of 'Women-church', I believe that all her work is implicitly devoted to this subject. See especially though, 'Women-Church – the hermeneutical centre of feminist biblical interpretation', pp.1–22 in *Bread Not Stone* and 'Epilogue Towards a Feminist Biblical Spirituality: The Ekklesia of Women' in *In Memory of Her*, pp.343–51.

26 Elisabeth Schüssler Fiorenza, 'Daughters of Vision and Struggle', a paper written for the Australian National Conference 'Towards a Feminist Theology', 18–20 August 1989, and published in *Conference Proceedings* obtainable from Elaine Lindsay, PO Box 140, Helensburgh, NSW 2508, Australia. Schüssler Fiorenza states at the beginning of this paper that she seeks, not to separate feminist strategies from each other, but to see them as 'different strands of a rope which only when intertwined and twisted together have the strength to bind the evil power of patriarchy'. Unfortunately though her own critique of feminist Exodus communities in conjunction with her stated preference for Women-church communities involved in struggle tends to divide the Women-church community into two opposing camps. By separating so completely these two strands, Schüssler Fiorenza has fostered the 'totalising either/or strategies' that she wishes to overcome. See my 'Response to "Daughters of Vision and Struggle" ' in *Conference Proceedings*.

27 *Ibid.* Schüssler Fiorenza notes that the expression, 'Struggle is a Name for Hope', is borrowed from a collection of poetry by Renny Golden and Sheila Collins.

28 *Ibid.* This is a recurring image in the works of Schüssler Fiorenza.

29 *Ibid.*

30 *Ibid.*

31 This National Conference, entitled 'Towards a Feminist Theology', was held at Collaroy, Sydney, 18–20 August 1989. It was to have been a National Conference of the Movement for the Ordination of Women (MOW) Australia but, on account of the expected presence of Elisabeth Schüssler Fiorenza, two other groups, Women and the Australian Church (WATAC) and Women-church (note 14 above), were invited to help organise the conference. Elisabeth Schüssler Fiorenza was finally unable to attend on account of illness, but the promise of her presence had the effect of making the conference truly ecumenical.

32 On Sunday evening 20 August 1989 a group of women and men singing 'Keep On Walking Forward' processed from St James to St Andrew's Cathedral, Sydney. The liturgy celebrated *outside* the cathedral was written and devised by Suzanne Glover.

33 The term '*ekklesia* of women', coined by Elisabeth Schüssler Fiorenza and translated at 'Women-church' by Diana Neu, probably first appeared in the context of the 'Women Moving Church' Conference held in the United States in 1981. The theological vision of Women-church seems first to have really taken hold in the Netherlands from where it spread. See Lieve Troch 'The Feminist Movement in and on the Edge of the Churches in the Netherlands: From Consciousness Raising to Womenchurch' in *The Journal of Feminist Studies in Religion*, Vol.5, No.2, pp.113–28.

34 Schüssler Fiorenza, *Bread Not Stone*, p.xiv.

35 See Schüssler Fiorenza, *In Memory of Her*, Part 111, 'Tracing the Struggles – Patriarchy and Ministry'.

36 Elisabeth Schüssler Fiorenza's opening words in a session entitled, 'Shaping Our Women-Church: Global Perspectives', at the Second National Conference 'Women-Church: Claiming Our Power', Cincinnati, Ohio, 9–11 October 1987.

37 *Bread Not Stone*, p.xiv.

38 The realisation that woman is 'the other' of the culture has become common feminist knowledge. Simone de Beauvoir was the first to articulate this clearly in 1949: 'She is defined and differentiated with reference to man and not he with reference to her; she is the incidental, the inessential as opposed to the essential. He is the Subject, he is the Absolute – she is the Other' (*The Second Sex* translated by H.M. Parshley, Penguin, 1972, p.16). In the same place, de Beauvoir points out that Emmanuel Levinas had already used the term 'other' with reference to the feminine, but he had used it uncritically. She says, 'When he (Levinas) writes that woman is mystery, he implies that she is mystery for man. Thus his description, which is intended to be objective, is in fact an assertion of masculine privilege' (p.16).

39 We can note the difference in meaning between 'women-identified men' and 'men-identified women'. The first term refers to men who identify with the oppressed group, while the second refers to women who identify with the oppressors. Patriarchal structures discourage the first way of behaving and encourage the second.

40 Schüssler Fiorenza says that men need to adopt a 'theology of relinquishment' whereas women need a 'theology of self affirmation': 'Whereas in a feminist conversion *men* must take the option for the oppressed and become women-identified, in such a conversion *women* must seek to overcome our deepest self-alienation' (*Bread Not Stone*, p.xv). 'Because the spiritual colonisation of women by men has entailed our internalisation of the male as divine, men have to relinquish their spiritual and religious control over women and over the church as the people of God, if mutuality should become a real possibility'. (*In Memory of Her*, p.345). These theologies of self-affirmation and relinquishment would contribute to the creation of the three mythologies I have advocated: male-centred, female-centred and one of male-female mutuality.

41 Janice Raymond, *A Passion for Friends: Toward a Philosphy of Female Affection*, The Women's Press, London, 1986, pp.24–27 and 64–70.

42 See note 8.

43 This is a recurring phrase in Schüssler Fiorenza's work and has become part of the literature. See, for example, *Bread Not Stone*, pp.20 and 75, and the title of Part 11 of *In Memory of Her*, 'Women's History as the History of the Discipleship of Equals'.

44 See chapters 5 and 7 of *In Memory of Her*.

45 See 'Neither Male Nor Female', chapter 6 of *In Memory of Her* and 'Discipleship and Patriarchy', chapter 4 of *Bread Not Stone*.

46 Schüssler Fiorenza says, 'Women as church have a continuous history and tradition that can claim the discipleship of equals as its biblical roots', *Bread Not Stone*, p.20.

47 *Bread Not Stone*, p.xxiv.

48 See Part 1, 'Historical and Theological Reflections on Women-Church', in Rosemary Radford Ruether, *Women-Church: Theology and Practice*, Harper & Row, San Francisco, 1985.

49 The Movement for the Ordination of Women is an international organisation fighting for the ordination of women in the Anglican communion. MOW in Australia began in Sydney in 1983 and became national in 1984. Women and the Australian Church, also a national movement and begun in 1983, is attached to the Catholic church.

50 The types of groups vary enormously. The Rippling Web (1983), for example, has no affiliation with any church denomination. Some groups identify with a particular denomination, but remain independent in most respects, the Grail, identifying with the Catholic Church, being one example. Other groups are not connected with any denomination but include women who remain committed to particular churches as well as women who are committed to none. So the groups themselves are independent. Examples of such groups are Magdalene (1973), Northcote Women's Group (1988), International Women's Development Agency, and New Vision for Women. All these groups are known for their publications and other public actions. Nobody knows, however, the number of Australian women's groups devoted to religion and spirituality, many of them unnamed.

51 Raymond, *op.cit.*

52 The construction of 'male' and 'female' in Western philosophy is succinctly traced by Genevieve Lloyd, *The Man of Reason: 'Male' and 'Female' in Western*

166   *Knowing Otherwise*

Philosophy, Methuen, London, 1984. This work includes a comprehensive bibliographical essay on the topic.

53 Patriarchy also divides men into categories of race, class, sexual preference, etc, but these categories do not serve women. They serve rather the interests of the ruling males. Women are divided into categories in the interests of all men, but men are never divided into categories in the interests of all women.

54 This resentment appears in some of the stories in K. Nelson and D. Nelson, eds., *Sweet Mothers Sweet Maids: Journeys from Catholic Childhoods*, Penguin Books, Melbourne, 1986.

55 In North America, in particular, religious sisters have been leaders in the feminist movement. Anyone familar with recent scholarly and political work in the area of religious feminism will know, for example, the names of Sandra Schneiders, Teresa Kane, Mary Collins and Joan Chittister, all religious sisters.

56 'Nuns: The Battered Women of the Church?', *National Catholic Reporter*, 21 December 1984, p.25, quoted in Elisabeth Schüssler Fiorenza 'Claiming Our Authority and Power', in *Concilium*, 180 (4/1985).

57 See, for example, Madeleine Sophie McGrath, *These Women: Women Religious in the History of Australia: The Sisters of Mercy Parramatta 1888–1988*, New South Wales University Press, Kensington, 1989; Kath Burford 'But Not Conquered: Pioneer Sisters of Saint Joseph and Clerical Patriarchy' in *Women-Church*, No.4, Autumn 1989. Australian women from various denominations are also telling their own stories concerning the issue of ordination and women's authority within the church. See, for example, Marie Tulip, *Women in a Man's Church: Changes in the Status of Women in the Uniting Church of Australia 1977–1983*, Commission on the Status of Women NSW, 1983; Barbara Field, ed., *Fit For This Office: Women and Ordination*, Collins Dove, Melbourne, 1989; Muriel Porter, *Women in the Church – The Great Ordination Debate in Australia*, Penguin Books, Melbourne 1989; Betty Feith, *Women in Ministry*, Kyarra Press, Melbourne, 1990.

58 A perusal of almost all histories of women's religious orders reveals that the sisters have been displaced from the centre to the margins in these accounts. One of the signs of this displacement is that the names of the sisters are omitted or made secondary while the names of the clerics and laymen are always faithfully recorded. So, for example, in 1983 the Brigidine sisters celebrated the centenary of their arrival in Australia by a number of activities including the publication of a centenary calendar. Of the six sisters who made this historic journey, the calendar records the name of only one, Mother Mary John Synan, the first superior. In the front of this calendar is a 600-word potted history recounting the 1883 journey made by the pioneer sisters from Dublin, Ireland to Coonamble, outback New South Wales. The protagonists are referred to only as 'six Brigidine sisters' while every male connected with the event is mentioned by name and position. So the account tells of Dr Murray, Bishop of Maitland, Rev. T. English, Parish Priest of Gunnedah, and Mr Cunningham, all of whom accompanied the nuns in a private coach. We know also that the travellers stayed at the home of Mr Hubert Kelly 'whose wife was sister to Sir Patrick Jennings', at Mr Field's hotel, at the 'beautiful home' of Mr Cuthbert Featherstonehaugh from whose family they received a most cordial welcome, and at the residence of Mr Sam Ryder of 'Calga'. Not only are the six women at the centre of the journey unnamed but so are all the women connected with this event, with one exception. So this account records that the pioneer sisters spent their last night in Ireland with the Dominican nuns in Dublin, and their first night in Australia with the Sisters of Mercy at St Patrick's Church Hill, that en route to Coonamble they visited the Dominican convents of Waratah and West Maitaland, and that when they arrived in Coonamble 'a sumptuous dinner was prepared by the ladies who also waited on the table'. We do not know the names of any of these women who offered hospitality to the sisters on their historic journey and who were probably more intimately connected with them than were the men whose names have been recorded. The one exception in this tale of omission is the recording of the name of Mrs A. Loughnan who read the address of welcome to the sisters. This brief unsigned account, almost certainly written by a Brigidine sister, is not unusually biased. Indeed, it is a typical patriarchal recording of history. Many nuns like many other women, having internalised an androcentric view of the world, easily accommodate the displacement of themselves from the centre to the margins of their own stories. Fortunately, an increasing number of sisters are aware of the omissions and remedying them. *Brigidine Bulletin*, No.2, 1990, under the heading 'What the History Books Don't Tell Us', records the following extract from a letter from Mother John Synan to Bishop Murray of Maitland, January 8, 1884:

> PS We had a great treat the evening of the 2nd bottling your Lordship's second barrel of wine. Many hands made light work and we had great fun. It is splendid and safely stored away in our cellar. I don't know how we would live at all only for the good wine.(p.16)

This extract is accompanied by Sr Chanel Sugden's delightful drawing of a celebrating nun.

59   Some examples are Sabine Willis, ed., *Women, Faith and Fetes: Essays in the History of Women and the Church in Australia*, Dove Communications, Melbourne, 1977; Sally Kennedy, *Faith and Feminism: Catholic Women's Struggles for Self-Expression*, Studies in the Christian Movement, Sydney, 1985; Hilary Carey, *Truly Feminine Truly Catholic: A History of the Catholic Women's League in the Archdiocese of Sydney 1913-1987*, New South Wales University Press, Kensington, 1987.

60   See, for example, Madonna Kolbenschlag, *Kiss Sleeping Beauty Good-Bye*, Harper & Row, San Francisco, 1988 [1979] pp.53-4.

61   Women working in jobs that serve the interests of patriarchy frequently bond and their very friendship can subvert patriarchy. Women are far more threatening to patriarchy, however, when they gather for the sake of their own interests.

62   Schüssler Fiorenza, 'Daughters of Vision and Struggle'.

63   Raymond, *A Passion for Friends*, pp.181-199. She says, 'I use *victimism* to describe a milieu in which women's primary female or feminist identity seems to be grounded in women's shared state of having been victimised by men' (p.181). See also Raymond's understanding of the closely related destructive phenomenon of 'therapism: the tyranny of feelings' (pp.155-160).

64   This is an expression that Jean Paul Sartre's character, Garcin, applies to his wife in the play, *In Camera*, translated by Stuart Gilbert, Hamish Hamilton.

65   Rosemarie Tong, *Feminist Thought*, Unwin Hyman, London, 1989, p.137. This is an excellent summary of the various types of feminist thinking, all of which have impact on religion.

66   For a discussion of the same topic, see Kolbenschlag, *Kiss Sleeping Beauty Goodbye*, pp.55–60.

67   More detailed accounts of obstacles and strategies appear in Raymond's *A Passion for Friends* and Kolbenschlag's *Kiss Sleeping Beauty Goodbye*. In her article, 'Daughters of Vision and Struggle', Schüssler Fiorenza briefly names some of the 'deadly sins' of Women-church, sins which effectively prevent female bonding: 'psychologism that does not allow for any critical debate, but infantilises women by "mothering" them; anti-intellectualism that understands serious intellectual work as male and therefore unfeminine; collectivism that does not recognise and respect creative leadership but usurps it by manipulating groups instead; horizontal violence that thrashes women who refuse to remain feminine victims; guilt-tripping and confessionalism that repeat the litany of patriarchal sins without ever doing anything about them; exclusivism that insists on Women-church as the gathering of the truly true feminists and dehumanises men as evil; dogmatism that draws its boundaries in doctrinal terms rather than welcoming a diversity of gifts and visions'.

68   As early as 1949 in *The Second Sex*, de Beauvoir noted women's difficulty in saying 'we': 'But women do not say 'We' except at some congress of feminists or similar formal demonstration; men say 'women' and women use the same word in referring to themselves. *They* do not authentically assume a subjective attitude', p.19 (with my emphasis). Is de Beauvoir aware, I wonder, of her own use of the third person in reference to women?

69   Compare with the morning prayers prescribed for the orthodox Jewish male, 'Blessed be God . . . that He did not make me a woman', and for the orthodox Jewish female, 'Blessed be the Lord, who created me according to His will'.

70   I am not here advocating an essentialist myth of the eternal feminine or the eternal female. Such a myth, with its univeralising and reductionist tendencies, restricts women rather than frees us. I *am* advocating the need to discover and create a mythology composed of culturally bound myths that celebrate women in their own right. I am also advocating that we become more critically aware of how male-oriented our myths and classics are, even those which are about women. Think, for example, of whose interest is being served in a fairy story like 'Sleeping Beauty'. Consider also the classics. Carol Christ points out (*Laughter of Aphrodite*, p.35) that the *Iliad* is about a conflict between two men, Achilles and Agamemnon, but that what prompts this conflict is the 'spear captive', Briseis, the raped woman and victim of the wars of men. *Her* tragedy is not dealt with. She simply provides the occasion for the conflict between men. This pattern is repeated in most classics of the west. Australian myths take their own particular male form. See Kay Schaffer's analysis of the 'typical Australian' and how the woman stands in relation to him (*Women and the Bush: Forces of Desire in the*

Australian Cultural Tradition, Cambridge University Press, Melbourne, 1988). Another sign of the lack of a female-centred mythology is that women in western cultures are generally reduced to using male surnames, either their father's or their husband's.

71 One of the ways of becoming aware of the depth and breadth of this awakening, impossible to document in any way here, is to browse in a feminist book shop where there is ample evidence of the constant rediscovery and creation of the female self. One example of a text that gives a hint of the magnitude of both the task and of what has been accomplished is Barbara Walker's *The Women's Encyclopedia of Myths and Secrets*, Harper & Row, San Francisco, 1983. In 1986 this work was honoured by *The Times Educational Supplement* as 'Book of the Year'.

72 Examples of the many works documenting this rediscovery are Marija Gimbutas, *The Goddesses and Gods of Old Europe, 6500–3500 BC*, University of California Press, Berkeley, 1982. (Originally published as *The Gods and Goddesses of Old Europe, 7000–4000 BC: myths, legends and cult images*, Berkeley, 1974); Monica Sjöö and Barbara Mor, *The Great Cosmic Mother: Rediscovering the Religion of the Earth*, Harper & Row, San Francisco, 1975; Pamela Berger *The Goddess Obscured: Transformation of the Grain Protectress from Goddess to Saint*, Beacon Press, Boston, 1985; *Woman of Power: Faces of the Goddess*, No.15 Fall/Winter 1990.

73 Joseph Campbell, *The Hero with a Thousand Faces*, Bollingen Series 17, Princeton University Press, Princeton, 1949. Almost all the heroes we are familiar with have a male face and the female only appears as assistant to or opponent of the male. Many women know, however, that despite the overwhelming predominance of male-centred myths there are many heroes with *female* faces, censored out of consciousness by patriarchy, and currently being rediscovered. See notes 71 and 72.

Bibliography
& further reading

Ackley, Susan. 'A Meditation on Diapers' in *Woman of Power* 12, Winter 1989.

Adelman, Penina V., *Miriam's Well: Rituals for Jewish Women Around the Year*, Biblio Press, New York, 1987.

Archer, Robyn, Diana Manson, Helen Mills, Deborah Parry, Robyn Stacey. *The Pack of Women*, Hessian/ Penguin Books, Melbourne, 1986.

Arendt, Hannah. 'Home To Roost' in *The New York Review of Books*, June 26, 1975.

Ashe, Geoffrey. *The Virgin*, Routledge and Kegan Paul, London, 1976.

Atkinson, C., Buchanan, C., and Miles, M. eds. *Immaculate and Powerful: The Female in Sacred Image and Social Reality*, Beacon Press, Boston, 1985.

Atwood, Margaret. *Surfacing*, Simon and Schuster, New York, 1972.

Australian Feminist Studies, GPO Box 498, Adelaide, 5001, South Australia, 1985-

Bachofen, J.J. *Myth, Religion, and Mother-Right: Selected Writings*, Princeton University Press, Princeton, 1967 [1861].

Beckett, Lucy, 'The Essential Feminine' in *The Tablet* 28, October 1989.

Bell, Diane. *Daughters of the Dreaming*, McPhee Gribble/Allen and Unwin, Melbourne/Sydney, 1983.

Bell, Margaret. 'Volunteers as Care Providers'. Paper from a conference on the Future of Women's Services, Sydney University, 1988.

Berger, Pamela. *The Goddess Obscured: Transformation of the Grain Protectress from Goddess to Saint*, Beacon Press, Boston, 1985.

Briffault, Robert. *The Mothers*, Macmillan, New York, 1931.

Bryson, Lois. *The Proletarianization of Women: Gender Justice in Australia* in *Social Justice, 1989*.

Budapest, Z. The Holy Book of Women's Mysteries Part II, Susan B. Anthony Coven No. 1, Oakland, 1980.

Burke, Christine. *Through a Woman's Eyes: Encounters with Jesus*, Collins Dove, Melbourne, 1989.

Burton, Clare. *Pay Equity in Australia*, unpublished paper of a talk to mark the 4th anniversary of the Sex Discrimination Act, Sydney, 1988. with Raven Hag and Gay Thompson. *Women's Work: Pay Equity and Job Evaluation in Australia*, AGPS Press, Canberra, 1987.

Caputi, Jane. *The Age of Sex Crime*, The Women's Press, London, 1987.

Carey, Hilary. *Truly Feminine Truly Catholic: A History of the Catholic Women's League in the Archdiocese of Sydney 1913–1987*, New South Wales University Press, Sydney, 1987.

Chernin, Kim. *Reinventing Eve: Modern Woman in Search of Herself*, Harper & Row, New York, 1988.

Chopp, Rebecca S. *The Power to Speak: Feminism, Language, God*, Crossroad, New York, 1989.

Commission on the Status of Women of the Australian Council of Churches, *Breaking the Silence: The Church and Domestic Violence*, Sydney, 1986

Rock-A-Bye Test Tube: Reproductive Techonology and the Churches, Sydney, 1986.

Women, Poverty and the Church, Sydney, 1986.

Concilium 182 (6/1985) Elisabeth Schüssler Fiorenza and Mary Collins eds. *Women: Invisible in Church and Theology.*

194 (6/1987) Elisabeth Schüssler Fiorenza and Anne Carr eds. *Women, Work and Poverty.*

206 (6/1989) Anne Carr and Elisabeth Schüssler Fiorenza eds. *Motherhood: Experience, Institution, Theology.*

Crisp, Louise, and Valery Wilde. *In the Half-Light*, Friendly Street Poets, Adelaide, 1988.

Christ, Carol P., and Judith Plaskow, eds. *Womanspirit Rising: A Feminist Reader in Religion*, Harper & Row, San Francisco, 1979.

Diving Deep and Surfacing: Women Writers on Spiritual Quest, Beacon Press, Boston, 1980.

Laughter of Aphrodite: Reflections on a Journey to the Goddess, Harper and Row, San Francisco, 1987.

Crumlin, Rosemary. *Images of Religion in Australian Art,* Bay Books, Sydney, 1988.

de Beauvoir, Simone. *The Second Sex,* translated by H.M. Parshley, Penguin Books, 1972.

Daly, Mary. *Beyond God the Father: Toward a Philosophy of Women's Liberation,* Beacon Press, Boston, 1973.

'God is a Verb' in *Women in a Changing World,* McGraw-Hill Paperbacks.

Gyn/Ecology: The Metaethics of Radical Feminism, Beacon Press, Boston, 1978.

Pure Lust: Elemental Feminist Philosophy, Beacon Press, Boston, 1984.

Downing, Christine. *The Goddess; Mythological Images of the Feminine,* Crossroad, New York, 1981.

Eisenstein, Hester. *Contemporary Feminist Thought,* Allen and Unwin, Sydney, 1984.

Field, Barbara ed. *Fit For This Office: Women and Ordination,* Collins Dove, Melbourne, 1989.

Ford, F., Ford, R., Loan, M., and Page, C., eds. *Out of the Darkness: Paths to Inclusive Worship,* Language and Liturgy Task Group, Commission on the Status of Women, Australian Council of Churches, 1986.

Franklin, M. A. ed. *The Force of the Feminine,* Allen and Unwin, Sydney, 1986.

and R.S. Jones eds. *Opening the Cage: Stories of Church and Gender,* Allen and Unwin, Sydney, 1987.

Frazer, Constance. *Other Ways of Looking,* Friendly Street Poets, Adelaide, 1988.

Friedan, Betty. *The Feminine Mystique,* Penguin Books, 1965.

Fuchs, Ester. *Israeli Mythogynies: Women in Contemporary Hebrew fiction,* State University of New York Press, Albany, 1987.

Gimbutas, Marija. *The Goddesses and Gods of Old Europe, 6500 to 3500 BC,* University of California Press, Berkeley, 1982.

Gilligan, Carol. *In a Different Voice: Psychological Theory and Women's Development,* Harvard University Press, Cambridge, Massachusetts, 1982.

Goldenberg, Naomi. *The Changing of the Gods: Feminism and the End of Traditional Religions,* Beacon Press, Boston, 1979.

Grahn, Judy. 'From Sacred Blood to the Curse and Beyond' in Charlene Spretnak ed. *The Politics of Women's Spirituality,* Anchor Press Doubleday, New York, 1982.

Grey, Mary. *Redeeming the Dream: Feminism, Redemption and Christian Tradition,* SPCK, London, 1989.

Grieve, N., and Grimshaw, P. *Australian Women: Feminist Perspectives,* Oxford University Press, Melbourne, 1985.

Grosz, Elizabeth. *Sexual Subversions*, Allen & Unwin, Sydney, 1989.

Gunew, Sneja. 'Male Sexuality: Feminist Interpretations' in *Australian Feminist Studies*, 5, Summer 1987.

Hampson, Daphne. *Theology and Feminism*, Basil Blackwell, Oxford, 1990.

Hampton, Susan, and Kate Llewellyn, eds., *The Penguin Book of Australian Women Poets*, Penguin Books, Melbourne, 1986.

Harding, Esther M. *Women's Mysteries, Ancient and Modern: A Psychological Interpretation of the Feminine Principle as Portrayed in Myth, Story and Dreams*, Harper & Row, San Francisco, 1987.

Harris, Maria. *Dance of the Spirit: The Seven Steps of Women's Spirituality*, Bantam Books, New York, 1989.

Harrison, Beverly Wildung. *Making the Connections: Essays in Feminist Social Ethics*, Beacon Press, Boston, 1985.

Harwood, Gwen. *Selected Poems*, Angus & Robertson, Sydney, 1988.

Heresies: The Great Goddess Issue, New York, 1978.

Holy Bible. Revised Standard Version, Thomas Nelson, Edinburgh, 1955.

Hurcombe, Linda, ed. *Sex and God: Some Varieties of Women's Religious Experience*, Routledge & Keagan Paul, London, 1987.

Johns, Anne. 'Images of God' in *Eremos Newsletter*, 20, August 1987.

Joseph, Alison, ed. *Through the Devil's Gateway: Women, Religion and Taboo*, SPCK, London, 1990.

Journal of Feminist Studies in Religion, PO Box 1608, Decatur, GA, 30031–1608, USA.

Keen, Sam. *Faces of the Enemy: Reflections of the Hostile Imagination*, Harper & Row, San Francisco, 1986.

Kennedy, Sally. *Faith and Feminism: Catholic Women's Struggles for Self Identity*, Studies in the Christian Movement, Sydney, 1985.

King, Ursula, *Women and Spirituality: Voices of Protest and Promise*, Macmillan, London, 1989.

Kolbenschlag, Madonna. *Kiss Sleeping Beauty Goodbye*, Harper & Row, San Francisco, 1988.

Lauter, Estella. *Women as Mythmakers: Poetry and Visual Art by Twentieth Century Women*, Indiana University Press, Bloomington, 1984.

Lerner, Gerda. *The Creation of Patriarchy* Vol 1, Oxford University Press, Oxford, 1986.

Leunig, Mary. *There's No Place Like Home*, Penguin Books, Melbourne, 1982.

A Piece of Cake, Penguin Books, Melbourne, 1986.

Lindsay, Elaine ed. *'Towards a Feminist Theology,'* Conference Proceedings, PO Box 140, Helensburg 2508 NSW, 1989.

Llewellyn, Kate, *Trader Kate and the Elephants,* Friendly Street Poets, Adelaide, 1982.

Lloyd, Genevieve, 'Selfhood, War and Masculinity' in Carole Pateman and Elizabeth Gross eds. *Feminist Challenges: Social and Political Theory,* Allen and Unwin, Sydney, 1986.

The Man of Reason: 'Male' and 'Female' in Western Philosophy Methuen, London, 1984.

Loades, Ann. ed. *Feminist Theology: A Reader,* SPCK, London, 1990.

Magdalene, Sydney, 1973-1987.

Maitland, S. *A Map of the New Country: Women and Christianity,* Routledge and Kegan Paul, London, 1983.

Mercer, Jan. *The Other Half: Women in Australian Society,* Penguin, Australia, 1975.

Matriarchal Study Group *Menstrual Taboos,* Flat 6, 15 Guildford St, London W.C. 1 (undated).

McCredden, L., McCarthy, M., McGinlay, A., and Morris, J. eds. *Women's Words: A Local Anthology,* Northcote Women's Christian Book Project, PO Box 51, Northcote 3070 Vic., 1989.

McFague, Sallie. *Models of God: Theology for an Ecological Nuclear Age,* Fortress Press, Philadelphia, 1987.

McGrath, Madeleine Sophie. *These Women: Women Religious in the History of Australia: The Sisters of Mercy Parramatta 1888-1988,* New South Wales University Press, Sydney, 1989.

Mellaart, James. *Catal Huyuk: A Neolithic Town in Anatolia,* McGraw Hill, New York, 1967.

Miller, Alice. *The Drama of Being a Child,* Virago Press, London, 1988.

Morton, Nelle. *The Journey is Home,* Beacon Press, Boston, 1985.

Mudflower Collective, *God's Fierce Whimsy,* Pilgrim Press, New York, 1985.

Murdock, Maureen. *The Heroine's Journey,* Shambhala, Boston & Shaftesbury, 1990.

Nelson, Janet, and Walter, Linda. *Women of Spirit: Woman's Place in Church and Society,* St. Mark's, Canberra, 1989.

Nelson, K., and D. Nelson. *Sweet Mothers Sweet Maids: Journeys from Catholic Childhoods,* Penguin Books, Melbourne, 1986.

Neumann, Erich. *The Great Mother: An Analysis of the Archetype,* Princeton University Press, Princeton, 1963.

New South Wales Women's Co-ordination Unit, *NSW Women's Policy Statement*, Parramatta, 1990.

Ortner, Sherry. 'Is Female to Male as Nature is to Culture?' in *Feminist Studies* 1 (2), Fall 1972.

O'Brien, Mary. *The Politics of Reproduction*, Routledge & Kegan Paul, London, 1983.

O'Donnell, Carol, and Philippa Hall. *Getting Equal: Labour Market Regulation and Women's Work*, Allen & Unwin, Sydney, 1988.

Pagels, Elaine. *The Gnostic Gospels*, Random House, New York, 1979.

Adam, Eve, and the Serpent, Vintage Books, New York, 1989.

Pateman, Carole, and Elizabeth Gross eds. *Feminist Challenges: Social and Political Theory*, Allen & Unwin, Sydney, 1976.

Perera, Sylvia Brinton. *Descent to the Goddess: A Way of Initiation for Women*, Inner City Books, Toronto, 1981.

Plaskow, Judith. *Standing Again at Sinai: Judaism from a Feminist Perspective*, Harper & Row, San Francisco, 1990

and Carol Christ, *Weaving the Visions: Patterns in Feminist Spirituality*, Harper & Row, San Francisco, 1989.

Porter, Muriel, *Women in the Church – The Great Ordination Debate in Australia*, Penguin Books, Melbourne, 1989.

Raymond, Janice. *A Passion for Friends: Toward a Philosophy of Female Affection*, The Women's Press, London, 1986.

Reekie, Gail. 'Feminism and Men's Bodies: More Thoughts on Male Sexuality' in *Australian Feminist Studies* 6, Autumn 1988.

Ricoeur, Paul. 'The Problem of the Foundation of Moral Philosophy' in *Philosophy Today* 22, 1978.

Rich, Adrienne. *Of Woman Born: Motherhood as Experience and Institution*, Norton, New York, 1976.

Roe, Jill. *Beyond Belief*, New South Wales University Press, Sydney, 1986.

Ruddick, Sara. 'Pacifying the Forces: Drafting Women in the Interests of Peace' in *Signs* 8(3), Spring 1983.

Ruether, Rosemary Radford. *New Woman New Earth: Sexist Ideologies and Human Liberation*, Dove Communications, Melbourne 1975.

'Sexism and the Theology of Liberation' in *Christian Century*, December 1973.

Mary, the Feminine Face of the Church, Westminster Press, Philadelphia, 1977.

'Motherearth and the Megamachine: a theology of liberation in a feminine,, somatic and ecological perspective' in Carol P. Christ and Judith Plaskow eds. *Womanspirit Rising*, Harper & Row, San Francisco, 1979.

Sexism and God-Talk: Toward a Feminist Theology, Beacon Press, Boston, 1983.

Women-Church: Theology and Practice, Harper & Row, San Francisco, 1985.

'Feminist Spirituality and Historical Religion', the Dudleian Lecture 1985–6, printed in *Harvard Divinity Bulletin,* 1986.

Russell, Letty M. *Human Liberation in a Feminist Perspective – A Theology,* Westminster Press, Philadelphia, 1974.

ed. *Feminist Interpretation of the Bible,* Basil Blackwell, Oxford, 1985.

Ryan, Edna and Anne Conlon. *Gentle Invaders: Australian Women at Work 1788–1974,* Nelson, Sydney, 1975.

Saiving, Valerie. 'The Human Situation: A Feminine View' in *The Journal of Religion,* April 1960.

Schaffer, Kay. *Women and the Bush: Forces of Desire in the Australian Cultural Tradition,* Cambridge University Press, Cambridge, 1988.

Schüssler Fiorenza, Elisabeth. *In Memory of Her: A Feminist Theological Reconstruction of Christian Origins,* Crossroad, New York, 1984.

'Feminist Theology as a Critical Theology of Liberation' in *Theological Studies* 36, December 1975.

Bread Not Stone: The Challenge of Feminist Biblical Interpretation, Beacon Press, Boston, 1984.

'Daughters of Vision and Struggle' in *Towards a Feminist Theology: Conference Proceedings,* PO Box 140, Helensburgh 2508, NSW Australia.

'Justified by All Her Children: Struggle, Memory, and Vision' in *Concilium: On the Threshold of the Third Millenium,* February 1990.

Semeia 28, 1983, Mary Ann Tolbert ed. *The Bible and Feminist Hermeneutics.*

Semeia 47, 1989, Katie Geneva Cannon and Elisabeth Schüssler Fiorenza eds. *Interpretation for Liberation.*

Shange, Ntozake. *for colored girls who have considered suicide/when the rainbow is enuf,* Macmillan, New York, 1975.

Sharma Arvind ed. *Women in World Religion,* State University Press of New York, Albany, 1987.

Shuttle, Penelope, and Peter Redgrove. *The Wise Wound: Eve's Curse and Everywoman,* R. Marek, New York, 1978.

Sjöö, Monica, and Barbara Mor. *The Great Cosmic Mother: Rediscovering the Religion of the Earth,* Harper & Row, San Francisco, 1987 (revised edition).

Skuse, J., M. Tulip, and B. Moore. *Liberation Theology and Feminism,* Commission on the Status of Women of the Australian Council of Churches (NSW), Sydney, 1975.

Spender, Dale. *Women of Ideas (and what men have done to them)*, Ark Paperbacks, London, 1983.

Spretnak, Charlene ed. *The Politics of Women's Spirituality: Essays on the Rise of Spiritual Power Within the Feminist Movement*, Anchor Books, New York, 1982.

Stanton, Elizabeth Cady, (and the Revising Committee). *The Woman's Bible* (6th printing) Coalition Task Force on Women and Religion, Seattle, 1978. [1898].

Starhawk. *The Spiral Dance: A Rebirth of the Ancient Religion of the Great Goddess*, Harper & Row, San Francisco, 1978.

Dreaming the Dark: Magic, Sex and Politics, Beacon Press, Boston, 1982.

Truth and Dare: Encounters with Power, Authority and Mystery, Harper & Row, San Francisco, 1987.

Stone, Merlin. *When God was a Woman*, Dial Press, New York, 1976. (also published as *The Paradise Papers: The Suppression of Women's Rites*, Virago and Quartet Books, London, 1976).

Summers, Anne. *Damned Whores and God's Police: The Colonisation of Women in Australia*, Penguin Books, Melbourne, 1975.

Taylor, Dena. *Red Flower: Rethinking Menstruation*, The Crossing Press, Freedom California, 1988.

Thiering, Barbara. *Created Second?: Aspects of Women's Liberation in Australia*, Family Life Movement of Australia, Sydney, 1973.

Deliver Us From Eve, ed. Australian Council of Churches (NSW) Commission on the Status of Women, Sydney, 1977.

Thistlethwaite, Susan. *Sex, Race, and God: Christian Feminism in Black and White*, Geoffrey Chapman, London, 1989.

Tong, Rosemarie. *Feminist Thought: A Comprehensive Introduction*, Unwin Hyman, London, 1989.

Trible, Phyllis. *Texts of Terror: Literary Feminist Readings of Biblical Narratives*, Fortress Press, Philadelphia, 1984.

God and the Rhetoric of Sexuality, Fortress Press, Philadelphia, 1978.

Tulip, Marie. *Women in a Man's Church: Changes in the Status of Women in the Uniting Church in Australia 1977-1983*, Commission on the Status of Women of the Australian Council of Churches, 1983.

'Religion' in Sneja Gunew ed. *Feminist Knowledge: Critique and Construct*, Routledge, London, 1990.
and Erin White *Women in the Church and the World: An Annotated Bibliography*, Catholic Education Office, Sydney, 1989.

von Franz, Marie Louise. *An Introduction to the Interpretation of Fairy Tales*, Spring Publications, Dallas, 1970.

Walker, Alice. *In Search of our Mothers' Gardens: Womanist Prose*, Women's Press, London, 1984.

Walker, Barbara. *The Women's Encyclopedia of Myths and Secrets*, Harper and Row, San Francisco, 1983.

Walters, Margaret. *The Nude Male: A New Perspective*, Penguin Books, Britain, 1978.

Waring, Marilyn. *Counting for Nothing*, Allen and Unwin, Sydney, 1989.

Warner, Marina. *Alone of All Her Sex: The Myth and the Cult of the Virgin Mary*, Quartet Books, London, 1978.

Wehr, Demaris. *Jung and Feminism: Liberating Archetypes*, Routledge, London, 1988.

Wex, Marianne. *Let's Take Back Our Space: "Male" and "Female" Body Language as a Result of Patriarchal Structures*, translated by Johanna Albert, Frauenliteraturverlag Hermine Fees, 1979. This project was originally shown in 1977 as a photo exhibition.

Wheeler, Lorraine. 'In Work Out of Pocket: Women Working in the Community Services Industry', Major Points Discussion Paper, Sydney, 1988.

White, Erin and Marie Tulip. *Women in the Church and the World: An Annotated Bibliography*, Catholic Education Office, Sydney, 1989.

Willis, Sabine ed. *Women, Faith and Fetes: Essays in the History of Women in the Church in Australia*, Dove Communications, Melbourne, 1977.

Woman of Power: Faces of the Goddess 15, Fall/Winter 1990, Cambridge Ma.

Woman's Mirror Cookery Book, The Bulletin, Sydney, 1937.

Women's Bureau. *Women's Work Women's Pay*, Department of Employment, Education and Training, Canberra, 1988.

Women Church: An Australian Journal of Feminist Studies in Religion GPO Box 2134, Sydney 2001 NSW, 1987–

Woodruff, Sue. *Meditations with Mechtild of Magdeburg*, Bear & Company, Santa Fe, 1982.

Winter, Miriam Therese. *Woman Prayer Woman Song: Resources for Ritual*, Meyer Stone Books, Oak Park, 1987.

Yeandle, Susan. *Women's Working Lives: Patterns and Strategies*, Tavistock Publications, London, 1984.

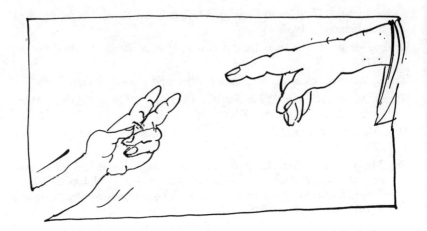

Index